SPECIAL AGENT MAN

MY LIFE IN THE FBI AS A TERRORIST HUNTER, HELICOPTER PILOT, AND CERTIFIED SNIPER

Steve Moore

D1113170

CHICAGO REVIEW PRESS

Published by Chicago Review Press, Incorporated
814 North Franklin Street
Chicago, Illinois 60610
ISBN 978-0-914090-70-0

Due to safety and security considerations for the FBI personnel mentioned in this book (especially those still serving), and at the request of the FBI, all names of FBI agents and other FBI personnel have been changed.

Library of Congress Cataloging-in-Publication Data
Moore, Steve.
Special agent man : my life in the FBI as a terrorist hunter, helicopter pilot, and certified sniper / Steve Moore. — 1st ed.
p. cm.
ISBN 978-0-914090-70-0
1. United States. Federal Bureau of Investigation. 2. Moore, Steve. 3. Intelligence officers—United States—Biography. 4. Criminal investigation—United States. I. Title.

HV8144.F43M66 2012
363.25092—dc23
[B]

2012014309

Cover and interior design: Visible Logic, Inc.

Printed in the United States of America
5 4 3 2 1

6/30

For Michelle, who cared more about my dreams than she did her own.

And for Meagan, Steve, and Madison; I am more proud of you than words can express.

Contents

Introduction

My brother-in-law Evan Easterly is a policeman in San Marcos, Texas, outside of San Antonio. One afternoon recently, I got a call from him. He had just responded to a bank robbery in which the robber got away, and Evan was standing inside the now-locked bank. I could hear voices in the background as the familiar process of interviewing the tellers and bank personnel began. I was absolutely at a loss as to why Evan was calling.

"Steve, do you know an FBI agent named Ryan March?"

I was floored. Ryan was one of my favorite people in the world; we'd been on the same SWAT team for five years. We went through SWAT tryouts, SWAT training, and countless SWAT operations together. As teammates, we depended on each other for our lives. We traveled all over the world with the team. But even beyond that, he was one of the most interesting, funny, and tactically competent people I had ever met. But he'd transferred to San Antonio several years ago, and we'd had had little contact since then.

"Ryan March?" I asked excitedly. "Yes, I know who he is. How do you know him?"

"He's standing right here, Steve; he responded to the bank robbery and he says he knows you."

"Evan, listen carefully," I said seriously. "The reason I know him is that he's a con artist who has posed as a preschool teacher and an FBI agent all over the world. Be careful. He's a very sick man."

"That's kinda what he told me you'd say." Evan said, deadpan. "Here he is," he added, handing his cell phone to Ryan.

"Hey, Steve, has your wife ever leveled with you about her and me?" was Ryan's opening gambit. It would be out of character for him to start a conversation with anything but a provocative joke.

Suddenly it all flooded back: all the memories, all the joy, all the pain, along with an aching longing to be back on SWAT with Ryan and the team. It wasn't the guns, it wasn't the excitement, it wasn't the cool operations—it was the people. Our conversation was all too brief, as Ryan had to get back to work. I longed to be in that bank, interviewing victim tellers and building a case. It had gotten routine before I retired, but now it would be incredibly refreshing. When we finally bid each other goodbye, Ryan finished with a quick "Miss ya, man." That's about as sensitive as SWAT guys get, but it said a lot.

One of the greatest privileges of being in the FBI was getting to work with the incredible people there. Obviously, in every situation there are exceptions, but I have never seen a more uniformly competent, overachieving group of people in my life. I was proud to be one of them, and never stopped hoping that I would measure up to the agents I worked with. There's a phrase in the FBI to describe the wide-eyed fascination that new agents come to town with; it's called "lights and sirens syndrome." It takes some people years to get over it. I'm not sure I ever did. I think that's because some people know that they belong in the FBI, that it's where they should be. Some are just grateful to be there.

I'm grateful, but like someone who finds a million dollars in a bag on the side of the road, I didn't want to call too much attention to myself for fear that a mistake had been made. I was always amazed at the mystique the FBI seemed to give me. Each time I pulled out the badge and said, "FBI. Special Agent Moore," the reaction was amazing. People went pale. They hyperventilated. They stuttered. I felt like whispering to the honest ones, "Look behind the sunglasses— I'm just a normal guy! I'm not really like you think I am."

Maybe that's why I wanted to tell my story. Since I never lost the lights and siren syndrome, I think I have a unique view of the FBI. I never forgot that I was blessed to be where I was, and I never, ever, stopped loving what I was doing there. So this is the story of an FBI career from a guy who didn't get jaded. From a guy who loved it as much on his last day as he did on his first. A guy for whom every case was the best case he had ever worked. Sure, there were times when I didn't love the FBI, but none when I didn't like the job of special agent.

I cannot tell you how many movies and TV shows I've seen about FBI agents. I've even written a couple of TV episodes. But in every one of those screen characterizations, agents are seen as fearless, emotionless near-automatons unfazed by death and risk. Jack Bauer (Kiefer Sutherland) of the television show *24* was a case in point. Every week, Jack would live another hour of an incredible twenty-four-hour adventure. What he regularly did in twenty-four hours, the average real agent doesn't do in twenty-four years.

When Jack Bauer was the head of the fictional Los Angeles Counter Terrorist Unit (CTU), I was the supervisor of al-Qaeda investigations for the Los Angeles FBI's Joint Terrorism Task Force (JTTF). Jack's job was to stop terrorism in L.A. and the United States. So was mine. Jack was a SWAT operator who carried a .40 caliber Sig Sauer P229. I was a SWAT operator who carried a 9 mm Sig Sauer P228—but I really wanted the higher-caliber P229. Bauer was a sniper, and so was I. Jack was an airplane and helicopter pilot for the FBI. So was I. Bauer was an undercover agent, and so was I.

But that's where the similarities end. Jack was fearless, and I felt fear—I just didn't let it stop me. Jack saw death and was unaffected. I saw death and couldn't get it out of my mind. Jack was cool, and I lived in a suburb and drove my wife and three kids around in a minivan. We had the same job; we just went about it in different ways. But my job was real.

So to the reader and to my fellow agents, I must confess: *I'm not Jack Bauer.*

(But I still want his Sig 229.)

1

"Hi, My Name Is Steve, and I'm Addicted to Adrenaline"

THE PREDAWN AIR was crisp and cool, and the breeze across my face refreshed me and wicked away some sweat that had soaked my black flight suit, even in the fifty-degree night. The streets were empty, the dutiful traffic lights just going through the motions.

I loved this time of the morning. I was exhilarated, I was happy, I was determined. My feet stood on a steel grate about eight inches off the ground, and the asphalt I saw between my feet was disappearing behind me at forty miles per hour.

I looked across at Ryan and saw the same excitement, the same contentedness, and the same intensity. He looked ahead, his goggles down, and he was in the zone. I loved the zone. The Chevy Suburban ahead of us suddenly slowed, the brake lights as bright as road flares. The team on the lead Suburban held on to the rails above the windows to keep from sliding forward. Four operators on each side. I looked back at the vehicles behind us:

two more Suburbans with eight operators each on the rails, the mount-out truck carrying any other equipment we'd need at the site, and a dozen police and FBI cars behind that. It was an exciting sight. LAPD black-and-whites blocked each intersection as we sped through.

Jeff Hughes, next to me, yelled over the rush of the wind and the sound of the trucks: "One-fourteenth Street coming up!"

All operators began going through their own personal checklist to ensure that they were ready to dismount. Helmet strap on, goggles down, balaclava pulled up, covering the face except for the eyes. I slapped the butt of the ammo magazine to check that it was seated into the Heckler & Koch MP5 submachine gun. A quick check that my muzzle light was working and a glance through the sight to make sure the red dot had reported for duty. A look down at my tactical belt confirmed that my Springfield .45 was secured and my reserve mags were locked down.

Jeff radioed in to the command post. "Thirties at yellow," he announced to the CP.

The yellow—the last place that the agents have the luxury of concealment and cover before the site of an operation—had been chosen from aerial photos and street diagrams two hours earlier at the SWAT briefing room in the garage/special operations structure of the FBI office in Westwood, just down the hill from a sleeping UCLA. The briefing had begun at 2:30 AM on the dot. Forty SWAT operators crowded into the briefing room.

To say that my teammates were my friends would be inadequate. We trained together, we worked together, and at times we depended on one another for our lives. I loved these guys. On the face of the Earth that morning, there was no place I'd rather be.

Five individual teams made up the entire Los Angeles FBI SWAT team. They were numbered: the Twenties, Thirties, Forties, Fifties, and Sixties. Each team consisted of between eight and ten operators, depending on staffing, and each thought it was the best team on Los Angeles FBI SWAT.

I, fortunately, was one of the Thirties, which actually *was* the best team on L.A. SWAT.

The Thirties were the primary team for this operation, and the Thirties' team leader, Jeff Hughes, got ready to begin the brief at the front of the room. Behind him was a whiteboard with a detailed drawing of an apartment floor plan, both the first and the second floors, as well as a map of the block, along with any environmental obstacles—fencing and the like. As Jeff got ready to speak, the SWAT secretary passed out a stack of twenty-page operational plans.

"Ladies!"

The room quieted down.

"In your packets you can see that we have a night-service warrant for Mr. Reginald 'Weezy' Stokes and his baby mama, Rachelle 'Shaazz' Washington. They reside within the confines of scenic Nickerson Gardens."

Several hoots followed. Nickerson Gardens is the largest public-housing project west of the Mississippi, with more than one thousand apartment units. The place has an armed-gangster-to-resident-population percentage probably as high as any place on Earth. It is not a safe place for anybody to be, really. An op at Nickerson Gardens carried with it more risk than other raids, which was fine by the operators, because nobody joins SWAT to be bored.

"Mr. Stokes and Ms. Washington have been running a business out of their residence in the fourteen hundred block of East One-fourteenth Street. It's a pharmaceutical business."

"A crack house?" asked somebody from the back.

"That's a vulgar term," Hughes scolded with mock propriety. "The Thirties are primary on this hit, the Forties are secondary, and the Fifties will cover perimeter."

"Dogs?" someone asked.

"None that we're aware of, which means there probably are."

After a full brief of the operational plan, the meeting broke into smaller individual team briefings, and we Thirties went over our specific mission.

"Hamlin will be the breacher. Looks like a solid-core door with no bars on it."

"No bars on a crack house in Nickerson Gardens? Are they crazy?" Bobby Hamlin wondered aloud. Hamlin was newer on the team than all of us and bigger than most of us, and his responsibility as the "breacher" would be to open doors for the assault team.

"The entry team will be three-two, three-six, myself, and three-one. Three-eight, three-three, and three-four will follow."

My call sign was Sam 36, or simply "three-six." It identified me as a member of the SWAT team and, more particularly, the Thirties team. That morning, I would be the second operator through the door. Ahead of me would be James Benedict, a former US Marine; behind me would be team leader Jeff Hughes, and fourth in the door would be my friend Ryan March, a former Army Ranger captain.

"Sparky, if we have a rabbit, he's yours," Jeff advised, using the nickname I was given after an aircraft incident. "Mark, you back up Spark." Mark Crichton was a bulldog of an operator who sometimes chafed at the bawdy behavior of SWAT. But if Mark was backing you up, you never had to check to make sure someone was there.

A SWAT operator in full gear has no chance of catching a rabbit—a fleeing suspect—in open ground. They wear approximately fifty pounds of gear, including a Kevlar helmet and tactical boots. But in a house, you can run but you can't hide. In my heart, I secretly hoped that somebody would run. It made things more fun.

The briefing adjourned at about 3:30 AM, and we moved into the garage area to stage our vehicles and gear. This was my favorite part of an op, and the thing I would miss the most, because this was my last SWAT operation. SWAT operators in the FBI spend approximately 25 to 30 percent of their time on SWAT training and operations, and the rest as regular FBI agents working cases, and my caseload had grown to the point where I could no longer do both. If I neglected my cases—the death penalty case of a man who machine-gunned a preschool class; the investigation of a nut who was planning to blow up an oil refinery—innocent people could get hurt. If I neglected my SWAT training, my partner could get killed (as an operator, your main job is to cover your partner). I couldn't quit my cases, and I wouldn't risk the lives of my friends. To this day, it is one of the most painful decisions I made in the FBI.

Breachers loaded their one-man rams, the "master key" for most doors. Best described as a three-foot-long, five-inch-diameter concrete-filled steel pipe with handles, the ram will open most doors very quickly. In case of a security-bar door, common in places like Nickerson Gardens, SWAT breachers also carry a hydra-ram, a mini version of the "jaws of life" used by the fire department. If needed, they also have torches, metal saws, and, everybody's favorite, a strong hook and chain connected to a truck. Other agents loaded CO_2 fire extinguishers, which seem to intimidate even the most aggressive guard dogs. Of course, if that doesn't work, a 10mm slug always will.

We rode inside the Suburbans to the staging area a mile from the Gardens. Once in the neighborhood, we got on the boards and headed out. Three minutes later, we were sitting at yellow, a block from the target location. The tactical operations center (TOC) a few blocks away provided the last intel brief before the hit, courtesy of the FBI's surveillance team, the Special Operations Group: "SOG reports lights on and movement in the target location."

It was 4:30 AM—did they ever sleep? I found myself taking a very deep breath and exhaling. At that second, the overall SWAT team commander, "Big Daddy" Dan Kurtz, came on the radio. This was it. I knew the next order by rote:

"I have control . . . all teams move to green and execute."

I snapped the condition lever from SAFE to BURST (which fires three rounds with each trigger pull), and Crichton, our driver that morning, accelerated briskly down the street, turning sharply onto 114th Street. As we turned onto the street, headlights were doused on all vehicles and we sped quickly down a narrow street with parked cars whizzing by on either side.

Stay in the middle, I silently begged Crichton.

The lead Suburban carrying the Forties came to a stop, followed by our truck. Silently, we dismounted from the vehicle and trotted toward the front door of the target residence, our rubber-soled boots muffling our steps. The Forties hurried to their perimeter position, moving around the side of the building, always careful to avoid the neck-high clotheslines endemic to the projects. I found Benedict and tailgated him to the front door as quickly and as quietly as I could. Behind me, I felt rather than heard Hughes keeping up. At the front door, Hamlin arrived simultaneously, carrying the ram. March, the number four operator, squeezed Hughes's shoulder, Hughes squeezed mine, and I squeezed Benedict's. We were ready.

I saw Benedict nod to Hamlin, who began a mighty backswing with the ram. He put his body into the incoming arc of the ram and hit the door perfectly, right above the door latch, and the door gave way as if blown into the room by explosives. Benedict leaped forward like a car at a drag race, and I struggled to keep up.

The lights were indeed on in the first room, which was the living room.

"*FBI! FBI! FBI! Get down! Get down!*" we screamed, as much a tension release as it was a warning to the occupants.

Benedict turned hard right deep into the room, clearing the corner in front of him as I turned left, clearing my corner. Hughes was by me so fast I never saw him; I only saw March enter out of the corner of my eye. Clearing the corner took less than a second, and I turned long to address the subjects in the room. Several fell to the ground, hands over their heads; others stood frozen, panicked. A tatted-up, muscular kid, probably eighteen years old, wearing only boxers and low-hanging basketball shorts, ran.

He sprinted right to left in front of me, directly up the narrow stairway, as we screamed uselessly for him to stop. The stairways in Nickerson Gardens are notoriously narrow. Maybe two to three feet wide.

"Rabbit!" I yelled, and started up the stairs as fast as I could move in fifty pounds of gear. I heard Crichton fall in behind me, and I heard his breath as we ran up the stairs. Halfway up the flight, we heard a loud *slam*.

Shit, he went to ground, I thought as I ran up the stairs. Why did he run? Why did he close the door? Was he running for a weapon in the room? Shitshitshit!

At the top of the stairs, I got bad news. The landing, all nine square feet of it, ended with three closed doors in a *U* pattern: one to my left, one to my right, and one dead-ahead of me. No matter which door he went into, we didn't have cover if he wanted to shoot through the door.

I had to think! What was the floor plan that morning? Which one was the bathroom—right, left, or long? Crichton was close behind me, but our bulky gear didn't give us enough room to stand in the hall together. He was on the top step before the landing.

Mark pointed two fingers to his eyes, then to each of the doors, quizzically: SWAT sign-language for *Did you see which door he went into?*

I answered his question with the unofficial SWAT signal for *I don't know*: I shrugged my shoulders and rolled my eyes.

It didn't matter. We had already been on the landing too long.

Just pick a door! I chided myself.

Nodding quickly toward the door on the left, Mark reached over to the knob. I locked the MP5 into my right cheek so I could see the red dot through the sight front of me. Silently mouthing and nodding, *Three, two . . .* , Mark sharply twisted the knob and threw the door open. I took one step into the room, heaving most of my weight against the door to ensure that nobody was behind it.

It was the bathroom. I could clear the room with my peripheral vision alone. It was empty. Two doors left. Fifty-fifty chance. My heart raced. It wasn't from the run up the stairs, either. What was the asshole doing in that room!

I nodded toward the room ahead of me, and Mark bladed himself between me and the wall so that he could reach the doorknob. I had both my hands full with my MP5. Again, I counted down silently, nodding with each count. Mark swung the door open and I lunged into the room, hammering the door against the wall with my shoulder, clearing the corners as quickly as I could. But before I even got to the last corner of the small room, I knew from peripheral vision that no one was in there. The room was empty save for a solitary ironing board. I cleared the closet silently, then moved back to the hallway, where Mark was already covering the last door.

There was no question now where the gangbanger was. He was behind that door. He had heard us breach the other two doors, and he had an idea of how long it would be before I got to his door. There would be no element of surprise. He would be waiting for me.

I knew his heart was beating as hard as mine was. The difference was that he knew what I was going to do and where I was going to be. I had no idea of anything. Mark positioned his hand near the doorknob, ready to turn it at my signal. Once he was ready, I had the quickest, slightest thought that I didn't want to go in. No, I mean I *really* didn't want to go in. But if I thought about that for more than half a second, it would become a debate in my mind. It was a case of mind over matter—or wisdom. I began the silent countdown, *Three . . . two. . .* I didn't want to get shot in Nickerson Gardens. Not on my last op.

On "one," Mark threw the door open and I burst in, hitting the swinging door with my right shoulder. I instantly saw not one but two males in the room, and the one I chased up the stairs was leaping from the closet toward a bed to my left. The male on the left stood in a corner screaming. Things were moving all over the place, and the world seemed to slow down.

I followed the gangster with my red dot in his leap toward the bed, shouting, "Get down! Show me your hands! *Show me your hands!*"

He dug his hands under the covers, under a pillow, as if he was reaching for something hidden. I could not enter the tiny room deep enough for Mark to enter without having my MP5 within reach of the gangster, so I was in the room alone. The second male in the room was a boy, maybe eleven, and he had his hands over his ears and was shrieking, "Don't shoot me! Don't shoot me!"

He was not a threat, so I could concentrate on the idiot on the bed. He stared at me, then down at his hands. His head was shaved; he wore nothing from the waist up, and he was tatted all over his arms and back. The bedspread on the bed was brown.

"Show me your hands!" I screamed again.

He looked me in the eyes and ignored my command.

That was three times. I had no choice. He could have a gun. He could shoot me; he could shoot Mark. It wasn't a decision anymore; it was a trained response.

Time slowed even further. Sound seemed to stop. I put the red dot just below the top of his head, because from years of range time, I knew that inside of twenty-five yards, the red dot was skewed high at this close distance. If I put the dot between his eyes, the round would likely impact his chin or neck. I checked behind the gangster to see where any bullets would go if they continued on through him. A miss from eight feet was not going to happen. Long rounds would go through the front wall of the apartment, not into the next room.

My trigger finger was on the side of the weapon above the trigger as we'd been trained. Any time you are on an op and touch the trigger with your finger, it is so you can shoot something or someone. I moved my finger to the trigger and began applying the measured pressure that I had practiced tens of thousands of times. I was surprised by how automatic and controlled my reactions were. I was about to end a life, and it was second nature.

When the finger began to move to the trigger, the gangster flinched. He threw his empty hands out from under the blanket and shouted, "Don't shoot!"

Sound returned to the room. I was immediately aware of loud screams from the kid in the corner, and they were almost instantly unbearable.

"Get on the floor! *Get on the floor!*" I shouted at the idiot on the bed. He threw himself on the floor.

"Hands stretched out at your sides, palms up!" I ordered, and he complied.

"Mark, can you get by me to cuff?" I asked.

Mark answered by sliding around me, grabbing the gangster's wrist, and in one fluid move twisting it behind his back as he dropped his full weight to his knees on the subject's back as if he'd practiced it a thousand times. Knowing Mark, he had. The gangster didn't allow us even the pleasure of hearing him grunt. Mark searched him, and he was clean. He then tore the sheets off the bed. Nothing. The idiot gangbanger had been playing chicken.

The kid in the room turned out to be his kid brother, and older brother the gangster was showing how tough he was. The kid brother was hysterical and had sunk to the floor in a sitting-up fetal position, rocking back and forth, sobbing, "Don't kill me for what my mama did! Don't kill me for what my mama did!"

Those sobs truly were heartbreaking. I can still hear them. The poor kid was in his pajamas, and tears streamed down his cheeks and dropped off his jaw. I was torn up. I tried to calm him down, not realizing initially that the guys in the black masks with the helmets and the submachine guns who just almost killed his brother were not going to relax him. I squeezed the remote microphone switch on my finger.

"Upstairs is clear. One in custody. Black male . . . any chance of sending a female agent up here? We've got a hysterical little boy." I realized that I had forgotten to breathe for about the last minute and a half. I was completely out of breath.

"Ten-four. We're code four downstairs," came the response.

Mark escorted Idiot down the stairs, and a female agent arrived almost immediately. As I walked downstairs I was suddenly aware that I had very little strength in my legs. I felt like I'd just finished a marathon. Once back in the living room, I covered the suspects during a cursory search until I was released.

I walked out the front door and squinted in the bright morning light. When had the sun come up? I spied Hughes, March, and Benedict sitting on a low wall near our Suburban, helmets in their laps, MP5s next to them. I took off my helmet and wordlessly walked toward them, the sweat inside my flight suit cooling rapidly in the light breeze. Under the flak vest, I was soaked to the skin.

"Hiding in the crapper, Steve?" March asked.

"Yup! Went in to rescue you and realized someone just forgot to flush," I answered.

I unzipped the pocket on the calf of my flight suit, retrieved my Blackberry, and powered it on, noticing that my gloved hands were shaking. I'd nearly shot somebody. On my last SWAT op.

A minute later, the phone rang. According to the phone, it was my wife, Michelle. I looked at my watch: a little after 6:00 AM. Her alarm had just gone off.

"Hello?" I said, trying not to sound hoarse.

"Oh, I didn't expect you to answer. You're finished already?" Michelle said in a chipper voice.

"We're done." I didn't, *couldn't*, tell her everything that had just happened, because I knew I couldn't adequately express it.

"Did it go OK?" she asked.

"I'm fine," I said, lying. I wasn't really fine. Something had happened that would stay with me a long time, yet something so "small" that I wouldn't even tell my friends. I knew that everybody on the SWAT team had experienced something similar or worse in their careers, most more than once. Nobody would bat an eye if I mentioned it.

Michelle's voice piped up again, sweetly. "We're out of cereal. Could you stop on the way home?"

"Sure."

2

Least Likely to Become an FBI Agent

WHEN I WAS in high school, had anybody shown me a video of my last SWAT raid, I would never have believed that the SWAT guy running up the stairs was me. I was easily the most unlikely SWAT candidate that I can imagine. I grew up a shy, polite, well-meaning, law-abiding, churchgoing kid. I didn't get beat up in the schoolyard, but neither was anybody afraid of me beating them up.

My dad, Lieutenant Kenneth Moore, was an investigator with the Office of Special Investigations (OSI) of the United States Air Force in San Antonio, Texas, when I was born. He had gone in to be a pilot, but weeks from graduation from "jets," a medical situation ended his military flying career. With years to go in his military commitment, he literally opened a catalog of jobs in the air force to determine what he was going to do with his life. The OSI intrigued him.

I'm grateful it did. He had no idea at the time, but he and I and our families were changed forever by his leafing through that catalog. I do not believe in coincidence. Why and how God moves

13

people in certain ways is beyond me, but I'm still glad Dad wasn't hungry when he perused that catalog, or I might this day be a chef. And I truly hate cooking.

My mom, Betty, had a movie-star face and figure and had been a cheerleader, homecoming queen, and so on, dating only the most eligible athletes at her high school in Salem, Oregon. Dad was not one of those guys. Not that he was ugly or insufferable; he just wasn't the quarterback of the football team, which was an important personality trait to my mom when she was eighteen. One thing Ken *was*, was persistent, and he apparently out-prayed the other guys. Mom, I think, didn't so much fall for him as just give in. Possibly against her will, she fell very much in love with him.

Dad was the grandson of a Baptist missionary and a Welsh coal miner and could not have come from a more conservative family. He seemed to excel at everything he tried. He was an Eagle Scout and faithfully attended Antioch Baptist Church (founded by his grandfather) and, later, Capitol Southern Baptist Church, where he met my mom. Mom was the granddaughter of an Arkansas circuit preacher, and her "Okie" dad had moved the family to Oregon to escape the dust bowl of the 1930s. They defined *poor* and ate mostly what they grew or killed. Her folks and the seven kids raised all sorts of crops on their tiny acreage in Salem and kept chickens for eggs and, well, fried chicken. Growing up, I was truly terrified by the realization that my mom, when she was a child, used to go outside, choose a chicken, and wring its neck, and an hour later would be frying it for dinner. This was what I grew up with, a mom who could take a whole bird and within a half an hour we'd be eating fried chicken and gravy. It was a way of life: with the exception of Thanksgiving, I have no recollection of eating anything but fried chicken at Grandma Bishop's house.

Dad was the number-one air force ROTC cadet at the University of Oregon in 1956, and a few weeks after he and Betty married the summer after he graduated, they turned their 1952 Chevy southbound for pilot training in San Antonio, Texas, stopping on the way at a thing called a "theme park" that had just opened the previous summer: Disneyland. Two years later, I was born, likely completing their bucket list.

After the air force, dad returned to Portland and applied for the FBI. When he was accepted, the family moved to Silver Spring, Maryland, and then to Phoenix upon his graduation.

In a tradition that is familiar to FBI or military families, Dad went ahead to his assignment and Mom returned to Oregon from our temporary digs in Maryland; packed up the house, two kids, and her single most valued possession, a Siamese cat, Bandit; and moved us to Arizona. As she was packing, she wrote dad a letter (remember those?) asking him about arrangements for the move. What should she do with her beloved Bandit? Dad, certain that Betty would understand a joke when she saw one, simply wrote, "Give the stupid thing away." When we arrived on the train (remember those?) in Phoenix, Dad looked around at the luggage and asked, "Where's Bandit?" You know how people say, "Someday we'll laugh about this?" Well, someday has never come for that one.

I was just four years old, and relocating to Phoenix was my sixth move. Our family motto was "Home is where the key fits." Moves across the country became second nature to me and my two-years-younger sister, Mary Kay. I eventually moved fifteen times before I went to college. The only families I knew who moved more than us owned camels.

Phoenix was a dream for my dad. He was making arrests, was in a small office with a minimum of bureaucracy, and had good cases. But he had made a serious mistake in the FBI Academy that caught up with him in Phoenix. When given the foreign language aptitude test, he did his best, just like Eagle Scouts always do. This was the worst thing he could have done. When the New

York FBI office convinced FBIHQ that they needed more speakers of the Czechoslovakian language to work counterintelligence in New York City, headquarters leafed through its language aptitude results and found Ken Moore at the head of the class. He was immediately ripped out of his ideal life in Phoenix and transferred to the Defense Language Institute (DLI) at the Presidio of Monterey to begin his study of Czech. (Years later, when I was in the FBI Academy, I was given the same language aptitude test. I was not an Eagle Scout—I tried scouting but quit after I earned my Sneaky Pragmatism merit badge. My failure on that test was so complete that I was brought before a board of agents to determine whether I had thrown the test. Of course, I had.) So, less than two years after arriving in Arizona, we had moved on to spend a wonderful year in Monterey, California, and then it was off to New York City.

I got to live in a fourth-floor walk-up in Queens, New York, and for me, the entire city of New York was one big theme park: riding the Staten Island Ferry and the subway, opening fire hydrants on hot, muggy days, and playing stickball in the streets. I still wonder why home plate and second base at Yankee Stadium aren't shaped like manhole covers. It was an adventure I still treasure. But after a year, Dad moved us to New Jersey for a more suburban setting.

After nearly half a decade with the New York field office, it was clear that Dad would be in New York for the rest of his career, but he badly wanted to go back West. To do so, he had to resign from the FBI, something he still regrets. We moved three more times in four years and ended up in Chicago. As I neared driving age, purchasing a car became my number-one priority. But I needed money to do that. I found a small fast-food restaurant that, rumor had it, would illegally hire fifteen-year-olds. This was a place where carhops still went out to the cars and made change with four-barrel, chrome, belt-mounted coin changers. This was not retro then. I worked every chance I got, and twelve-hour days were not uncommon.

I would have earned enough for a car more quickly had I not spent nearly all I had on flying lessons. Since my dad told me bedtime stories about flying in the air force, I was desperate to be a pilot. I had to work almost twenty hours to earn enough for one flight lesson, which meant that I could fly only once or twice per month. But after a dozen hours, I was finally released to fly solo on an evening when light snow flurries were starting to fall, visibility was four miles, and the ceiling was two thousand feet. But I was flying a plane all by myself. I was ecstatic.

After this milestone, I started paying more attention to girls than to airplanes, and my money began to go toward more ground-bound transportation. I bought a 1969 GTO with the Ram Air IV engine. Why Dad let me do that I will never know. Owning that car introduced me to every policeman in our little suburb of Buffalo Grove, Illinois. I was once stopped with a carful of friends as we were all cheerfully downing beers as I drove. This, however, was a different era. The policeman asked me to walk to his car with him. He questioned me repeatedly about what we were doing, how many beers I had had, and things about my life and high school. I know now that what he was doing was trying to determine whether I was a bad kid doing the usual thing or a good kid doing an unusual thing. Apparently he was sufficiently convinced that I was a good kid making a bad mistake that he simply followed me home and made me leave the keys to the car looped over the antenna all night. The world has certainly changed since then.

It was not until several years later that I realized the value of the grace that the officer gave me that night. He is one of those officers (and there are several) for whom I would like to throw a party at this point in my life. Had he and others done what I deserved, I never would have been in the FBI.

Somehow, I made it through into my senior year without getting arrested or screwing up my life in other ways. My dream of becoming an air force pilot took a huge step forward when I received a congressional nomination to the United States Air Force Academy. Once I had that on my horizon, I gave up all other options, notions, and life plans. But during a military physical, one eye was not 20/20, and my dreams of flying for the air force were dashed. I cannot put into words the devastation that one exam did to my life at the time. I fell into a yearlong depression, where partying and working on cars were about the only things I had the energy for.

At that point in my life, my dad was working for United Airlines, and we could hop airliners like hobos hop freight trains, so when my college-bound musical-prodigy sister jetted off to the West Coast to check out the Conservatory of Music at the University of the Pacific (UOP), I tagged along. Upon seeing the campus, the fraternities, and the distance from my depression and the Chicago winters, I decided that this would be my new start. At UOP, I entered a wonderland of fraternities, parties, and, oh . . . classes. I joined a fraternity, Alpha Kappa Lambda, almost immediately and within a semester had been named "Social Czar." The Social Czar was an elected office that wielded mighty power in a frat, because the Czar planned the parties. I dated popular girls and picked up a job with United Airlines at Stockton Airport to make ends meet. Things were great—except for my grades and the occasional skirmish with the police.

One morning at 3 AM, the fraternity was having an intimate party with about three hundred close friends. Our thin-skinned, light-sleeping neighbors complained to the police, who didn't just arrive, they invaded. I was the most senior (coherent) fraternity officer, so I went outside to negotiate. This was 1979, the heart of the disco years, and everybody in the world had hair down to their collars. I hadn't seen an ear for a decade. Except on the policeman I met outside, whose car was parked on our lawn. He had a flattop haircut and, looking back, he reminds me so much of the drill instructor in the movie *Full Metal Jacket*, R. Lee Ermey, that I have trouble remembering anything else about him. His opening gambit was likely intended to soothe me, but in my somewhat inebriated state, it instead incited me:

"*Son*, this party is over," he said. "'Son'?" I heard, my eyes turning red.

"No, officer, this party is not over," I argued.

The officer kept his cool. How he did it, I do not know. Had I been him, I would have punched me. "Son"—there he went again—"if the music isn't off in ten minutes, I will arrest everybody in that house as soon as they leave the front door."

I found this to be a ridiculous bluff. "That's ridiculous!" I snorted. "There's three hundred people in there." He was looking at me like a drill sergeant looks at a new recruit, but I foolishly continued, "How are you going to get three hundred people to jail? Where are you going to find a jail that can hold three hundred people!"

And then I delivered the coup de grace: "You don't even have enough handcuffs for three hundred people! How many pairs of handcuffs do you even have?"

He slowly moved his face toward me until his nose was almost touching mine, and he stared directly into my eyes in a very intimidating manner. "Son, I know I have at least *one*," and to prove it, he held it up to my face with one finger. There was no question in either of our minds whom that one pair of handcuffs was meant for.

I turned toward the house and screamed, "*Party's over!*"

During my last year of college, my easy life unraveled. I had run out of energy, sleep, excuses and options. It had all seemed like a game until my senior year, when the reality of graduation sobered me up. I had lost interest in studying law in my junior year—the same year

I had the pleasure of meeting that Stockton police officer—and I didn't really know what I wanted to do with my life after I graduated. Initially, I decided on continuing in a management training program with United Airlines, but in January 1980, just five months before my graduation, United began a massive contraction and all management training programs were canceled. I swallowed the bitter pill of continuing to work as a ticket agent and ramp agent ("bag smasher") until I could find more appropriate employment, but eight weeks before graduation, United laid me off.

Then, a funny thing happened. My shift at United had run from 5:00 AM until 7:00 AM, six days a week, for more than two years. At union scale, I made more in those two hours than my friends did in six hours at minimum wage. But I was paying a price I was unaware of. Living in a fraternity meant that lights didn't go out until after midnight on any night, and didn't go out at all on Friday or Saturday. I awoke every morning at 4:00 AM, returned to the frat for breakfast at 7:30, and then went to 8:00 AM classes. I would occasionally nap in the afternoon, but in actual fact, I was sleeping less than four hours a night for more than two years. (Airlines don't have holidays.) On my day off, Tuesday, I would usually sleep all day, thinking I had caught up. Most Friday and Saturday nights there were parties, so I frequently didn't bother to sleep at all those nights.

Now, suddenly, I was sleeping eight hours a night. It was if my mind suddenly cleared from anesthesia. Colors became brighter, my mood drastically improved, and alcohol was no longer necessary for me to enjoy a party. I could study and remember what I had read. I didn't fall asleep in class every day. I discovered amazing things; I didn't like how my girlfriend treated me, so we broke up. I discovered that most people don't go through life craving sleep. And I remembered that God had been a big part of my life until somewhere in high school.

I realized that I had let my relationship with God completely deteriorate. It was not that I had ever ceased believing in God, but I had certainly wanted him to keep his distance, because I had some things that I wanted to do that I didn't think he would approve of. Now, I had the chance to rekindle our relationship, and I took it, becoming involved for a short time with Bible studies on campus (boy, were they surprised to see me) before I graduated. In reality, the layoff was a blessing in disguise.

After graduation, I didn't want to stay in Stockton and try to hold on to college life, which I considered pathetic. I had nowhere else to go but home to my parents—which I found only slightly less pathetic. In fact, it was devastating and humiliating. I spent six months living at home, fighting depression, and sending out résumés sometime seventy-five at a time. A friend from United at Stockton got me a job throwing bags at Oakland Airport for the summer, so at least I didn't need to borrow money. When that job ended in August, my dad found a friend at Lockheed Missiles & Space, a defense contractor in Sunnyvale, who said he would get me an interview, but likely just for an hourly, menial job. But even that was better than the twin joys of daytime TV and self-loathing.

Lockheed was simply a miracle. After several interviews (which I thought excessive just for an hourly job in the document reproduction office), I was offered a job I couldn't have imagined: government security representative, a salaried management position. Lockheed made spy satellites, and the work was highly classified. My job was to monitor government-mandated security policy and practice for classified programs. I dealt with the organizations that ordered the reconnaissance systems, the "birds" that Lockheed built. I worked with the air force, the National Reconnaissance Organization (NRO), and the CIA in developing and implementing security plans to keep the design programs secret. It was interesting work, to say the least. I was making great money and I found that when I wasn't living in a frat, I could really excel at things I put my mind to. I was promoted three times in two years, and my salary nearly doubled in the same time frame. But at the end of those three years, I realized that the "gee whiz" element of the job had worn off, and my single enjoyable challenge was advancing in the department. I really didn't live for the job; I lived to leave every day. It was my first bout of career-ADD, a malady that afflicts me still. After a few years of doing the same thing, I began to yearn for something more. I looked in every direction, and my dad encouraged me to apply to the FBI.

The FBI? I thought. I might as well send in an application to be a Supreme Court justice. I knew that the Bureau received more than ten thousand applications per year to fill between zero and one thousand agent slots, depending on the economy and the need.

But Dad kept bringing it up. Finally, on St. Patrick's Day, 1983, as much to prove to him that I was noncompetitive as to actually try to get a job, I applied to be a special agent. I thought it would be interesting if I just got a *letter* from the Federal Bureau of Investigation, even if it was a rejection letter.

I did, and it was.

The reason for my rejection, they said, was "lack of full-time work experience." The FBI requires three years of such for agent candidates who do not have a law degree and are not CPAs. But I felt that they certainly had better reasons to turn me down. I actually did have three years of work experience, and I called the person who signed the letter in order to point that out to her.

To my stunned surprise, I got a letter two weeks later from the FBI scheduling me for a written exam. I was elated but still doubted that I had a chance. There were, according to Special Agent Karen Whitfield, twelve thousand applicants on the FBI's candidate list who had taken the written test and were currently *qualified*. The next fiscal year, they were going to hire only one thousand. Quick math brought me back to reality. Not having anything to lose, however, I took the test. I was told that I would have to be ranked in the top one or two thousand candidates to even be asked to interview. With those odds, I put the FBI out of my mind and went on with life.

I had found an awesome church nearby and had been asked to run the junior high school group. In July 1983 a dozen counselors and I took two hundred middle-schoolers to a church camp in the Sierras. On Thursday of that week, I got an "emergency" phone call. Remember, these were the days before cell phones, and there was only one phone at the entire camp.

The call was from my folks. Much to the surprise of everyone who knew me, I had nailed the written test. I was ranked 612 out of 12,000 applicants. I didn't know how that could be possible; I still don't know how that was possible. But I didn't want a recount for fear that they had made a horrible miscalculation.

The interview the next week with a panel of agents was not too difficult, but they did their best to trip me up and get me flustered. They pressured me on questions about my background in the fraternity, my mediocre grades, and why I thought I had what it took to be an FBI agent. I was shocked when I sailed through to the next phase. I started to allow myself to get excited.

But then I almost lost everything. I was called in by my recruiting agent, Whitfield, for a standard "big-picture" discussion of my background, prior to an extensive, detailed investigation by the FBI.

Whitfield slid a piece of paper under my nose, which said, in part, ". . . under penalty of perjury I swear and/or affirm that I have not . . ." and below that was a long list of a things that I had never done—*and some that I had*. It's not as though I had ever advocated for the overthrow of the government, spied for the Soviets, etc., but when it got to "illegal use of controlled substances," my heart stopped. I looked up at her and asked her to define "controlled substance" and then "illegal use." I began to sweat. I had smoked marijuana, and unlike a future president, I actually inhaled. I agonized over what to do for about ten seconds as I pretended to be reading the list carefully. Then, with nothing to lose (I thought), I started to sign the sheet—then stopped.

As casually as I could fake it, I asked her, "If somebody *had* done one of those things, would they still be eligible for the FBI?"

"It depends on which *thing* it is," she said, pretending that she hadn't heard that same question a hundred times. "For example, murder is a disqualifier."

"You guys are strict," I ad libbed, trying to break the tension only I felt.

"Murderers generally take too much sick leave," she parried.

"How about . . . marijuana? Just curious," I said, lobbing the question as if my curiosity was that of a social scientist.

"Well, it would depend on the amount of use and how long ago it was," she returned, knowing exactly where the conversation was headed.

"Hypothetically, what if it was about five years ago, and just recreational use," I said.

"Likely, that would not be a huge problem," she allowed.

"Really?" I asked incredulously.

"Unless, of course, you lied about it and swore in writing that you hadn't. That would be perjury, and we're really sensitive about perjury."

I looked down in horror at the sheet I had almost completely signed.

"Steve," she leveled with me, "do you think we could staff the FBI with agents with the creativity, curiosity, and life experiences we need if we disallowed everybody who had experimented with things like that?"

After a short pause, I blurted, "I think I screwed up the form."

"Then tear it up, and let's talk," she with a wry smile.

Three months later, I received a letter from the FBI offering me the position of special agent candidate. But you really do not consider yourself "hired" by the FBI until you have been given a date to report to the FBI Academy for training, known as the "class date." My class date was listed as December 11, 1983. The last sentence of the letter stated, "This matter is confidential and no publicity should be given to this appointment." Cool! It was already sounding exciting! Of course, as soon as I opened the letter, I began giving it as much publicity as I could.

3

Quantico Theme Park

ON SUNDAY, DECEMBER 11, 1983, I reported to the San Francisco field office of the FBI and was sworn in as an employee. Not as a special agent but as an employee. I wouldn't be an agent until I graduated from the academy—*if* I graduated.

At my swearing-in, the special agent in charge (SAC) of the San Francisco office was gracious enough to have a photographer standing by, and we took photos with my mom and my dad, my grandparents, my sister, my brother-in-law, and several people I didn't even know. When everything was over, an FBI agent drove me directly to San Francisco International Airport, where I boarded a nonstop to Washington. The agent even waited in the boarding lounge to ensure that I actually got on the plane. The FBI leaves nothing to chance. Apparently, years ago, an agent candidate had gotten drunk in an airport bar and missed his flight. It was a short career.

The cab ride from Dulles Airport to Washington, DC, that night was magical. There are few things more moving to me than the sight of the Washington Monument, the Lincoln Memorial, and the Capitol Rotunda, all spectacularly lit as you enter the city.

It was doubly so during that cab ride, knowing that I was entering the city to begin service to the United States for the next twenty-five to thirty years of my life.

Arriving at the hotel near Georgetown, I was too excited and hungry to sleep. I headed to the only place to get some food within walking distance, the hotel bar. The small, dark bar was nearly empty, though the Washington Redskins were playing the Dallas Cowboys on Sunday-night football. There was only one other person sitting at the bar as I watched the game, munching on peanuts and waiting for my nachos, and she was without any doubt a Dallas Cowboys fan. She had a nearly *debilitating* Texas drawl and screamed every time Dallas made a first down. I also noticed that she was good looking. She was blonde, about my age, and unmarried, according to her left hand.

We began talking about the game. Being an adopted San Franciscan, I was the sworn enemy of the Dallas Cowboys and mentioned that to her. She took the bait.

For the next hour and a half, we bet rounds on quarter scores, first downs, and sometimes even individual plays. Her name was Loren Thornton, she said, and she was an assistant district attorney from Corpus Christi, Texas, and she was in Washington for a conference. I, after being told to keep my FBI affiliation confidential, told her that I worked for Lockheed Missiles & Space and was out there for a program review. Loren was drinking Glenlivet single-malt scotch, neat, and *only* Glenlivet, thank you very much. I was drinking beer. Whatever was on tap was my brand. Due to the disparity in the cost of the drinks, it seemed to me that I had the most to lose financially. Fortunately for me, the Cowboys were having a bad night, and I rarely had to buy a drink; the 'Skins took the 'Boys 35 to 10.

A little tipsy, Loren and I bade each other good night. We had had so much fun that I thought she would think it odd if I didn't at least ask for her number or something. I saw no reason to, though, because I would be occupied for the next four months and she was returning to Corpus Christi. But when she didn't even bat an eye at that, my feelings took a hit. My first sacrifice for the FBI.

The next morning dawned snowy. I got dressed in my darkest suit, a crisp white shirt, and my reddest tie, went downstairs for breakfast, and began to anticipate the most exciting day of my life. That day, I would begin to become an FBI agent. I grabbed a five-minute ride to the FBI building on Tenth and Pennsylvania Avenue. I was in a state of absolute giddy disbelief as I walked down underneath the building to a large reception area on the first (underground) floor, just past where the bomb-blast deflectors are.

I found several dozen of my future colleagues, all with their luggage for the academy and all wearing dark gray suits, crisp white shirts, and very red ties. It was as quiet as a church.

After what seemed like hours sitting and standing around in that room, two agents entered, also dressed in dark suits, white shirts, and red ties. They were to be our class counselors. The forty-two of us were escorted into a classroom with sloped theater-type seating. I was one of the last ones to walk into the room, because I didn't want to be one of the first.

As I walked in, I scanned the class to see who I was about to spend the next few months of my life with. There in the middle of the room was Loren, the Cowboys fan from the night before. We made eye contact and smiled, realizing that we had started our friendship by lying to each other's faces.

After a brief orientation, we were off to Quantico, Virginia, and the FBI Academy. It would be an understatement to say that our class was eclectic. We had several Special Forces soldiers, military pilots, policemen, lawyers, a couple of CPAs, a third-grade schoolteacher, a psychologist, a CIA case officer, and several assistant district attorneys. There were only a few of us (like me) who had no specific specialty that was going to do the FBI any good. The class ranged in age from twenty-four to thirty-five. The vast majority were married and most had kids. I was the second-youngest in the class at twenty-five. And I felt like it. In the class of forty-two, I counted about eighteen women.

The initial physical performance testing was scheduled for the very next morning. It was a rigorous morning that left everyone exhausted. We were tested with sit-ups, push-ups, pull-ups, a sprinting relay, several other events, and a two-mile run. Points from 1 to 10 were awarded for each event. You were not allowed to zero any event, and you had to score an overall minimum—I believe 23 out of 50 possible points. At the end of the first exhausting day, our class of forty-two had been reduced to forty.

Each day at the academy was broken down into different curriculum blocks. Most days, we would spend at least three hours on the firing range with our pistols, shotguns, and rifles. Other days we stayed in the classroom, where we would study federal law, rules of evidence, basic investigation, about 250 federal laws that we were to enforce, abnormal psychology, FBI procedure, basic forensics, and so on. Several times a week we would practice defensive tactics, a combination of tae kwon do, boxing, wrestling, and getting our butts kicked. It was enjoyable, at least for the guys, but it was a rare day when at least one agent candidate didn't come back to class bloodied and/or black-eyed for our next classroom session.

With the exception of the firing range, my favorite place at the FBI Academy was a bar known as the Boardroom. It was not fancy in the least, but it did serve beer on tap and a range of well drinks. It was only open in the evening till eleven, but it was absolutely the best place in the world for me during those four months.

In the FBI Academy, there is at all times a session of what is known as the National Academy. The National Academy is a large class of police executives and high-ranking officers who come to Washington for an extensive law enforcement executive course. It is kind of a graduate school for cops. But executives or not, a cop is a cop. So in the Boardroom at any given time are probably thirty to fifty policemen and twenty to thirty FBI agent candidates.

One of my favorite memories of the Boardroom was the day that the Dirty Harry movie *The Enforcer* was playing on the big TV. In the movie, Tyne Daly plays Harry Callahan's (Clint Eastwood's) partner. Halfway through the movie, the two are engaged in a gunfight on Alcatraz Island against a group of thugs, and the cops and agents in the Boardroom were shouting at the screen at every mistake in tactics or shooting. At one point in the film, Daly dramatically takes cover to reload. As she does, she ejects the spent brass from her gun into her right hand and puts it in her pocket— an *unforgivable* sin in law enforcement. Instantly, an indignant, angry scream of "*No!*" erupted from fifty cops, and beer was thrown at the TV. It took several minutes for order to be restored.

During those first eight weeks I had begun to hang around with a tall, thin redhead named Patty Muller. I say "hang around" because dating among class members was strictly prohibited. However, within weeks of arrival, half the single people were dating the other half of the single people. Heck, even some of the married people were dating. The academy during those first few weeks was very similar to the proverbial "remote desert island." This was common for all classes, it seemed. The Bureau preferred a "don't ask, don't tell" policy.

But someone must've realized that Patty and I were dating. This became frighteningly obvious during one of our boxing classes, when I was taken from the guy I was paired with for boxing, who was about my size and weight, and was told to box *Patty*. This, I thought, was not a great idea. I should have known they were on to us the previous week, when we were instructed to wrestle each other. That time it backfired on them, of course, because I loved it.

However, *boxing* her was something completely different. Even though we wore the big gloves and the headgear, it still hurt to get hit in the face.

When the whistle blew to start our first round, I began tapping on Patty's headgear and thumping her lightly on the shoulder with my boxing gloves, halfheartedly. She was doing the same back to me. This went on for the entire thirty-second round, after which our boxing coach pulled me aside. He told me in no uncertain terms that he had been watching me and had realized that I was not putting anything into my punches.

"You need to give her realistic training," he ordered.

Through my mouth guard I mumbled, "Why camp a *girl* gib her reearistic craiming?"

"Because the people we arrest are called 'bad *guys*,' not 'bad girls'! Do you want the first time she's punched in the face to be in an alley when she's trying to arrest somebody? If that's the case, we won't know until she gets punched whether she collapses into a pool of tears while the bad guy grabs her gun and kills her or whether she can actually take a punch and stand up and defend herself!" He whispered so loudly into my ear it hurt. But what he said made some sense.

"What you're doing is essentially *killing* her!" he hissed dramatically. Then, he made a point that was, if anything, just as compelling. "And if you don't punch her, I will use you as my boxing demonstration partner for the rest of the month."

I had seen what he had done to his other "partners." It was less a demonstration technique than a method of unofficial discipline. I nodded.

I went back to Patty with a new plan in mind: hit her. I decided to start hating myself right then so that I wouldn't lose any time later. I didn't want to get beat up totally by the instructor, so I warned Patty that he had said I needed to punch a little harder. She nodded, but I'm not sure she understood what that meant. For about fifteen seconds I continued the tap-tap-tap sparring I had done previously. At that point, the instructor walked around behind Patty so that I couldn't avoid seeing him. He made direct eye contact with me with a grave and threatening stare. I knew what I had to do, and I took a deep breath and exhaled and took a jab at Patty's headgear about twice as hard as I had on any given punch yet to that point.

The speed of the jab and its unexpectedness caught Patty completely by surprise, and she wasn't quick enough to block it. I, too, was surprised by the force with which it caught her squarely on her right cheekbone. Her head jerked sideways, and I instantly felt like a punk. I had connected better than I wanted to. I leaned forward to see if she was okay, placing my gloves on each of her shoulders.

I never saw her glove coming at me until it was too late to duck. It was a classic right hook, and a good one, connecting with the force of an earthquake and making the world spin. I looked up at her and saw her dancing in a Muhammad Ali "float like a butterfly" footwork celebration. But she was blurry; I couldn't focus. I thought I had a concussion, but Patty showed me that my contacts had come out and were on my cheek. As I later learned, Patty had older brothers, and that wasn't the first punch she'd ever taken . . . or thrown.

But my favorite part of the academy was firearms. I reveled in shooting, even though it was something that I had very little prior experience with. We shot skeet, we shot shotguns, and we fired M16s out to several hundred yards.

I remember the day we were given our Smith & Wesson model 13 .357, brand-new, still in the box. It was the coolest thing I had ever gotten. The gun room itself was one of my favorite places in the academy. It smelled of Hoppe's 9, a gun-cleaning solvent that permeated every surface in that entire room. It had a sweet smell that was so intoxicating to some of us that we used to joke that if women wore Hoppe's 9 instead of Chanel No. 5 they'd get more action from the agents.

One of my better friends at the academy was Larry Page, who would go on to a spectacular career in the FBI. Larry had been a member of Delta Force, an army special operations team. He later became a member of the FBI's elite Hostage Rescue Team as well as a sniper. Years later, he transferred to Los Angeles and was my supervisor. He was better than me at just about everything at the academy, but I tried to close the gap. He was also friends with Patty Muller, and after Patty and I stopped "hanging out," she and Larry began "hanging out."

Unwittingly, Patty almost caused Larry and me to face an early departure from the academy. In the twelfth week, each class took a major firearms test: we had to qualify with firearms to continue in the FBI. Patty's shooting lane was between Larry's and mine. Neither of us could avoid noticing that Patty had significant problems with the shotgun. FBI shotguns fired either double-aught buckshot or monstrous rifled slugs that weighed an ounce apiece. With either load, the shotgun kicked like a mule, but with the slugs, it was worse. Nobody in the class enjoyed firing the slugs, because we ended up bruised every time. But it was much harder on hundred-pound women, for whom the blow was substantially greater by comparison; they tended to flinch before firing, making it almost impossible to put the round into the target with any consistency from fifty yards. Larry and I watched every day as Patty missed the "kill" zone in the target, or even missed the entire target when firing the shotgun.

Unfortunately, part of the crucial twelve-week test that determined your future in the FBI required firing two rifled-slug rounds from fifty yards and putting *both* of them into the target. If Patty had ever achieved that feat in the previous twelve weeks, it was news to Larry and Me.

The last firearms practice before the test was the Monday of the twelfth week; the following day we would have our test. Because Monday was simply another warm-up for the test, the targets were not important to Larry or me. Incredibly, each of us decided, and neither told the other, to fire one round into our own target and one round into Patty's target to build her confidence. Neither of us knew, either, that Patty had spent the weekend practicing with a firearms instructor and had gotten the shotgun down perfectly and was looking forward to proving it.

Unaware of all this, on the whistle Larry and I each fired one round into our target and then put our second round into Patty's target. To our horror, at the whistle ending the test, Patty had *four* rifled slug holes dead center in her target. Larry and I each had one. It didn't take an FBI agent to figure that one out. But they had one anyway: the instructor.

As usual, the instructor walked down the line to check our targets. Larry and I looked at each other frantically, realizing what we had done. We were terrified. Cheating could get you thrown out of the FBI. Even cheating for the benefit of someone else.

As the instructor passed my shooting position, he noted that I had uncharacteristically missed one round. He looked at me quizzically and asked, "Partying this weekend, Moore?"

I nodded nervously.

He then walked the short distance to Patty Muller and stared downrange at her target. Looking back at her dubiously, he asked, "How many rounds did you fire, Ms. Muller?"

"Only two, I swear!" she said in panic. She was truly confused.

By this point the instructor was also confused. He took two steps farther to Larry Page's shooting position and stared downrange, noting that the Delta Force Ranger had also missed the target—but only once. He looked back at my target, then at Larry's, then at Patty's.

You could almost see the exact moment he figured it out. "I would like to see Mr. Moore and Mr. Page at the bleachers at the back of the firearms range in ten seconds." This was bad.

This firearms instructor was a legend in the FBI. Benjamin "Big Ben" Sheffield had been a firearms instructor at the academy since it converted from swords to muskets. He could shoot skeet with a pistol. There was nothing I didn't think he could do with the gun. He was also six feet, seven inches tall and likely a good 225 pounds and spoke with a resonant bass voice. I believed that he could crush rocks into gravel in his baseball mitt–sized hands.

Larry and I jogged back to the bleachers at a good pace because of the tone we had heard in Sheffield's voice. We watched Big Ben walk into the central firearms control booth as we waited, discussing what had happened. Despite our concern, we could barely keep from laughing when we realized that we had both had the same idea at the same time. We were especially cracked up by the genuinely confused look on Patty's face when she found four large slug holes in her target. But as we saw Sheffield walking slowly toward the bench where we waited, we sobered immediately. He had a shotgun in his right hand.

"Do you suppose he's going to execute us?" Larry asked.

This didn't help: I started to giggle. I forced myself to think that he might actually execute us, and that calmed me down. Without a word, Benjamin stood directly in front of Larry and me. He held up the shotgun horizontally in both hands, chest high (eye level to us) as if he were giving us a profile view of the weapon. He then spoke to us much like a college professor beginning a dramatic lecture.

"This, gentleman, is a Remington Eight-Seventy, pump-action, twelve-gauge shotgun. It has an eighteen-inch hardened-steel barrel and a blued finish," he said calmly. "It has a single-bead front sight and a seven-round magazine, and it fires rifled slugs at a velocity of one thousand six hundred feet per second. But if either of you ever again does anything like you just did, I will make it into a necktie for you."

Neither of us was too sure he wouldn't do it.

"Get back on the line," he said sternly.

We had survived! To this day, Larry and I both believe that he was pleased that we had done what we had done but could not allow it to go unpunished. It is a desirable quality in the FBI for its class members to look out for one another. But I was relieved to be allowed to stay in the FBI after that.

Also around week twelve, a somewhat painful FBI tradition and rite of passage takes place: new agents are issued transfers to their first offices. This is when they find out where they'll spend the next few years of their lives. When agents "enter on duty" in the FBI, they are asked which of the fifty-nine offices they would prefer to be transferred to after the academy. This is known as their office of preference (OP). I now believe this question was asked simply for FBIHQ's curiosity and amusement. It does not mean you are going to be assigned to that office, and in fact many people believe that telling the FBI that you want to go to an office will guarantee that you will *not* be sent there.

I listed my OP as Sacramento, because I had gone out a few times with a pretty blonde water-skier at Sacramento State University just before I went to the FBI. Plus, it was not far from where my family lived and not far from where I went to college, so I would have a built-in group of friends.

The location of an agent's first office transfer is a source of unlimited angst among the trainees. For single guys like me it was difficult enough, but many in the class had wives or husbands and children. The stress is not relieved until week twelve; every few weeks, we would hear the screams from other classrooms as earlier classes received their "orders." No "upperclassmen" would tell us the drill, except to say that everyone in our class would get the letter at the same time. This only heightened the fear. We were on pins and needles.

On Thursday, March 1, about an hour before lunch, without any fanfare, in the middle of a lecture on abnormal psychology, our class counselor, an FBI supervisory special agent, strolled into the room holding a stack of envelopes. He walked slowly, wearing a sly smile, as if he had just heard the most important secret in the world. He was as conspicuous as if he had been holding a severed head. Nobody paid any more attention to the lecture, and any hope of education of any type for the rest of the day was lost. A loud groan and a few nervous comments were heard in the room. We were terrified. I expected our letters would be handed out to us so that during lunch we could bring them back to our rooms and find out where we were going to be living for the next few years of our lives and tell our loved ones. That would have been hard enough. But we weren't going to get off that easily.

"We have a little tradition here at the academy," said Frank Germann, our counselor, with the feigned civility and implied threat of Strother Martin in *Cool Hand Luke*: *What we have here is a failure to communicate.*

"We shuffle the letters, and everybody gets to open theirs in random order—in front of the class," he said, chilling the audience. Before opening, we were to remind the class where we transferred in from, where we hoped to be transferred, and where we thought we would actually be transferred.

As he spoke these words, he began to shuffle the letters. Another groan went up. Finished shuffling, he wrote on the whiteboard the words *farthest* and *nearest to guess*. What that referred to, we were told, was the agent transferred the farthest from his or her home and the agent who guessed the nearest to the actual office of transfer.

With that, everybody was asked to contribute a $5 bill, and each winner would receive approximately $100.

With the sensitivity of an executioner, Germann called the first name.

"Loren Thornton." My friend from Corpus Christi went to the front of the room and said that she wanted any city in Texas and believed she might get El Paso. She opened her letter nervously, took a long read, looked up, and quietly said, "Mobile, Alabama."

The disappointment on her face was obvious, but she finished with "Well, at least I know where that is, and it's not too far from Corpus."

She got a small round of applause. According to the official contest reference document, the *AAA Road Atlas*, the distance from Corpus Christi to Mobile was 684 miles, and she was in the lead for "farthest" transfer.

We slowly and agonizingly went through the next dozen names, each future agent reacting with excitement or disappointment. When Bill Clement realized he had been transferred to Erie, Pennsylvania, he pantomimed an elaborate samurai seppuku ceremony, kneeling on the floor and ritually disemboweling himself with an imaginary sword. Had I been transferred to Erie, the sword might not have been imaginary. Another close friend, Tim Beck, was transferred to Seattle, and he was ecstatic. He would find out upon arriving in Seattle that he was assigned to the Coeur d'Alene, Idaho, Resident Agency, the satellite office of a larger field office, which was heaven for him. There was no place on Earth he would rather be. Some people did get their dream transfers. Then it was my turn.

It was not easy to walk to the front of the class, and I had less riding on it than anybody. I still hoped for Sacramento, but I had tracked where previous classes sent their agents, and the two classes before ours had each sent an agent to Sacramento, and I could not believe that they would still have any openings there. The only office in the West that had not received an agent in several classes was Salt Lake City, Utah. I therefore told the class that I wanted to go to Sacramento but that I was sure I was going to Salt Lake City instead. Over the last four months they had noticed my love of good draft beer and laughed at the thought of me going to a theoretically dry state. I opened the letter and won $100. I was the first and only person to guess his exact office. Anton Kowalcyk (of late the legal attaché in Warsaw, Poland) won the other hundred dollars for being transferred from Portland, Oregon, to Alexandria, Virginia.

As the long winter went on and receded, with transfer orders received, spring in the air, and just a few weeks left in the class, our attention moved to the future. We had a lot to keep us busy besides the academy. I had joined the Quantico Marine Air Base Flying Club. They had a few Cessnas and Pipers and even a couple of surplus navy trainers. I hadn't flown enough hours to qualify for the navy planes, but I grabbed a Piper Archer any clear weekend. I brought my classmate Ricky Madera along frequently. Ricky had flown many different types of aircraft in the air force, from F-4 Phantom IIs to KC-135 aerial tankers to the NASA "Vomit Comet," a converted KC-135/Boeing 707 aircraft that the space administration used to provide weightlessness training to astronaut candidates. It created the weightlessness by diving to a substantial speed, pulling up into a steep climb, and then gradually "pushing" the aircraft over into a dive, reproducing the feeling you might feel on a roller-coaster, but amplified immensely. If the pilot pushed too hard, people were thrown into the ceiling, negatively weighted. If he or she didn't push hard enough, people sat on the floor with a queasy feeling in their stomachs, feeling lighter but certainly not weightless. There was a trick to getting perfect float-around-the-cabin weightlessness. Ricky had been a pilot of those airplanes and flown hundreds of weightless parabolas, so he certainly knew the trick. And he showed me that trick in the Piper Archer. We had riotous fun, going into weightless parabolas all up and down the Potomac River.

We would dive down, picking up a bunch of speed, and do a two-*g* pull-up, and then, once established on the up arc, Ricky would begin pushing over. We knew we were at perfect zero *g* when we could spin a camera between us and it neither floated toward the ceiling nor fell to the floor. It was immense fun. Sadly, we had to stay buckled in, so we couldn't float around the cabin. The only glitch in the whole routine was that the Piper Archer was a carbureted aircraft, meaning that it depended on gravity to deliver fuel to the engine. Each time we did a zero-*g* parabola (which lasted about twenty seconds), the engine would quit. But the engine started quickly once positive *g*s were applied. It was a great way to deal with the stress of the final weeks of the academy.

My parents came out for the graduation in March, and the ten members of the class who were the sons of FBI agents ("lega-cies") received our badges and credentials from our fathers. Our graduation took place one year and one week after I mailed my application to the FBI, an amazingly quick turnaround time as far as the FBI goes.

Surprisingly, the most significant moment of the academy for me came as I departed. During our time at the FBI Academy, we were not allowed to keep our pistols when we were not on the range. Each weapon corresponded to a small poker-chip medal-lion; when you went to the range, you traded your medallion for your weapon and then swapped back at the end of the day. This created a very simple inventory system for the range masters.

After the graduation, I went to the gun vault and waited as a class of trainees picked up their guns to go the range. As I had done so many times, I traded my gun chit for my Smith & Wesson Model 13. This time, however, I was in a suit, I was wearing my holster, and instead of walking to the range with an empty gun and loading it on the line, I was handed a box of fifty rounds of ammunition and allowed—told—to load the weapon right then and there.

As I did so and holstered the weapon, it occurred to me that as of that moment I was an FBI agent. An unfamiliar, cautious elation swept over me. I'd made it. I had done something that I had dreamed of but never believed down deep that I would ever achieve. Still, "strapping on the gun" drove home the reality that I was in a dangerous business, and theory and imagination were about to become reality. I had no idea what the future held, but as I walked out of the academy that day, I left behind schoolkid notions of what the FBI would be, unaware that it would be more than I had ever bargained for.

4

Not My Dad's FBI

FROM DAY ONE, the FBI was magic for me. My first day at an FBI office held the same excitement as when, at the age of six, I stood with my family waiting to catch the tram from Autopia parking lot to Disneyland. I sighted the federal building on State Street in Salt Lake City from several blocks away, much as I had spied the Matterhorn when we were still a mile from "the Happiest Place on Earth." My life's dream was about to come true. I was about to walk into an FBI office as a special agent. It was almost too much for me to take in.

The reality of being in an FBI office startled me. I expected to find an office that looked like the War Room in *Dr. Strangelove*. Instead, I found what appeared to be a normal office. I was introduced around, then shown my desk. It was hard up against a desk occupied by my first training agent, Baxter Christiansen. I looked around the desk for a phone and did not see one. Baxter pointed to the one on his desk and said, "It's right here." In 1984 in Salt Lake City, FBI agents shared phones: one for every two desks. This was incomprehensible to me. In my previous job, at Lockheed, I had one desk, two phones, and a secretary. Welcome to the federal system, I thought. At least the phone was push-button and not a dialer. I was then given the keys to my Bureau car, which was very exciting . . . until I saw it.

Sadly, it was not the Aston Martin DB6 I had hoped for. It was a 1978 Plymouth Volaré station wagon, "The car," according to Plymouth ads of the late 1970s, "that has America singing!" I had no idea what America could be singing, maybe "Queen of My Doublewide Trailer." I could only assume that it had once been a vibrant lemon-yellow color, but it had since faded into baby-food pureed banana. At that point in its history, the FBI still tended to order its cars with few options, if any. In "Hoover's Bureau," any standard AM radios, known in the Bureau as "good time" radios, were removed from the cars prior to being given to agents. My dad had told me the story of his time in Phoenix in the early 1960s when the first American Motors cars were delivered to the FBI with standard air-conditioning. Hoover initially ordered that the aircon on those cars be removed—nationwide—because it was not fair for some to have it and some not. Thankfully, the ones in Phoenix avoided the neuter-ing, but they were driven only by the most senior agents.

My Volaré would certainly not have offended Hoover's sensi-bilities. There were no carpets on the floor, only standard rubber mats. It did have an AM radio, but it didn't have an antenna, so that resolved any distraction issues. The windshield was cracked from top to bottom. When I started it, it sounded like a muffled Harley-Davidson motorcycle, and it purred on five working cylin-ders out of six. I made my decision then that nobody could see me arrive for interviews or investigations in this vehicle for no other reason than credibility. I would park a block away and walk to the location. I was then given my radio call sign. Salt Lake City was the FBI's smallest office at the time, with only thirty-eight total agents (before I retired, I would supervise a *single squad* of nearly as many agents), so elaborate call signs were unnecessary. I was simply "Thirteen." Great. Oh, the benefits of being the new guy.

The formalities over, I joined the entire office for a quickly called all-office briefing. The meeting was in a wide open bay, in which stood a large chart of the United States, perched on an easel. Just like in the old movies, it had pins in it, and a red line went from pin to pin. This was exciting. This was what I had expected to find in an FBI office. I was about to be involved in a case for the first time. It would be my first experience with the dichotomy of serious cases: excitement and glamour are often mutually exclusive.

The briefing set the stage. Christopher Wilder was a thirty-nine-year-old multimillionaire from Florida. He was a successful race car driver who had weaknesses for Porsches, photography, and young girls. The difference being that he didn't torture his Porsches or kill his cameras. He had been charged with and convicted of numerous sex crimes in his native Australia. He had also spent time in a mental institution, where he received electroshock therapy, before he immigrated to the United States, apparently able to conceal his past. Upon settling in this country, he made a fortune in real estate. On February 26, 1984, a female model hired to work the Miami Grand Prix (in one race of which Wilder was competing) disappeared. Eight days later, on March 5, Wilder's former girlfriend, a Miss Florida contestant, also disappeared. A number of other unexplained disappearances began to be linked to Wilder, and on March 15, he discovered that he was a suspect and fled. But he didn't *just* flee. Apparently realizing that he would eventually be caught, the sociopath Wilder embarked on one of the sickest crime rampages in US history. Rather than simply run, he set out on a cross-country trip to live out a sadist's ultimate fantasy, luring a different girl into his captivity every one to three days. Each of the women, ages sixteen to thirty-three, would be sexually tortured, at least one was methodically blinded, and all but two were brutally murdered.

On March 18, 1984, the exact day I graduated from the FBI Academy, Wilder was posing as a fashion photographer in a Florida shopping mall and lured a twenty-one-year-old girl to his car in the parking lot to "sign a release" to use photos he had taken of her for a nonexistent show. She was never seen alive again. Each time he kidnapped a victim, he used her car to travel to the next victim's location in a roughly westbound direction. Each time he found a new victim, he would leave the previous victim's car in the parking lot of the mall in which he obtained his next. He would dump the previous victim along the way, usually forcing the new abductee to help him dispose of the previous victim's body as part of the psychological torture. As I listened to the briefing, my ears began ringing. This wasn't a sick movie; this was real.

The pins on the maps in the FBI squad bay were the location of victims and therefore the direction of travel of Wilder. From the route, law enforcement could determine what freeways Wilder must have used and even predict his possible routes. Each day, they were looking for a different car, however. I was stunned by the evil that I was seeing on my first days in the FBI. Nearly thirty years later, I can still feel the horror with which I took in the briefings.

On March 29, eighteen-year-old Sheryl Bonaventura was taken from a mall in Grand Junction, Colorado, along a route that could have taken them to Salt Lake City. For the next three days, every FBI agent and every police officer who could walk was posted in the malls around Utah. I had in my mind the hope of saving a life, of stopping this man or at least being a part of the effort that did so. We were out in force in "soft clothes"—casual attire rather than our usual suits—throughout the malls from well before opening to well after closing.

We listened to our radios, hoping that if we had not seen him, somebody else had. There couldn't have been a mall in Utah that day that was not absolutely lousy with law enforcement. On Sunday, April 1, at the end of the day (an early day because the malls closed sooner on Sundays), the news was passed to all of us that a teenage girl had gone missing in Las Vegas that day. If he was in Vegas, he had gone through Utah. While it was a relief that no one was taken in our jurisdiction, it was a crushing blow that he had been there and we did not find him.

Wilder, for his part, continued all the way to the West·Coast, taking another sixteen-year-old girl out of Torrance, California, one of the only victims to survive. He then headed back east through New Mexico, taking more women, until in New Hampshire, near the Canadian border, two state troopers spotted Wilder as he pumped gas. When they approached, he dove into the car to get a .357 Magnum. In the ensuing gunfight, Wilder was killed. I felt he suffered too little—at least before he died.

Three weeks later, on May 5, the decomposing body of Sheryl Bonaventura, the victim taken from Colorado, was found near a freeway in southern Utah. Being low man on the totem pole, I was assigned to represent the FBI at the autopsy. Only a fortuitous and unscheduled out-of-town assignment saved me from working that autopsy.

The tragedies disturbed me, but I loved the work. I woke up before my alarm just about every morning, eager to get to the office. I even got rid of the Volaré in a very unusual way. David Spencer, the principal firearms instructor in Salt Lake, called me into his office and asked me if my dad had been an FBI agent. I told him he had. "Was his name Ken Moore?" he asked.

I was delighted. "Yes! Do you know him?"

"He and I were in the same class at the academy," he said, smiling. After that, David seemed to look out for me, something that I learned was part of FBI life: a never-ending loyalty to your friends. I'm not sure I always measured up, but I tried.

As the principal firearms instructor, David had a nearly new Ford Bronco sitting in the FBI garage that he used only for toting ammo out to the range. He made me a deal: if I would bring the ammo out to firearms in the Bronco, I could drive it as my car the rest of the time. In one short conversation, I had gone from driving the worst car in the office to my favorite. An FOA with a new car was unheard of.

The moniker "first office agent," or FOA, is the FBI term for "rookie." It is descriptive, ubiquitous, and pejorative. As I had been told more than once, the job of the FOA on a big case is to make coffee for the "real FBI agents" who are working it. Of the thirty-eight agents in the office, roughly 50 percent were very senior agents with decades under their belts, and the other half were FOAs with months under their belts. There was a reason for this unusual ratio: the office-of-preference list.

As you might guess, the lists are of different lengths depending on the office. There are, for instance, very long lists of agents who have Hawaii as their OP and very short lists of people who have Gary, Indiana, as their OP. The size of the lists for some offices, however, will surprise you. There is usually no list at all for sunny Los Angeles or picturesque San Francisco; you just change your OP to either of those and call the moving van. The reason for this is the high cost of living in those cities; cost-of-living salary adjustments do not make up the difference, so transferring to those offices represents a de facto pay decrease.

Salt Lake City, Utah, was the preferred retirement spot for a sizable number of FBI agents who were Mormons, members of the Church of Jesus Christ of Latter Day Saints. Because the list was so long and the office so small, only the most senior agents ever obtained their OPs to Salt Lake. FOAs came in directly from the academy and transferred out after two years, which meant that about half the slots in the office were occupied by sub-two-year agents and the other half with twenty-year-plus agents. It was not a good combination.

The two don't mix well. One group is as eager and wise as a litter of puppies, and the other group is predominantly (though there are exceptions) as jaded, burned out, and reluctant as an old, skinny stray dog that has been kicked once too often.

The agents that the FBI really depends on and, I would hazard a guess, do 90 percent of all the work that gets done are the agents with between two and twenty years of experience. These agents generally know what they're doing, have the energy to do it, and have not been beaten down so much by bureaucracy or simply exhausted by so much success or failure that they've stopped caring about making a difference. FOAs want to be them but aren't there yet; they simply don't have the experience.

The older agents are known as GS-13s (their pay-grade) or KMA agents. KMA stands for "Kiss my ass," as in "If you piss me off, all I have to do is submit my retirement papers and I'll be at home in an hour collecting a fat pension, and I'm only staying because this job gives me a car and a gun, so if you're here to tell me to do something I don't want to do—kiss my ass." (There are a significant number of senior agents for whom the excitement never wears off, but there are still enough burnouts that it is noticeable.) Not surprisingly, KMAs have the seniority to get the good cases, cars, equipment, and assignments, and FOAs get "nothing" cases and menial, unpleasant duties. But sometimes they're wrong about what cases are nothings.

One warm summer afternoon months into my time in Salt Lake, I was handed a "nothing" lead. A lead is simply an investigative request from another office. It can be anything from a records check to a request to locate and arrest a subject. The ones that said "Locate and Arrest" never went to FOAs, at least in Salt Lake City. That's the good stuff, and those are kept by senior agents. FOAs' leads say things like "Obtain birth certificate for John Q. Criminal and forward to New York office" or "Surreptitiously collect the trash from the cans at the curb of John Q. Criminal in Orem, Utah, and determine from contents whether he currently has strep throat." But the one in my hand said "Locate and Arrest." Simply because it was given to me, an FOA, I knew it was garbage before I even read it.

The lead read in part:

Title: LESTER CLEOPHYS RIGGS, AKA "SHORTY";
DAMIEN DURELL IVEY, AKA "D.D. YO" (Deceased)—VICTIM;
UNLAWFUL FLIGHT TO AVOID PROSECUTION (UFAP)—MURDER;
OO: BA

Synopsis: Request to locate and arrest subject LESTER CLEOPHYS RIGGS, AKA "SHORTY"

Details: Subject RIGGS is a member of the BOUNTYHUNTER BLOODS, a gang in the Baltimore area. On May 22, 1984, RIGGS attacked victim, a member of a rival gang, in an alley behind a local bar. IVEY was shot-gunned execution-style and died at the scene. According to confidential sources, RIGGS has fled to Salt Lake City where he is believed to have family.

SALT LAKE CITY at SALT LAKE CITY, UTAH:

Conduct logical fugitive investigation to locate and arrest subject LESTER CLEOPHYS RIGGS.

ARMED AND DANGEROUS

When I saw that the subject was a member of the Bountyhunter Bloods, a black gang, I knew immediately why I had gotten this lead. It was junk. A black gang member hiding out in Salt Lake City? That was unlikely. There were very few African Americans in Utah, and inner-city gang members did not come to Salt Lake City to hide out.

I called the agent in Baltimore for more details. He sounded truly convinced that Shorty was in Salt Lake City. But the agent also sounded young, maybe an FOA. I realized with embarrassing self-awareness that even *I* didn't trust FOAs. The last bit of information the Baltimore agent entrusted with me was that Shorty was allegedly scheduled to fly to New York that very night to try to broker a truce between the two gangs. The agent knew only that it was a nonstop flight from Salt Lake to New York. As I hung up, I was crestfallen. First, a black gang member hiding out in porcelain-white Salt Lake. Then, he was to take a nonstop flight from Salt Lake to New York. A nonstop between Salt Lake City and New York City? That was like a direct flight between the Vatican and Las Vegas. Who would even *have* such a flight?

It turned out that Continental Airlines would. Okay, so *one* thing checked out. I arrived at Salt Lake City International Airport and found the Continental Airlines desk. These were the years in which you could simply walk up to a ticket counter, show an FBI badge, and find out who was on a flight. I miss those days. Within minutes, I was told that there was a Lester Riggs booked on the flight.

I was astounded. Gang members didn't use their real names, did they? I had a dilemma. There was enough information in my hot little hands to call my boss, Danny Klaus, who held the dual roles of assistant special agent in charge (ASAC) of the Salt Lake City office and supervisor of the FOA squad. It was my *duty* to call him and say, "Danny, this is Steve Moore. Listen, I got a lead this morning about a murder suspect that an informant says is hiding out in Salt Lake. It looks like it's a good lead, and I may have him pinned down to a flight at Salt Lake International tonight. He's A&D, so I know you'd want some senior agents with me at the airport."

Then Danny would send five or six GS-13s to the airport to "assist" me, and they would interrogate me on the case, thank me for my assistance, take away the lead, and send me for coffee. (See, the FBI doesn't just do it to the police; they do it to each other. It's instinctive behavior.)

So I called. Not Danny, but my fellow FOAs Randy Dinwiddie and Matt Aagard. Randy picked up, and I talked fast. "Okay, listen. I've got a lead for an eighty-eight: UFAP-murder. And it may be the real deal. Get Matt and Kalb and get out here." I used the FBI case number for a fugitive investigation, 88, and the abbreviation for unlawful flight to avoid prosecution.

Randy asked the right question: "Why do *you* have the case?" If this was a good case, he knew instinctively, none of us would have it. Why should he waste an evening on a BS lead?

"They made a mistake—they thought it was a crap lead, but it may be real. The guy is supposed to take a flight out of Salt Lake tonight at five, and someone with his name is booked on the flight. I need you guys to help me out."

"On our way," he said.

While I waited for the cavalry to arrive, I met with the ticket agents on duty for Continental that night. They agreed that when anybody identifying himself as Lester Riggs presented himself for check-in, they would give me a subtle signal. I suggested rubbing the side of their nose, like in the movie *The Sting*. They liked that; they thought it was cool. This was super-agent-type stuff to them.

Matt, Randy, and Ed Kalb arrived in about twenty-five minutes, and we had an impromptu meeting in a vacant baggage claim area. Among the four of us, we had a total of nearly *two years* of FBI experience. What could go wrong? I briefed them on the case, and we set up a plan to take Shorty into custody if he showed. Our guess was still that this was not going to happen, however. We took our positions and waited. Incredibly, at 4:15, an African American man joined the line at the Continental counter. He carried only a briefcase, no suitcase, for a cross-country trip. He wore a button-down oxford shirt, khaki pants, and loafers. His hair was neatly cut, and he had the demeanor and look of an accountant. I was sure it couldn't be "him."

As he completed the transaction with the person in front of our unidentified black man, the ticket agent smiled as usual and then looked toward the next customer, and he was—black. You could see the realization on his face that *This might be him.* All expression went out of his face, and he stood staring at the customer for two beats before he asked for the man's ticket. He then executed what was likely the worst, most obvious subtle sign I have ever seen. Rather than brush the side of his nose, he appeared to be putting out a fire on his right cheek. I nodded, stood up, and made eye contact with Matt and Randy, who were on the next floor up at the top of the escalators next to the screening area.

Now, *we* were excited. I pulled my radio from behind my newspaper and transmitted.

"Matt, it's him."

"Okay, point him out when he gets to us," Matt replied.

"Matt, he's *the* black guy in the airport," I chided. "This isn't going to be complicated."

Riggs passed me, went to the second floor, and made it through screening. I hid the radio in my back pocket under my suit coat and trotted toward the concourse, where Riggs was looking for his gate. Matt, Randy, and I converged on him silently from behind, grabbing him quickly by the arms and elbows.

"Mr. Riggs, FBI," Matt said quietly into Riggs's ear.

Riggs, to say the least, was thunderstruck. But he didn't ask *What's this all about?* which led me to believe we were on the right guy.

"OK, OK," he said nervously but politely.

At the gate, Matt and I searched him for weapons and had him sit down on a gate chair. With Riggs's permission, Randy began to search the briefcase. Riggs turned out to be soft-spoken, polite, and educated. I searched his wallet and found a Utah driver's license, but the name wasn't Lester. It was Martin Riggs. I handed it to Randy, who went to a pay phone to call the office to run his name, as the radios were out of range of the office. In the next ten minutes we had the story: Martin was Shorty's uncle, and Shorty had convinced him to go to Baltimore in his stead to try to negotiate with the rival gang his safe return to his neighborhood. Shorty, he said, was still in Salt Lake City.

My excitement at that moment was hard to contain. We were going to get the fugitive! But then I realized what I was going to have to do, and my heart sank. I *had* to report this to the office. Now this wasn't just a "maybe" that we could explain away; this was a "certainty" that left no room for a gray area. With Randy watching Riggs, Matt and I walked to the concourse to discuss our next course of action.

"I should probably call the ASAC," I said, bouncing it off Matt. Matt had more than twice my field experience; he had been in the Bureau eight months longer than I had.

"If we call him, we might as well go home," Matt warned. It was my case to decide, but Matt made a powerful argument. "The GS-13s will arrest this guy, hand him to us for the paperwork and getting him into the jail, and then they'll go home. No fucking way."

Suddenly I had that same feeling I had had when I was talked into ditching high school and driving out to the quarry to swim, a mixture of excitement and dread. The excitement was intoxicating.

"Listen," Matt assured, "we bring a UFAP-murder subject back to the office in cuffs, and what are they gonna say? Bad dog?"

"What if he's not there?" I asked, playing devil's advocate.

"Then no harm, no foul—we could say we knew it was a BS lead."

"OK," I said, "let's go." I dismissed the memory that I almost didn't get to graduate because of ditching school for the quarry.

The decision was made. We were going to arrest the guy ourselves. We left in two cars: Matt and Randy, the two senior FOAs (an oxymoron), and Riggs, followed by Kalb and me. We drove to the location without speaking, wondering if we were about to enjoy the first major milestone in our careers, or simply end them. I was plagued with doubt. While this wasn't technically against any FBI rules, it was certainly against our bosses' rules in Salt Lake City.

The house that Shorty was holed up in looked like a movie set. It was located in one of the few seedy sections of Salt Lake City and reminded me of Norman Bates's home in *Psycho*, except that it was only a one-story, likely built in the 1920s. The windows were boarded up, and the plywood had been on the windows for more than one season, judging from the weathered appearance. But the front door, under a large porch, appeared operational. It didn't look like the house had any electricity.

We parked a block away from the house. On the hood of one of the cars, Matt, by virtue of his seniority, drew up our plan. Randy and Ed would cover the sides of the house. I would cover the rear of the house, and Matt would go to the front door with Martin Riggs. As I moved to the back of the house minutes later, still wearing my suit coat, each footstep crunching on the overgrown, ankle-high dead grass sounded like an avalanche. It was a bright summer day, and it was difficult for us to see inside the house through cracks or window openings. Once at the back of the house, I transmitted to the group that I was in place. Randy and Ed did the same. Matt then went to the front door with Riggs. Upon hearing their feet clunk on the porch, my throat seemed to tighten. This was a feeling I would experience innumerable times in my FBI career.

From my position in the back, I clearly heard the loud knocking on the front door. I heard Martin Riggs call Shorty.

"Lester, it's Martin!"

I then heard footsteps inside the house moving toward the front door. If my throat had not been tight by that time, it certainly was now.

"Martin?" came a voice from inside the house. "I thought you were on a plane!"

"Something happened," Martin replied truthfully. "I need to talk to you, it's important."

I heard the footsteps move farther toward the front door and distinctly heard the sound of a latch being opened. This was it. We were going to get him. I heard the squeak of the door as Shorty swung it open just a crack.

"So what the hell hap—"

He didn't finish the question before he saw Matt behind Martin. Matt lunged for the door, but Shorty had already slammed it shut and turned the bolt. With stark terror, I heard Shorty running directly toward the back door I guarded. Pointing my .357 at the door and getting a sight picture, I expected Lester to make a run for it right then. The doorknob turned and my heart stopped. But the door had been nailed shut, and when Lester pulled on it, nothing happened. He started to jerk mightily at the door and was able to peek out the door frame as the door came slightly ajar. That's when he saw me.

"Stop right there!" I screamed, not able to think of anything more clever.

He abandoned his attempt to open the door, and I heard him run back into the depths of the house. I tugged on the doorknob and knew that I could not open it without a crowbar. I made a radio call to the others, as if the preceding events had not been loud enough for them to hear. Randy and Ed reported that they could hear him moving around but had no idea where in the house he had hidden. There were no lights in the house, and the windows were boarded up. Likely it was nearly pitch black in there.

"Well, *that* sucked," Matt transmitted, completely redundantly. I had Randy cover the rear of the house from a corner where he could see both one side and the rear and went around to the opposite front corner, where Ed had moved to cover the front and the other side. Matt, with Martin in tow, strolled up to Ed and me and announced, "I've got a plan. Just go back to your positions. This will work." We did so, and I motioned Randy back to his original position as well, hoping that Matt's plan was good. Prior to the FBI, Matt had been a prison guard at one of the worst federal prisons in the country, the US Penitentiary in Marion, Illinois. Marion was the maximum-security prison that replaced Alcatraz as the home of the worst of the worst. Matt was, if nothing else, a student of human nature, and he seemed to understand Shorty very well.

Matt returned to the porch with Martin and began to shout into the house: "Shorty, my name is Matt Aagard! I'm an FBI agent! This isn't Andy and Barney out here." For some reason, I liked that. "In the back of the house is Special Agent Moore. Say hi to Shorty, Steve."

"Hi, Shorty!" I obeyed.

"Moore has killed two men in the last year," Matt lied. Wow—I was a badass! "Special Agents Kalb and Dinwiddie are on the sides of the house. Say hi, guys!"

Kalb and Dinwiddie said hi.

"Here's the thing, Lester. None of us are married," Matt explained. *What?* I asked myself incredulously. I couldn't wait to see where *this* was going. "I'm the only one with a girlfriend, and she's in New Jersey. We have no. Place. To. Go. Tonight. There is nothing that we would rather do than camp out here. In a little while, in fact, we're going to order a pizza."

That was Matt's plan? Tell him we were going to wait him out?

"Matt," I called on the radio, "That's it? That's what we're going to do?"

Matt replied matter-of-factly, "Yes, we're gonna order pizza. Remember, we don't bluff. Martin says Shorty doesn't have any food in there, and he might not have eaten at all today. When he gets hungry, he'll come out."

Five minutes had not gone by when we heard a voice from inside the house: "Uncle Martin! Is that really the FBI?"

"Yeah, son, it is," Martin said. A long pause followed.

"OK, I'm coming out. I don't have a gun!"

From my post in the back, I heard the front door open. Randy ran around to help Matt cuff Shorty, who was indeed hungry. We assured him he was going to get to the Salt Lake County Jail in time for dinner. But returning to the office after we dropped Lester off at the jail was *much* more frightening than the arrest had been. I called Danny Klaus's secretary from the jail and told her to show Danny the communication from Baltimore and tell him we had found the guy and arrested him. I told her to tell him it happened so fast we couldn't call for reinforcements.

After dropping Shorty off at Salt Lake County Jail, the four of us returned to the office, more terrified than we had been at the house. Our fondest wish was to get into the squad bay without being noticed. But as soon as we entered the office, Klaus stepped out into the hall, his face as grim as a marine drill instructor. And he had been a marine.

"Into my office. All of you." That was the last thing he uttered for the next twenty minutes that did not actively damage his vocal chords and our ears. Klaus went through every possible negative scenario as a result of our "irresponsible" actions. We were reminded of our short tenure in the FBI and our assumed incompetence, which, he said, we had proved "beyond a shadow of any doubt." He listed for us the people who could have been killed or injured as a result of our decisions. He didn't mention us.

So Kalb helped him out. "And I suppose we could have gotten killed, too."

"Who the hell cares about you fucking idiots?" was Klaus's response. He finally dismissed us with several graphic threats and reminded us that we were on probation. But no sanctions! We had gotten off with an (impressively ferocious) admonishment. We felt like we had new life. We decided that we were going to go out for beers to celebrate.

As I was completing the paperwork for the day and tying up loose ends, I had occasion to walk toward the senior-agent squad bay. Before I got to the door, I could hear Klaus speaking, and I did not want to be in his presence again for a few days, at least. But I was curious as to what he was telling them. I snuck up to the door, and for the next few minutes I listened as Klaus gave the GS-13s a detailed rundown on what "his boys" had done.

"Hell," he said, bragging, "they captured an A&D UFAP-murder subject." Our activities at the airport were—according to him— "good investigation," and we were able to "flip" Martin Riggs and get him to hand Shorty over to them.

"Listen," he told them, "if you guys ever have an A&D fugitive you need to grab, give me a call; I'll have my boys go out and get him for you." That night, over our beers, we toasted ASAC Klaus and thanked God we weren't still sitting around that house.

The next morning when I came in to work, I found a cigar, a box of bubble gum, and a note on my desk. They were from Klaus. The cigar, the note said, was congratulations on the arrest. The Double Bubble was earned because I was now "officially a gumshoe."

Klaus was a character. He used to walk into the squad bay every morning around nine, unlit cigar in his mouth, and loudly ask everyone in the room, "Are all the criminals in Salt Lake City locked up?" We would look at him and know the inevitable response: "Well, then what the *hell* are you doing sitting in here!"

If we weren't arresting people, Klaus insisted that we be out developing informants.

Informants are a necessary evil in law enforcement. They are people who are motivated in some way to give law enforcement information on criminal activities. The flaw in the arrangement is that no law-abiding person can be effective in providing information on criminal activity; because they're law abiding, they don't know what crimes are going on. So by necessity, you are dealing with criminals. This makes them very difficult to handle. They tend not to have the wisdom of Solomon or the character of Mother Teresa. And by virtue of what you're paying them to do, they've already proved that they will betray friends. Dwayne Monson was my first informant. Dwayne was a money launderer with whom I traded (his) freedom for information. Dwayne liked the excitement of being an informant.

But Dwayne, like all informants, was not easy to manage. The very first time I asked him to get me some information, I learned a lesson the hard way. I had heard through witnesses that a crook I was investigating had a Beretta semiautomatic pistol in his possession. This would be an extra felony count I could add. Also, it would be important to know if I eventually needed to arrest him. So I gave Dwayne his first task. A very simple task: "Get me the serial number on Ed Lang's Beretta 92SM." How hard could that be?

The very next Saturday I got a call at home. It was the FBI office switchboard, and they said they were talking to someone who called himself "Hot Air." Every informant had to have a code name. Hot Air was the code name I had given to Dwayne. They put the call through, and of course it was Dwayne.

He excitedly blurted, "I found the gun; I've got the serial number!"

"Dwayne," I congratulated, "good job!"

He read the number over the phone, and I told him to make sure he disposed of the paper he had written it on.

"Don't worry, Steve, I didn't write it down," he assured me.

"Did you memorize it?" I asked.

"I was reading the number off the gun, Steve."

"Dwayne! Did you steal Lang's gun?" I blurted.

Dwayne replied quickly, "No way."

That was a relief. I was afraid he had stolen Lang's gun; I could get in trouble if my informants committed a crime.

"It was in his truck, so I grabbed his truck."

Oh my God.

Before I could ask the next question, he continued. "Don't worry, I made it look like it was stolen," he bragged.

"Dwayne, it *was* stolen!" I shouted, fighting off the urge to vomit.

Dwayne obviously felt he had done a great job and his work wasn't appreciated. But he was able to return the truck to its original location, and Lang believed that he had been the victim of a vandal. I left it at that.

Informants cause other types of problems, too. I worked another informant who was known as a "truck stop cutie." A cutie is a prostitute who works at truck stops, bouncing from sleeper cab to sleeper cab turning tricks. Because of this clientele, she tends to know what stolen goods are coming in and out of an area as well as whether fugitives are moving in and out of the city. My truck stop informant gave me very valuable information several times. Among those tips was the location of a man wanted for theft from an interstate shipment. She described the truck he was driving, the new identity he had assumed, and where we could find the truck. I verified that there was a warrant for him out of Kansas City and that it was a felony warrant, and I set up the arrest. It went flawlessly, and my partner and I drove him to the Salt Lake County Jail.

But the story did not have a happy ending. Without notifying me, the court released the guy on bail, and he had figured out how the FBI located him. It was my truck stop cutie informant, "Easy Red." Within two hours of his release from jail I got a frantic call from Easy. She said that the man I had arrested had found her and beaten her up. I rushed out to the motel where she was staying, and she let me into her room.

What I saw appalled me. There was blood in the sink and all over the room, and Easy was holding her upper two front teeth in her hand. On the floor was a puppy that appeared to be dead. It was her only pet and likely the only thing she had any affection for. The truck driver had come over and punched Easy's lights out. Then he stomped on the puppy. Miraculously the dog turned out to be alive, but I didn't give it much hope to survive. I was horrified.

Easy needed to leave the motel immediately. She also needed to get some medical care and to bring her dog to a vet. Because time was of the essence, I went to an ATM and pulled money from my personal account. (Getting informant money from the FBI can take twenty-four hours or longer.) I drove her to a nearby motel, where she checked in, and then we dropped off the dog at the veterinarian (it survived with broken legs), while we took Easy to a free clinic. That was where I left her.

She had gotten her immediate needs taken care of and did not want to be in the presence of an FBI agent longer than she needed to. When I put in for reimbursement for the money I had spent on the informant, I was originally denied. I was told that I had spent the money without authorization and that because I had given personal cash to a known prostitute—in a motel room, without a witness—that I could be in serious trouble. Danny Klaus, who knew I had simply had to act in an emergency situation, verified everything I said, ran interference for me, and also got me reimbursed. But I never again met with a female source without a witness.

❂

Soon after arriving in Salt Lake City, I learned of something in the FBI known as a "special." Specials are cases that are so large and need so many resources that agents are pulled from other offices for periods from a month to a year to work the cases. The beauty of these cases is that they are all *big* cases. Even if you have a small role, it is a small role in a very exciting investigation. It is an ideal way for new agents to gain valuable experience in cases they might never see in their home office. I was always on the lookout for an interesting special.

In late September 1984, I learned that the FBI was canvassing for agents to spend the winter in Idaho or Montana working against a criminal organization I had barely heard of: the Aryan Nations (AN), a white supremacist group. Within twenty-four hours of applying, I had been chosen for the assignment and given another twenty-four hours to leave for Montana. That is not a long time when you're going to be gone for an entire winter and need to do things like store your car, forward your mail, and reassign your cases. But I got it done.

As I left Salt Lake City in my Bronco, stuffed to the windows with suitcases and FBI gear, I knew I was going on an adventure, but I didn't yet understand the extent of that adventure. When I returned to Utah early the next year, I was not the same person who had left.

5

I Didn't See the Train Coming

UPON MY ARRIVAL at the FBI office in Butte, Montana, a canvas went out for six volunteers to work undercover in Sandpoint, Idaho, near the Aryan Nations' main headquarters in Hayden Lake. We were told that this was a potentially dangerous assignment, but frankly my only fear was that I wouldn't be chosen.

Two weeks later, I was in Idaho's wood panhandle, fifty miles south of the Canadian border. I had arrived in the field just before midnight on a moonless night, pulling carefully off the remote road onto a soggy trail surrounded by unharvested hay five to six feet high. A two-cut rut ran through the center of the field, invisible unless you were actually on it. Though the truck sat high on its suspension, the tall hay all but obscured it as it sat on the glorified four-wheel-drive trail through the field. I couldn't be seen from the roads nearby and was essentially invisible.

This is an ideal make-out spot, I thought. It's Saturday night, I've got a new truck, and it has a bench seat. Perfect.

But on the seat next to me, sadly, was not the pretty girl I would have preferred but rather a Colt M16A1 assault rifle with a thirty-round magazine, a round chambered, and the safety on. Another thirty-round magazine rattled around on the floor mats as I drove up to the spot.

I pulled out a small pair of binoculars and confirmed with a quick glance at the objective that nothing had changed since I last saw it twenty hours before. One of the jobs of the six undercover agents was to covertly surveil Aryan Nations subjects and weapons caches. I was excited, on pins and needles.

Long hours passed, and every few minutes I checked the target—a self-storage unit with a roll-up door. Inside that miniature garage was a .50-caliber machine gun and ammunition. The fifty-cal is a military weapon designed to shoot down airplanes and blow sizable holes through tanks. The bullet it fires is one-fifth of a pound, one-half inch in diameter by almost two and a half inches long, and it moves downrange at more than two thousand miles per hour. It fires ten of those rounds per second and is accurate to three miles. That's two pounds of slugs per second. It is a horrendous, brutal weapon.

This particular weapon belonged to members of the Order—also known as the Silent Brotherhood—a splinter group of the white supremacist AN. Earlier in the year, the Order had used high-caliber weapons and submachine guns to begin a murderous crime spree. Just six months before I parked in the field, the Order had robbed an armored car of $3.6 million in Ukiah, California, carrying out the assault with military tactics and precision. Some of that money was used to purchase the .50 caliber in the shed. A .50-caliber machine gun would make quick work of any Brinks truck—or my Ford Bronco, for that matter.

Money was just a means to an end for the Order. Just four months before—June 18, 1984, to be exact—a controversial radio talk show host in Colorado, Alan Berg, was machine-gunned to death in his driveway after a show. As he arrived home, a man appeared from nowhere and opened up on Berg with a .45-caliber Ingram MAC-10, which had been converted to a submachine gun. Berg was hit approximately ten times in the head, shoulders, and face before the MAC-10 jammed. He was dead before he hit the ground. Berg, who was Jewish, had recently been sparring on air with members of various white supremacist groups, including members of the Order. The tactics and the weapon used immediately cast suspicion on the Aryan Nations.

At the Ukiah armored-car robbery, a Glock pistol had been dropped at the scene and was traced to a member of the Order. The Aryan Nations and the Order were both based at a military-style compound near Hayden Lake, Idaho, complete with an armed-guard tower that made it look like a German POW camp. The compound was just about thirty miles from where I was sitting. Within days of the Berg murder, the FBI acted, assigning dozens of agents to the Pacific Northwest to bring down the group. We knew that if the Order was going to initiate another attack or robbery, it would be preceded by retrieving the fifty. There was no way that this weapon could be retrieved in daylight without arousing suspicion.

I heard a noise. I clicked off the AM radio and quietly but quickly cranked the window the rest of the way down. I sat motionless, holding my breath, listening. But the sound of my pounding heart in my ears made it difficult for me to determine whether any sound was coming from outside of the truck. I heard only the wind in the trees and a faint unidentifiable hum.

Then a glow appeared behind my truck. A light was moving through the woods behind me, throwing eerie, deep shadows from tree to tree. It wasn't coming from the direction of the road, but the rapidly moving shadows made it difficult to determine where it *was* coming from. I was not supposed to be relieved from my shift. Nobody was supposed to know I was here. If the other agents were going to head that way, they would have radioed. I slowly reached for my M16.

As I did, a painful, disorienting, terrifying sound erupted like a bomb in my world—a painful, angry noise that made it impossible to think and caused my entire gut to vibrate—and it seemed to be no more than twenty yards from me. At that second, a blinding burst of white light—almost blue-white—lit up the interior of the Bronco like a flashbulb. I squinted but was instantly night-blinded. In the rearview mirror I saw only the blinding ball of light that appeared to be very close and moving closer. I grabbed my rifle and decided to bail out of the passenger door, but before I could, I realized the sound and light were coming from that direction. I threw myself onto the bench seat, out of sight.

I carefully raised my head to peer out the window and saw a huge freight train rolling along toward my Bronco at a good clip. The sound blasted through me again—a train horn? As the train curved past my right door at high speed, the horn silenced momentarily, the noise of the train itself seeming to catch up with it; then the horn went off again, causing me to jump just as high the second time. The train flew by, seemingly an arm's length away. The truck rocked from the turbulent air, and I struggled to catch my breath. The force of the passing freight hit me like a linebacker. I felt as if the wind had been knocked out of me. As the train rattled off into the distance, I struggled to regain my composure. The only good news I could find was that I had maintained bladder integrity.

A wave of relief and giggles swept over me, followed closely by a wave of self-recrimination and embarrassment. Real FBI agents don't get scared to the point of nearly soiling themselves just because a train goes by. Who was I kidding? I wasn't a real FBI agent. In the suburbs where I was raised, most train tracks were simply abandoned relics of a time when the public had the patience to sit and wait for a mile-long freight during the morning commute. In the field, even with all the rain, an experienced agent would have realized that here, where trains are the lifeblood of the timber industry, rarely do tracks go unused. And these tracks were silver, not rusty. A real agent would have known the train schedule and looked at the tracks.

I took a deep breath, staring toward the target once again. I feared I was an agent only because the FBI seemed exciting and I could talk my way through interviews better than other guys. I was the guy they shouldn't have taken. Had they known me, I would never have gotten in. I was sure I wasn't what FBI agents had to be. I was not fearless. I thought that by graduation from the academy, the FBI would have made me into a real agent. All through the academy, I wondered when they would teach me how to defend myself against anybody with just a flick of my wrist. I wondered when I would learn to know at a glance everything that had happened at a crime scene. When were they going to make me such a trained weapon that I didn't have to be afraid of anything? When would I stop being just a normal guy and become an FBI agent?

I put the binoculars to my eyes again; still nothing going on at the shed.

I hadn't reached that point yet. I thought I must have been doing something wrong. I must have missed that day at the academy.

Days passed, and the cadence of the case increased. A week after staking out the shed, I found myself motoring through a Currier & Ives scene. The *clunk-whir* of the wipers blended with the muffled crunch of tires plowing through deep snow. The paradox of experiencing such beauty and at the same time dealing with such ugliness was almost disorienting. The snow was falling so heavily that I could see only a few yards ahead, and the wipers were creating snowy, stratified drifts on the edge of the windshield.

I love snow. I love driving in snow, and I love the fresh, crisp air it brings. But right then, it was a distraction. Like a kid in third grade looking out the window and daydreaming while the teacher delivers the lesson, I was having trouble concentrating on the deadly business in which I was engaged. Then the FBI radio in the Bronco kicked in:

"Is he on Bennett?"

"No, McTavish. One south of Bennett!"

It was as if the teacher had just called my name and asked what I was doing. In third grade, I always had Walter Mitty daydreams: I was a fighter pilot or an FBI agent engaged in some exciting, dangerous act of heroism. I would play in the snow pretending to be a secret agent. Ironically, there I was, an actual agent on a case, doing the things I had dreamed of, and I was imagining I was out playing in the snow.

Driving through the quaint town of Athol, Idaho (population 350), does nothing to dispel the feeling of being in a Christmas card. Athol's quaint two-block-long downtown consists of ancient two-story brick buildings and an antediluvian train station that in any other town would already have been converted into a museum. In my cynical mind, I wondered where the town's name came from. Was Athol named for a mean-spirited Idaho settler with a lisp?

The radio once again interrupted my reverie and took me back to the reason I was there:

"Left turn signal for a westbound on Smylie . . . RIGHT turn! Right turn! He's eastbound now on Smylie! He signaled left and turned right!"

Crap, I'm *west*bound on Smylie, aren't I? I think. He's coming right back at me.

"OK, I gotta turn north here, or he's gonna see me again. Can you keep him, Rob?" I ask.

"Yeah, but I'm getting a little toasty here. This guy's really hinky! Hey, Barney, where y'at?"

"Two behind you, Rob. Don't go with him on this turn, I'll take the eye and you can bail out. He hasn't seen me in a while."

Surveillance language is a mix of easy slang and verbal shorthand. When calling out the movement of a car you're following, there's not time for extended explanations. Much like Mandarin, the meaning and urgency of surveillance slang change with inflection and tone. "Hinky" is one of those great words that can mean so many things based on the situation and the inflection of the user. It can mean "suspicious," "furtive," "paranoid," "astute," "scared," or "obsessed." For instance, "He's really hinky" is an observation that the subject suspects he is being followed, whereas, "Man, is he hiiiiinkyyyy!" indicates that the subject not only is suspicious but is looking directly at the agent who is speaking (who, by the way, is embarrassed that he got so close).

Likewise, "burned" means to be completely detected by the person you're following. There are various degrees of burned, and there are many words to describe the extent to which an agent has been burned, much the same as Eskimos have dozens of words for snow. For instance, "I'm feeling a little toasty here" or, "Does it seem warm out here to you guys?" means the agent likely feels he has been too close to the subject for too long and is hinting for someone else to take the eye, or primary surveillance position closest to the subject. "I am hot" is not bragging. It indicates extreme "detected-ness," as in "The bad guy just flipped me off. I'm *totally* hot." If the subject is "hot" or "burned," he's on to the surveillance.

The most egregious form of burning, of course, is the infamous bumper-lock, the act of traveling so close behind the subject that a rear-end collision is a distinct possibility. This results in the rare situation where both the agent and the subject are referred to as "burned up." It is either the surveillance technique of an idiot or a new agent, or an intentional means of letting the bad guy know he's being watched, a.k.a. intentional harassment/warning.

Most of the time, important surveillances are conducted with the help of an aircraft. The aircraft makes it easier for the grounders, or ground surveillance teams, by keeping the eye on the vehicle and providing traffic control for them. Such as: "He's pulled to the side of the road! Everybody sit down!"—in other words, "Pull over and park where you are." Pulling to the side of the road is a common trick used by those who suspect they are being followed. If there is no plane, the surveillance team has to stay close enough that they have to pass the subject of the surveillance or be seen pulling off. Do that twice, and the bad guys have the description and even license plate numbers of the following surveillance cars. An airplane, used well, can keep the surveillance team blocks or even a mile away from the subject.

The lexicon of a good, experienced surveillance team is really an art and puts truckers' slang to shame. For example: "OK, he's four back in the number-one left pocket at a stale red-ball, two ahead of a mini-Winnie. You've got three for cover. Careful, number one's a motor."

Translation: "The subject has reached a red light that is likely to go green at any moment. He's the fourth car back from the light in the leftmost of two left-turn lanes. He is behind a van-based motor home, and the first vehicle in the turn lane is a motorcycle traffic policeman, and the nearest FBI agent is well hidden, three cars behind the suspect."

Certain phrases are easily understandable, however. Conveniently, "Oh shit!" still means "Oh shit!"

The man we were following, Gary Yarbrough, was truly hinky that day. The astute, "knows what he's doing" kind of hinky. He had spent the past half hour driving in unpredictable course changes and generally engaging in dry cleaning—trying to identify and/or lose a surveillance. And he was good at it.

Gary Yarbrough had every reason in the world to believe that the FBI would be following him. He was an ex-con who had recently robbed an armored car and a bank and bombed a synagogue. He'd also provided logistics and weapons for the murder of Alan Berg. The only thing he didn't know was how much the FBI knew. But by this point he certainly knew we knew *something*.

In 1984, Sandpoint and the surrounding areas were wildly remote. It was the ideal place for those who did not enjoy the benefits of society to hole up. There was no way to infiltrate the city and surroundings with covert FBI agents for very long without their cover being blown—though that rarely stopped the FBI from trying. Our plan for six of us to covertly surveil different locations and people and blend into the community to gather intelligence lasted about ten days, when we noted that we were being followed far more than we were following anyone else. The word was out: the FBI was in town.

Yarbrough and others discovered Sandpoint, Idaho, in the twentieth century; fittingly, the town is a few hundred miles from Butch Cassidy's Hole in the Wall hideout, as the crow flies. A small-time felon from Arizona, Yarbrough became entranced by the charismatic, paranoid ramblings of "Pastor" Richard Butler, founder of the Aryan Nations in Hayden Lake, Idaho, and, later, Robert Matthews, who founded the AN splinter group the Order.

Matthews was a young, handsome Mormon who believed that "racial purity" was the key to the survival of the United States. He used his charisma, looks, and contagious enthusiasm to attract a group of capable, racist young men who wanted to do something more effective for the cause than just march in parks in Nazi uniforms. These were not knuckle-draggers. These were intelligent, though dangerous and sick, people. Matthews based the goals and plans for the Order on a book called *The Turner Diaries*, a novel by William Pierce, written under the pseudonym Andrew McDonald.

In this fictional diary of one Earl Turner, Pierce outlines the overthrow of the US government by Turner and a group of like-minded men known, unsurprisingly, as the Order. The book begins at the moment the US government confiscates all civilian firearms as the result of a law written by—wait for it—a Jewish congressman. The book includes a truck-bomb attack on FBI headquarters in Washington, DC, an eerie presage of the later attack on the Murrah Federal Building in Oklahoma City by Timothy McVeigh, a known fan of *The Turner Diaries*. Complete "racial cleansing"—genocide—and the execution of whites married to blacks round out the light-hearted tome. The book also postulates the funding of the group by the use of armored car and bank robberies. Matthews had been using the book as both instruction manual and script.

Matthews's Silent Brotherhood sought to emulate *The Turner Diaries* and began, as described in the book, with bank and armored car robberies, the bombing of a theater and a synagogue, and, of course, the murder of enemies such as talk show host Alan Berg. Their war chest at this point contained $3.6 million, and their stated goal was the establishment of a white homeland that would consist of the states of Oregon, Idaho, Washington, and Montana. Certainly they had no chance of succeeding, but with time on their hands, a festering hatred for Jews and nonwhites, and several million dollars to spend on weapons and explosives, they could kill a lot of people while failing. Yarbrough was the group's sergeant at arms and was believed to hold all their weapons and much of the money.

A wiretap told us that this particular morning Yarbrough was going to take his daughter to a medical specialist in Spokane, Washington. Yarbrough's daughter required kidney dialysis, but coded phrases in the conversation led those on the wire to believe that Yarbrough might have been using the trip as camouflage for other meetings or activities. Was he meeting with Matthews? When Yarbrough's jacked-up 4x4 popped out onto the road right on schedule, he was in the company of not just his daughter but also his wife and another child. The presence of the family could simply have meant further camouflage for his activity. We laid well back as the Yarbrough SUV negotiated the snow-covered streets and stoplights of Sandpoint before jumping onto I-95, direct to Spokane, about an hour away.

Twenty minutes into the trip, Yarbrough turned abruptly from the road into the town of Athol. For the next thirty minutes, he executed a series of unexpected turns, wrong-way trips down one-way streets, and red-light running to determine whether he was being followed. If he was just going to the hospital, he was going to a lot of trouble. We did our best to stay well back, but the weather had kept the surveillance plane grounded, and we were on our own with poor visibility.

What we didn't know was that Yarbrough believed there was a warrant out for him and was prepared for an attempt to arrest him at any time. He never traveled unarmed, and he had no intention of surrendering—especially in front of his family. Aryan men don't do that. They fight to the death for their "kindred folk." On this day, unbeknownst to us, Yarborough carried with him a MAC-10 submachine gun identical to the one that killed Alan Berg. It looks like an Uzi but is smaller and can be concealed under a winter coat. Like all the members of the Order, he had sworn that he was not going to be taken alive.

The agents following him were similarly well armed but unaware of Yarbrough's mindset and suspicions. Finally, Yarbrough left Athol, and forty-five minutes later, we were approaching the Spokane city limits and discussing what to do for lunch after Yarbrough went into the hospital. At that moment, Yarbrough veered onto a freeway off ramp at the last second, barely making an exit.

He did it so suddenly that Rob, the closest agent to him, couldn't make the exit in time. Barry White, a KMA agent from New York with the call-sign "Barney," was far enough back to make the exit with him, and I followed second in line. But Yarbrough ran the stop sign at the end of the exit, and we were suddenly well behind him. Trying to catch up in the heavy snow, we slid all over the place and lost sight of him. We were in nowhere land—no stores, no service stations, just spectacular, snowy pine forest. We sent another agent, Moose, ahead to the hospital in case Yarbrough showed up, and we split into two directions and tried in vain for about five minutes to find him.

Barney spoke up first, over the radio: "Hey, Steve, it's not worth it. We know where he's going."

"Barney, he can't be too far up here. What if he doesn't go to the hospital?"

"Then we tell them"—the case agents—"we lost him. If they wanted him followed so bad, they should have put more than four cars on him."

Actually, Barney was right. But wisdom comes with experience, and I didn't have any of that. The thought that I was following a truly bad man was intoxicating to me. It was an exciting game. The upside was possible glory, and I didn't see a downside.

In reality, most of the equation was downside. Sometimes on fourth down it's smart to punt. Rob got off the freeway at the next exit and was coming from the other direction on the frontage road, hoping to see Yarbrough go by. But the trail was cold. The chances of finding him now were almost nil. Once you're more than a minute behind the subject on a surveillance, you might as well be there on a different day.

"Rob, I'm just gonna drive around for a few minutes and see what I can find. I'll take south of the bridge," I offered.

Rob replied, "I'll take north."

Barney was strangely quiet on the radio.

"Hey, Barney," I queried, "where are you?"

The reply came a few seconds later. I imagined that his microphone had fallen on the floor and he was retrieving it by the cord. "I'm a ways down the road. I'll just sit here and see if he comes by."

I heard Styrofoam squeak in the background during his transmission. Most likely he had found a drive-through McDonald's in the next village, and the delay was him taking the lid off the coffee cup without spilling.

Rob and I began our more-or-less methodical search. Between the two of us, we had nearly a year of field experience as FBI agents. And there we were searching in a snowy forest for an armed man who was, for all intents and purposes, one of the most dangerous men the FBI was investigating at that time. In a way, that's the kind of mental attitude the FBI recruits for: an overriding personal confidence. The danger, of course, is that sometimes the confidence overrides experience. The snow seemed to be picking up, and the defroster was barely keeping pace. I was wearing a red ski jacket and using the sleeve to keep the driver's side window clear. Under the ski jacket I wore a sweater, and under that was something the

Bureau liked to call a ballistic protective undergarment, or BPU. Most people just call them bulletproof vests. But they're not always. Depending on the caliber of the bullet, they sometimes just slow them down a little.

I U-turned in the road and noticed that the sharp profile of the tire ruts I had just left in the snow were already being softened by covering snow. These tracks would be covered up in five to ten minutes, max, which meant that any visible tracks had to be less than ten minutes old. At the next four-way intersection, the stop sign was already covered in snow. While deciding which way to turn, I noticed recent tire tracks in the snow on the road perpendicular to mine.

"Rob?" I asked.

"Go."

"Rob, what's your twenty?" I radioed, requesting his location.

Rob drawled back, "I'm not completely sure. But I think I'm way east of you right now."

No one was out in this weather if they didn't have someplace they *had* to go. Since getting off the freeway, I'd seen no other cars but Rob's and Barney's. But here were tire tracks that couldn't have been more than five minutes old or they would have been completely covered.

"Rob, I'm south of the bridge. Did you drive south past the bridge?"

"Nope."

Turning left, I began following the ruts. Certainly, I thought, I'll never find who they belong to. Or I'll find that they go to a VW parked in somebody's front yard. Most likely, though, Yarbrough will show up at the hospital at any second, and I'll feel a little silly. But I've got nothing else to do right at this second, and I'd rather be doing this than sitting outside a McDonald's sipping coffee with Barney. As I continued down the road, I contemplated how we would explain losing Yarbrough to the boss.

I radioed the agent at the hospital. "Hey, Moose, has he shown up yet?" I asked.

"No. No sign."

I was beginning to feel like we'd screwed up big time. If he knew he'd lost us, he could have been anywhere doing whatever he intended. He had beaten us.

The tire tracks in the snow made an abrupt left turn into the woods.

I stopped in the middle of the road, cranked down the window, and looked at the trail as the cold invaded the truck. The trail was big enough for my truck, but barely. Too narrow to be a road or somebody's drive. Likely it was an abandoned logging trail or a fire road. What were the odds that someone would drive down such an unlikely path on a day like this? But the ruts were clearly visible and recent. A vital part of me did not want to drive down that road. But the part of me that wanted desperately to be a real FBI agent lobbied for going down the road. I wondered, should I make a radio call to tell the others where I am and what I'm doing? I turned onto the fire road/logging trail, thinking, what are the odds he'll be down here anyway?

Looking back twenty-five years later, I realize that the part of me that said *Don't drive down that road* was the real FBI agent. The voice telling me to follow the trail was the excited, inexperienced twenty-five-year-old, unaware of how much he was risking, and for how little, in the grand scheme of the investigation. If I had been the experienced agent I wanted to be, I would have called to tell the others where I was and what I was doing. But at the time I thought, Nah, they'll just tell me to come on back.

I crept down the road at a walking pace, the truck swaying from rut to rut, far enough to tip the rearview mirrors into the branches of the trees on either side of the trail. After going about a hundred yards, I stopped and looked ahead. I couldn't see any exhaust from a vehicle, no movement, no color except for the brown and green of the fir trees and the white of the snow. I continued for another hundred yards or so and still saw nothing. My self-doubt began whispering into my ear; I was sure I was wrong. A little sheepishly, I decided to give up, find a place to turn around, and go back. I couldn't back up the entire way; I needed a wide spot in the trail. Up ahead, the trail seemed to tee into another trail, and I thought I could do a three-point turn there.

I got to the *T* and swung left, concentrating on not putting my right front fender into a tree, and went about a truck length, and as I threw the truck into reverse and looked over my left shoulder to back up, I realized that I was driver's door to driver's door with Gary Yarbrough. We were so close I don't know how our driver's-side mirrors didn't smack each other. His beard and his hair were redder than in the pictures. His hands were below the window frame and his window was down. I saw in a glance his wife's face and the faces of his children, all deadpan. Not a scintilla of emotion showed on their faces. Yarbrough, however, glared at me with apparent hate. I was semiparalyzed.

Three weeks later, as a fugitive, Yarbrough would write a letter to members of the Order in which he described the incident. He described me, my red ski jacket, and my brown Ford Bronco. After driving down the logging trail, he had parked facing a direction from which he could see back down the trail and turned off the engine, holding the MAC-10 in his lap and sure he had lost the surveillance. He watched as I slowly drove through the woods toward him, and he pushed the weapon's safety to FIRE. As I pulled even with him, Yarbrough suspected that he was being blocked in for arrest; a maneuver a con like Yarbrough would know as the "felony car stop." The entire time we were opposite each other, his gun was held below the window line pointing directly at me, and I never saw it. Had I opened my door, he said, he would have machine-gunned me. Maybe some rounds would have hit the vest, but all it would have taken was one in the face to make the vest superfluous. Because I hadn't notified anybody of where I was, it would have been a while before it was determined that I was missing and certainly hours (at least) before I was found. Nobody would have heard the shots in the snow-muffled forest through rolled-up windows and the drone of their own heater fans.

Yarbrough told his followers/associates in his epistle that the agent who pulled up next to him "looked like a fine young Aryan." He explained that it would have been a tragedy to kill a "misguided kinsman," even if he did work for the "Zionist Occupation Government" (ZOG). He also said that I looked "terrified" and that this let him know that I wasn't a hardened ZOG agent bent on arresting him. He claimed that he had shown me grace. Of course, when this letter made its rounds and eventually into the hands of the FBI, and then my surveillance team, I had to laugh at that description. With false bravado I angrily demeaned Yarbrough's characterization of me being "terrified." But now, all these years later, I have to tell you that I can still see the look on his face, and I'm still scared at what almost happened.

Dry-mouthed and startled, I carefully put the Bronco back in drive and headed down the road, keeping the Yarbrough truck in my rearview mirror. I saw the plume of exhaust when his engine restarted, and I watched as he drove out the way he came in, this time directly to the hospital, it turned out. What is that saying? "Good judgment comes from experience, and experience comes from bad judgment"? Only six months in the FBI, and I was already gaining experience.

"Hey, guys. I found him," was all I could say into the radio without my voice breaking.

The Aryan Nations case was an octopus with tentacles reaching from Seattle to Los Angeles to the East Coast and just about everywhere in the Northwest. Our little team in Sandpoint had a mushroom's view of the case, even though we had at least one of the main players in our sights. After the hospital trip, our surveillances picked up, but Gary disappeared.

The Bureau feared that he might be meeting with Aryan Nations members somewhere in Idaho or Montana or that fugitives might be meeting with him in his home in the woods. Our six-man team was told to procure a pickup truck and uniforms from the US Forest Service and drive out into the woods to Yarbrough's home and figure out just what was going on. Two Coeur d'Alene agents and Moose drove to the house. Less than a half an hour later, the truck pulled back into the dirt parking lot in front of the ski lodge we were renting to use as lodging and headquarters. Moose entered the room without his usual smile.

"He shot at us," he said quite matter-of-factly.

As they had approached Yarbrough's property, they found that a log had been rolled across the road to deny access. Moose got out of the cab to move the log when pops were heard. Looking in the direction of the house, they saw what appeared to be Yarbrough firing at them from a position near the garage, about a hundred yards away. Quickly beating a retreat, they ensured that they were not being followed and returned to the lodge.

Clearly, Yarbrough could not have made a worse mistake. He had opened the door for us. Now warrants could be sworn out, his remote hideaway could be searched, and, we hoped, much evidence collected. It seemed to me that time was of the essence. A surveillance perimeter was set up around Yarbrough's property. I was tasked with going up with our pilot and taking the aerial photos of Yarbrough's house. Though not an FBI pilot, I was a private pilot, and they felt I would be the best choice, since having an extra pilot aboard is never a bad idea.

From the air, I actually laid eyes on the property for the first time. Sitting in a small, idyllic clearing of fir and aspen was Yarbrough's A-frame. A large ditch ran behind the house, and in the driveway was the dark SUV I'd followed so many times. I snapped photos as my pilot, Special Agent Garth Sheets, flew several circuits around the property. This being 1984, we returned to Coeur d'Alene and had the photos developed in the most expeditious way that the FBI in Coeur d'Alene had at their disposal: one-hour photo. Once the photos were done, we got back in the plane and returned to Sandpoint.

The FBI's Hostage Rescue Team (HRT) had been called up from where it had staged in Boise, Idaho, to lead the raid. Things were getting exciting. HRT was a high-speed, low-drag paramilitary team of former special operations military types who had become FBI agents. As a new guy, I was somewhat in awe of them. The word was that HRT wanted to go in under cover of darkness, as so much time had already passed that exigency did not demand an immediate hit. That much I could understand. What happened next caused me to shake my head.

Tom Philips, the assistant special agent in charge of the Butte office of the FBI, strode into the room. It was rumored that the Butte office of the FBI existed only because the FBI didn't own Devil's Island and it needed a place of exile. While not true of every agent there, Butte had been the penal colony of the FBI. It mattered little that some agents fought to get to Butte for the hunting and fishing; it remained a disciplinary post. To be a manager in Butte was something like being a trustee in a gulag. I soon learned that Philips was not an exception to this rule.

The first time I saw Tom was my first day on the AN case. All agents assigned to the case were mustered at the Butte office, as it was at the time the headquarters office for Idaho, Wyoming, and Montana, where this case was largely based. Dozens of FBI agents, along with police and sheriff's deputies from cities embroiled in the case, milled about in the turn-of-the-century stone office building that was the FBI office. We awaited a briefing on the case from Rich Manson, the case agent. But before Rich could get up and tell us about the case, ASAC Philips wanted to make a few welcoming remarks (that is, take some credit for the investigation). Rich stood around awkwardly for several minutes waiting for Tom to come out of the bathroom. When he did, I was embarrassed. For the entire FBI.

Tom bore a striking resemblance to Alfred E. Neuman of *Mad* magazine fame. But he didn't look as sophisticated. That day, he wore a western snap-front shirt and a bolo tie, both of which unfortunately accented his petite chest and arms as well as his basketball-round gut. His jeans hung off his hips, accentuating his gut and blocking sight of the too-large oval rodeo buckle holding the ensemble off the floor. I was horrified. I silently begged God for this to be a joke. I can't describe his cowboy boots to you, because as my eyes were following the outfit down that direction, it became painfully obvious that Tom had neglected to secure his Levi's zipper, and it had bloused out about two inches wide, allowing about half of his shirttail to protrude from the opening like . . . well, it just protruded.

A stunned silence engulfed the room, which Tom might have mistaken for respect. He strode to the front of the room and turned to face the audience with his hands on his hips and his feet about two feet apart in his best Barney Fife stance. But all eyes were fixed on the zipper. Snickers started. Muffled laughter was heard. People left the room red-faced, but Tom continued to speak. I have no idea what he said. Grown men were weeping before he finished. He strode out of the room, confident that he had made an impression. Yes. He had.

It was not until 10:00 PM that night that the raid briefing began. An outer, tactical perimeter would be established by non-HRT agents. Once this perimeter was established, HRT would tactically enter (crawl into) the site.

By 11:00 PM, it was eighteen degrees Fahrenheit outside. An overcast sky prevented any moonlight, and the forest around Yarbrough's house was as dark as the inside of a closet. A 360-degree perimeter was established around the house. I took up a position lying in the tall grass, which had been exposed during a recent thaw. The house was brightly lit inside; the yellow light and the smoke emanating from the fireplace reminded me of a Christmas card, minus the snow.

HRT's entry to the scene was nearly impossible to detect, even though I knew they were coming. For nearly an hour, they silently belly-crawled closer and closer to the house, tightening the noose. Once they were in position, there would be no chance for Yarbrough to escape. This, I thought, was what the FBI was all about: doing things that other organizations simply did not have the resources to accomplish. This was the FBI at its best.

That's when I heard the car. Lying about five feet from a double-rut car path, I realized it was headed right toward me. Within seconds, my position was completely lit up by headlights. I tried to put my body as deeply in the grass and frozen ground as I could and hoped the car would not run over me.

The road into the raid site was barricaded, and agents were stationed to monitor any approaching vehicles. There was no way a random car could enter without being stopped. But no calls had been heard from the checkpoint. Were they OK? The car passed, and as it did, I risked turning my head to see what it was. It was a late-model brown Plymouth four-door with a whip antenna on the trunk. An FBI car. This was not part of the operational plan. This was improvising. This might be bad news.

The car drove to within twenty yards of the front door of the house, and two men exited the vehicle. One was Tom Philips. Two men then exited the house from the front door, facing Philips from about twenty yards away. One appeared to be Gary Yarbrough. The next sound I heard was from Philips's megaphone.

"This is the FBI! We have you surrounded. Come out of the house with your hands up." It was an almost comical send-up of old gangster movies.

At that point, the men who had just exited the house ran back inside and slammed the door. Philips had unilaterally decided that the whole thing was taking too long and that the element of surprise was overrated. The reason he was assigned to Butte was becoming crystal clear.

Mere seconds later, I heard a faint scraping sound from the direction of the house, and the radio crackled to life: "Someone's going out the back window!" At that point, all bets were off, and I realized a critical flaw in the planning. If somehow—say, because the ASAC gave away the element of surprise—the occupants of the house got outside into the darkness and tried to break through the perimeter, we could do little about it, because with agents 360 degrees around the house, the noise in the bushes might have been Yarbrough or it might have been your best friend, and you wouldn't know which until you shot him and checked the body.

An hour went by. Noises were heard in the trees, in the bushes nearby, and in the brush all around the house. On the radio, agents were calling out bogies from all compass points, but there was little that could be done. Stress levels were off the chart. Every agent was silently cursing Philips. With children and Yarbrough's wife in the house, the situation did not lend itself to an assault. At approximately 1:00 AM, HRT made contact by bull-horn with a woman in the house who claimed to be Yarbrough's wife. She said that Gary was not there. She allowed the agents to approach the front door, and by 2:00 AM, HRT had negoti-ated entry into the house, entered, and searched for Yarbrough or any AN members. None were found. Within a half an hour, Yarbrough's escape was confirmed by radio. The frustration in the HRT operator's voice was palpable. We were called up to the house. Agents emerged from the bushes and converged on the house to conduct what was, to this day, the most successful search I have ever been a part of.

The inside of that house was the stuff of search warrant dreams. We found a hidden room off a walk-in closet on the second floor. As sergeant at arms of the Aryan Nations, and with $3.6 million to spend, Yarbrough had amassed a frightening collection of weap-ons for the group. I could not have been happier to be assigned to the search team for that room. The experience helped me really understand the immensity of the cases that the FBI dealt with.

Hanging from the ceiling were rows of new, unfired automatic and semiautomatic weapons. They were expensive, brand new, exotic, unfired weapons such as 9mm Heckler & Koch MP5s, the weapon most associated with Navy Seals and FBI SWAT teams. A large picture of Adolf Hitler was posted in front of candles, near a stack of police scanners. Weapons were all over the place, along with thousands of rounds of ammunition and ammo cans full of who knows what. In the corner of the room, however, was an incon-gruous sight. An overstuffed recliner sat in a corner segregated by clear plastic sheeting on all sides. An intravenous pole stood next to the chair. It was the room in which Yarbrough's daughter took her therapy. Next to the shrine to Adolf Hitler.

The search of the room took hours. My section included half a dozen military ammunition cans. I knelt down and began to go through the cans. The first one I opened contained a fist-sized wad of wire attached to small metal tubes. I dug farther, trying to figure out what these things were. Then, with sudden concern, I recognized them. They were blasting caps, detonators for high explosives. They appeared to be electric detonators, so they could be ignited by small currents of electricity, as small as the irritating snap of static electricity you conduct when you touch a door knob (or an ammo can) in a very dry environment, like the inside of a heated house in winter.

I carefully took the caps out of my lap and called over other agents to get advice on how to handle them. I placed them several feet away, and while the other agents discussed what to do with them, I dug deeper into the ammo can. Under the blasting caps was a small homemade cardboard "shelf." I pulled it out and found what appeared to be several blocks of modeling clay a little larger than bars of soap. With horror, I recognized them immediately. Plastic explosives. C4. I had stumbled onto a bomb lacking only a power supply and a switch. Yarbrough stored this thing mere feet from his daughter's therapy chair. A bomb that size would have leveled the house. Explosives Ordinance Disposal (EOD) experts were summoned from Fairchild Air Force Base near Spokane.

With the blasting caps and C4 separated for their (and my) own good, I continued with the ammo cans. Most of the rest contained ammunition. But each one was like opening a Christmas present. I had never had as much curiosity or trepidation about opening packages.

Eventually, I came to a fairly large can. Opening it, I was stunned to find a MAC-10 submachine gun/pistol. I pulled the gun from the can and examined it to determine whether it was loaded or not. Immediately I noticed that it had a brass .45-caliber shell casing wedged between the bolt and the breech. It was a classic "stovepipe" jam, so named because it appears that the gun has sprouted a chimney. The empty casing took the gun "out of battery," so it was not in immediate danger of firing, but I "safed" the weapon by removing the magazine, which contained several unfired rounds. I remembered almost immediately that the disc jockey from Denver, Alan Berg, had been murdered by Aryan Nations members wielding a .45-caliber MAC-10. The crown of the barrel and the breech gave off the unmistakable aroma of detonated gunpowder. It had jammed while firing, and had not even been unloaded or cleared, much less cleaned. Therefore, it likely still bore valuable fingerprints, and I handled it carefully. I marked the gun with my initials, indicating who had recovered the weapon, then called over the search team leader and showed him the MAC 10. Several days later we would learn that this was the Berg murder weapon.

On the deck of the house, agents found an entire case of dynamite, within feet of a child's tricycle. The dynamite, stored outside, had begun to deteriorate, or "sweat" nitroglycerine. The extremely unstable nitroglycerine pooled at the bottom of the crate of dynamite. Unlike plastic explosive, just about any jarring or shock (such as being hit by a tricycle) could have set off the entire case of dynamite, which would certainly have left a large crater where the house once stood. When the EOD experts arrived from Fairchild Air Force Base, they wouldn't risk even moving the dynamite from the deck. They literally burned it in place (along with a sizable portion of the wood deck), which was the only safe way to dispose of it in that condition.

In a theme that would continue throughout my career, the search, and the most exciting and memorable events in my career, occurred between midnight and dawn. With the search of the hidden room completed by about 4:00 AM, I went back downstairs to find a truly bizarre scene. A dozen agents were milling about, logging evidence. HRT operators were rotating into the warm house from twenty-degree temperatures outside. Some exhausted agents sat on a couch trying to stay awake. Yarbrough's wife Betty did not really know what to do. Her husband was somewhere at large in the cold woods wearing only a T-shirt, her kids were sleeping on the living room floor, and dozens of federal agents were systematically disassembling her house and, likely, her life as she knew it. At a loss, she decided to do what Gary would have wanted her to do: resist. So she grabbed a 35mm camera with a flash attachment and began wandering through the house taking photographs of all the agents, taunting them.

Instead of objecting, the agents posed for her. They helped her, ensuring she had the camera set right and the flash timed carefully so that the photos would come out well. They gave her pointers on flash photography. They stood together and even put their arms around one another's shoulders in the pictures. When the last photo on the roll was taken, she began to rewind the film in the camera. One of the HRT guys offered in a very gentle voice to help her with the film. Now used to the agents being helpful with the camera, she handed it to the HRT agent. He immediately popped open the back of the camera and pulled out the film like unspooling a long ribbon, destroying the entire roll. He closed the camera gently, handed it back to her, and then in a very stern, raised voice, said, "Now make some coffee!"

I don't know what switch flipped in her brain right then, but she went from defiant Aryan woman to dutiful hostess without a word. She proceeded to make pot after pot of coffee for the agents, then carried mugs around on trays serving the men who were searching her house. She became truly charming. I just made sure that I wasn't the first to drink the coffee.

Though I didn't know it at that moment, this was the beginning of the end for the Order, if not the Aryan Nations. With the finds we made in Sandpoint, we had enough evidence to obtain warrants for the remaining members of the Order. For the next few weeks, we continued to search for Yarbrough, Matthews, and the other members. This involved several flights in the FBI Cessna Turbo 210 aircraft assigned to the case with a pilot who would become a longtime friend, Ryan Jones. Ryan was possibly the best pilot I'd ever flown with and certainly the best instructor. Along with another pilot assigned to the case, Norm Kemp from Los Angeles, he taught me formation flying over the course of several off-days on the case.

A few weeks later, the next shoe dropped on the case. On November 24, Gary Yarbrough had been lured to a motel in Portland, Oregon, with Bob Matthews by an FBI informant. Agents and SWAT teams set up on the motel covertly during the morning rush hour, and all went well until a local TV broadcast about the FBI activity at the hotel near the airport. Matthews was watching TV.

Suddenly, before the agents were ready to assault their room, Yarbrough jumped out a second-floor window, directly into a group of FBI SWAT agents. Matthews ran out the front door of the room onto the second-floor walkway, sprinting toward the stairs. A running gun battle ensued in which an agent was shot and Matthews's hand was mangled by an FBI shotgun blast.

Little more than a week later, the FBI located Matthews in a cabin at Whidbey Island, Washington, and after a two-day stand-off and gun battle, the cabin caught fire, apparently ignited when an FBI flare landed on its roof. It was never clear whether Matthews was killed by gunfire or the fire, but his body was found in the ashes. The rest of the Order were rounded up one by one, until only a few were remained outstanding. Eventually, *all* of the Order members were captured, tried, convicted, and sentenced. The sentences ranged from 40 to 252 years, with one man sentenced to life without parole for the murder of a Missouri policeman who was gunned down trying to arrest him. Yarbrough was sentenced to 75 years. (He remains in prison. Two Order members, David Lane and Bruce Pierce, the driver and the shooter in the Berg murder, have already died in prison.)

For all intents and purposes, the case was over, and I returned to Salt Lake City with the New Year.

6

I Swear I Didn't Know She Was Dead

I DIDN'T FEEL that I was released from the Aryan Nations case so much as I was paroled from it. It was one of the biggest reliefs of my life. I felt I had not relaxed in three months. I had at times thought that I might not get home from that one. As winter gave way to spring and skiing gave way to golf, I became aware of another FBI special that I could not pass up.

I had been trying to get into the FBI Aviation Program on at least a part-time basis. Salt Lake City needed a copilot, but I didn't have enough flight hours. Finally, I was given the opportunity to take a five-week assignment as an FBI copilot trainee in San Juan, Puerto Rico. This would get me officially into the program and provide five weeks of flying in a tropical paradise while getting the experience I desperately needed. This was certainly the polar opposite of the Aryan Nations special. Instead of arctic cold, we had tropical humidity. Instead of constant danger, I was flying in blue skies above the bad guys. This was truly a working vacation for me. We flew just about every day, worked hard, and did a good job, but it was a needed respite.

This special was very similar to the AN case in one way. The Puerto Rican separatist group Los Macheteros (Machete Wielders) were intent on having a section of US territory—in this case, Puerto Rico instead of the Pacific Northwest—secede from US control. They, too, had begun with a series of multimillion-dollar bank heists and followed it up by striking out at adversaries and the US government. Among their other violent acts, they had killed American servicemen in two separate machine-gun attacks.

The adventure of this special became evident within minutes after touching down in the airliner in San Juan. I had been told that an agent would meet me at the baggage area to pick me up. He did, grabbing my bags and urging me to hurry because I was due in the air in a few minutes. There was no way they were going to send me off on a four-hour surveillance minutes after I arrived, I thought. But I didn't want my first act in front of the other pilots to be a refusal to fly, so I went along with the plan.

The agent had double-parked in the red zone outside of baggage claim. He tossed my bags into the trunk, handed me an aircraft headset, and drove like a maniac to the other side of the airport. Driving up to a parking lot, I could see on the other side of the fence that a Cessna R182 aircraft, with the telltale FBI antenna package installed, sat with its engine running.

The agent who picked me up told me, "Ricky's waiting for you."

"Ricky?" I asked. "Ricky Madera?"

"He says he was in your academy class."

I ran to the plane holding my headset, excited about what Ricky had in store. I had not seen him since the days of flying zero-g parabolas over Virginia. I jumped into the airplane buffeted by the prop wash.

With a familiar big smile, he shouted, "Get in—we're late!"

I climbed into the seat. Late for what, I had no idea.

Within minutes we were several thousand feet above the ocean between San Juan and the US Virgin Island St. Thomas, and I was mesmerized by the scenery. With a moment to talk after we leveled at cruise altitude, Ricky explained that we were en route to St. Thomas to pick up some other agents. Ricky, a native of San Juan, spied a bright white cruise ship between St. Thomas and St. Croix and pointed to it. "There! That's the ferry from St. Croix to St. Thomas."

I nodded, thinking he was just pointing out something interesting.

"I guess those guys are running late, too. The guys we're picking up are coming on the ferry from St. Croix."

I started to say *oh*, but before the word left my mouth, Ricky had rolled the aircraft sharply into a near-vertical right bank. As I soon remembered, Ricky had been an instructor for the air force in F-4 Phantom fighters, and he had just entered a classic strafing dive. Within seconds our nose was pointed down at a forty-five-degree angle, and the aircraft reached redline airspeed, making a whistling noise I rarely heard. Pulling an extra g and leveling a few dozen feet above the water, Ricky approached the boat from its port side at approximately two hundred miles an hour at what I estimated to be about twenty to thirty feet. It was obvious that the boat was much taller than thirty feet, maybe fifty or sixty. When I was absolutely sure that there was no way to avoid a collision with the boat, Ricky initiated a very robust pull-up, pulling somewhere between two and three gs, and rolled the aircraft into another near-vertical right bank. We passed over the top of the ship looking straight down on the deck. Past the boat, he rolled wings-level again and pushed back over to an altitude of about thirty feet, causing a momentary, yet strangely familiar, zero-g ride, and leveled again just above the swells. Had this been 1942, that would have been a perfect torpedo run.

After a second he looked over at me and asked, "Did you see them?"

"Did I see who? Ricky, I don't even know who I was looking for!"

"The agents. They were the ones looking up at us."

"Ricky, everybody who didn't dive for the deck was looking up at us."

"Yeah. It was those guys," he said with that familiar, mischievous grin I hadn't seen since Quantico.

"The only thing I saw," I protested, "was my life flashing before my eyes."

"And you're still awake?" he dug. Ricky laughed hard at that.

If you cherished boredom, Ricky was not the guy to hang with. I would love to tell you what happened during the rest of that flight, but I am afraid that the statutes of limitations have not run out, and I still have a pilot's license to protect. I think it is safe to say that for the next half hour the airplane was operated to the full extent of its legal limits. At least.

Finally, landing at Charlotte Amalie Airport in St. Thomas, I noticed two other R182s with the FBI antenna package. We picked up the agents, who were impressed with the buzz-job on the ferry. Two of them were pilots, the rest ground team members coming back from their day off. The other two pilots and their passengers boarded their aircraft, and two passengers climbed aboard ours. We flew home in a tight three-aircraft formation, pitching out over San Juan International. It was great fun. Taxiing in to the FBI hangar at the Puerto Rico Air National Guard base, I was somewhat surprised to see what appeared to be the wreckage of several jets on the perimeter of the hard stand.

"Ricky, what's that?"

"That's why you're here, Steve. Those are the National Guard fighters blown up by the Macheteros." Good reminder that this was more than just play.

Ultimately, I was assigned to what had become known as the dawn patrol. For five weeks, I was airborne by 5:30 AM, usually landing by 10:30 AM. And after a few hours of paperwork and other responsibilities, I had the balance of the day to kill. I spent a lot of time at the beach and the weekends scuba-diving. At the end of five weeks, I jumped at the chance to fly one of the planes back to the mainland with Ricky because it was having engine "issues," and the nearest FBI overhaul facility was in Pompano Beach, Florida. Ricky and I set out on the thousand-plus-mile overwater trip at six the next morning. The airplane was packed with all of my gear, as well as Ricky's and my guns. A little over halfway to Florida, it was Ricky's turn to be flying and I was napping when he woke me up with a disturbing question.

"What was the oil pressure when you were flying, Steve?"

That's a horrible question to hear when you're flying over water. It told more than it asked. "Dead center in the gauge. Perfect . . . why?"

"Oh," Ricky said, trying to sound as casual as he could, "it's not dead center anymore."

The oil pressure was very low. My eyes flew to the oil temperature gauge. If the oil temperature was rising, it would indicate that we had lost *all* the oil, and the engine was beginning to fail. Thankfully, the oil temperature was good at that point. But we were over water, and the nearest land was over the horizon.

"I think we should land when we get a chance," Ricky declared in a truly epic display of understatement. In truth, the airplane had already decided it was going to get on the surface of the earth soon. We were just being allowed some input as to where. After referring to our charts, we found that the nearest airport was Norman's Cay, a remote strip on the northern part of the island of Exuma in the Bahamas, and we thought we had a decent chance to make it there. Honestly, I thought Exuma was a skin disease.

On approach to Norman's Cay, I saw no less than six aircraft in the water just short of the runway. All seemed to be the size and type of aircraft preferred by smugglers. I was not loving what I was seeing about this airport. Nor was I loving the thought of landing a plane containing semiautomatic firearms in a foreign country that does not allow firearms or—worse—the thought that smugglers might learn that US federal agents had landed at "their" strip.

After the immense relief of making it to an airport, we were confronted with an aircraft whose belly was coated with oil from the engine to the tail cone. It was literally dripping off the bottom of the aircraft. Nobody seemed to even look in our direction, not even the customs official. The safest thing to do from an aviation standpoint was to leave the aircraft there, arrange transportation back to the mainland, and send mechanics and a pilot to retrieve the aircraft. But the safest thing to do from a *personal* standpoint was to fill the plane with two gallons of oil, get the hell out of there, and see how far we got before it ran out of oil again. Since most of the rest of the flight was nearly within gliding distance from land of some type or another, we chose option two. We eventually made it to Pompano Beach, Florida, late that afternoon after seeing much of the Bahamas.

The US customs official asked, "Did you land in any other countries en route?"

"Nope," Ricky lied, "nonstop."

Several months after my return from San Juan, I was swept up in a case that had begun nearly a year before, when I was still up in Idaho following Gary Yarbrough.

Six days before Christmas in 1984, it was snowing in Orangeville, Utah. Orangeville is the city nearest Utah's most productive coal mine, the Wilberg Mine. Wilberg is not like the mines many people are familiar with, in which the miners go deep underground via a vertical shaft. Wilberg is seventy-six hundred feet up in the mountains of central Utah, and the shafts are horizontal. But they are long. Some are miles long. At the coal face that night, miles into the mine, were twice the usual number of people: two general mine foremen, the mine manager, and the vice president of operations for Emery Mining Corporation, the owner of the mine. Twenty-eight people in all. They were there because the mine was trying to set the US coal mine record for production in twenty-four hours. It would be a feather in the mine's cap, but the union, the United Mine Workers (UMW), strongly opposed the bid on safety grounds. What went wrong that night was a mystery for nearly three years, but the consequences were cruelly obvious within a few hours.

A fire somehow started in a tunnel known as the Fifth Right longwall during an operation on which the twenty-eight miners were working. Fed by the forced-air ventilation system, the fire grew out of control almost immediately. Hours later, a single miner stumbled from Fifth Right after somehow traveling a half-mile in pitch black, smoke-filled conditions by feel alone. But the fire beat the remaining twenty-seven miners to the entrance of the tunnel, cutting off their escape. Though heroic efforts were made to save them, it was hopeless. With the fire completely out of control and cave-ins occurring, it became obvious that the fire would spread to the rest of the mine, endangering the miners still in the other shafts, and burn for *years* unless deprived of air. The decision was made to seal the Fifth Right shaft, and the missing miners were entombed.

Human nature being what it is, suspicion immediately fell on the one miner to escape. How did he get out when so many others couldn't? Did he have a head start? Did he know something?

The miner who escaped was a member of the UMW who had spoken out about the hazards of the record attempt and tried to keep it from happening. Whispered allegations began to be bandied about that the union had attempted to cause an accident to prove their point and embarrass the mine management but that the plan had gone horribly wrong. If this was true, the deaths were

murder, and this was a violation of a new federal law, "destruction of an energy facility," and the FBI was called in to investigate
alongside the Mine Safety and Health Administration.

As an FOA, I was involved in the investigation initially only in
an ancillary role. The special agent in charge (SAC) of the Salt Lake
City field office, Leigh Thomas, and the case agent needed to make
frequent trips to the mine to investigate, make appearances, and
assure people that the FBI was "all over" this case. The drive from
Salt Lake City took several hours, but by plane, it was less than an
hour. The Salt Lake City office had two planes at their disposal, and
two agents (one of which was me) who flew them on a part-time
basis when case work allowed or required. With my newfound status in the FBI Aviation Program, I flew as copilot on these trips in
a Cessna 210, a six-passenger, 180-miles-per-hour plane.

It was because of that plane and that case that I fell out of the
SAC's graces. One rainy night, the SAC demanded that the Salt Lake
crew (I was the only copilot) fly him to the mine so he could be at a
press conference in the morning. I pointed out that the weather was
too poor to fly and that we would be in forecast icing conditions—
for which the plane was not equipped, which made the flight illegal.
Flying a light plane at night, in ice, in the Rockies, is near suicide. I
suggested we wait until daylight and see if the weather cleared.

The SAC said no, and I exercised my right to decline a flight
based on safety. He never forgave that.

It was not until almost a year later, November 6, 1985, that the
mine was finally opened and the recovery of the bodies and the
investigation inside the mine could begin. Anytime there is a death
during the course of a crime (or suspected crime) that the FBI is
investigating, the Bureau must witness the autopsy and attest to
the identity of the body. This time there were twenty-seven deaths.
Guess who the SAC chose to be the FBI's representative at the
autopsies? The pilot who wouldn't fly.

I had never been to an autopsy before. At 4:00 AM on November 7, I reported to the Salt Lake County Coroner's office/morgue. It seemed eerily appropriate to be at a coroner's office before the sun came up. Outside the coroner's office sat a refrigerator-truck trailer emblazoned with the logo of a Utah grocery chain. The compressor was running, and it took little imagination to conclude what its cargo was.

The morgue was in the basement of the University of Utah's (U of U's) hospital, located in the rear of the building so that it was not conspicuous. From the outside, it looked more like a loading dock than anything else. In a way it *was* a loading dock. Ambulances and hearses would make deposits and withdrawals right there at the back door. Entering the facility, I was immediately confronted with a sweet, somewhat sickening smell similar to that of spoiled meat, which I had been warned about by experienced agents. But it was at a level that I could deal with. All the lights in the morgue were off, except those in occupied offices.

Hearing voices, I walked to the doorway of a large office off the main examination area and found two sheriff's deputies and an "old friend," Max Jones. Max had been my fingerprinting instructor at the FBI Academy. Max had testified in major trials and had become one of the world's premier experts in identifying bodies. It was Max who ran the hastily created identification lab at Dover Air Force Base to identify the more than a thousand victims of the Jonestown mass suicide in Guyana. He knew his way around a corpse. Part of my job was to identify the bodies, which meant fingerprinting them, and I was grateful for the help.

It was then that I met Steve Sweeney, the Salt Lake County coroner. He was an unusually gregarious person for a coroner. Not in the least like the dour, macabre individual you might expect. He was a young doctor, possibly in his early thirties. He was tall with an extremely dry sense of humor. Within a few minutes two of his many assistants arrived. These two were U of U students studying anatomy. They were attractive and also incongruously upbeat and in good humor at four in the morning.

I struck up a conversation with one, Angie, asking her what it was like working there.

Sweeney answered the question for her. "Are you kidding? Angie's more comfortable in this place than I am. Some nights when she's partying too late—"

"I don't party, Steve," she protested. "I meet people in social settings."

"Whatever." Sweeney continued, "Whenever she's meeting people in social settings and gets too drunk to go home and she has an early shift, she just comes back to the office and sleeps here. On the gurneys!" I do not think I could do that.

There were four examination tables in the autopsy area, and each one had a small rim around it to contain and channel any bodily fluids into a central drain. The bodies we were to examine had been in the mine just a few days short of ten months.

An hour later, the first body bag was rolled in on a gurney, and we hoisted it onto the autopsy table. Steve unzipped the bag from top to bottom and spread the sides apart. I expected that we would be seeing very little of a recognizable body. I was wrong. When the mine was sealed off to stop the fire, the air in the remaining half-mile shaft was consumed by the fire itself until the flames finally died out due to the lack of oxygen. Oxygen is an essential element for decomposition. The bodies, therefore, had been kept in an airless container for almost a year, much as if they had been in Tupperware.

The body we saw was almost completely intact, showing no obvious signs of trauma, and it looked as if it had been spray-painted with flat black paint. This was from the soot and ash from the fire as well as from the coal dust. Strapped to this miner's chest was what is known in the mining industry as a self-rescuer, a small oval oxygen generator about the size of a lunch pail that is flat on the top and bottom. What looks like a vacuum cleaner hose sticks out of the top of the container, and at the end of this hose is a snorkel-like mouthpiece. The self-rescuer provides approximately one hour of oxygen. The mouthpiece was still in the miner's mouth.

Sweeney methodically removed the self-rescuer and pulled the mouthpiece out of the victim's lips. The lips remained in the same shape as if the mouthpiece was still between them. This is a picture I will always remember. Startlingly, when the shoes and socks were removed, the feet were as pink as if he had just come out of a shower.

Sweeney continued removing the clothing and personal effects from the miner. This was difficult for me to experience in many ways, but mainly because it identified this body as a "someone." Had it just been an inanimate "thing," it would not have bothered me as much. But I realized this person had been expecting to come home after work and see his family. When they found and removed a wallet and some dollar bills out of the victim's pocket, it was all the more real.

Autopsies begin with a large "Y cut" to open the chest and torso of the corpse. Y cuts start at the front of each shoulder and meet in a large *V* at the bottom of the center of the sternum. From there the stem of the *Y* is a vertical cut from the base of that *V* to the top of the pubic bone. This leaves three skin flaps that can easily be folded over and up. The speed and relative nonchalance with which these cuts were made were strikingly harsh to me. While in no way was the autopsy disrespectful, careless, or sloppy, it was jarring to a neophyte like me. With the Y cut completed, the bone saw was brought out—a small, high-speed radial saw with a blade approximately three inches in diameter. The sound of the saw is very much like that of a dental drill. With the skin pulled back from the chest, the bone saw made quick work of the rib cage, allowing the front to be removed as a single piece, much as you would remove the front of the rib cage of a plastic model of a human skeleton. Once the chest was "cracked" everything was right at hand. The coroner took samples of all fluids, especially the stomach contents; samples of all the organ tissue, including slices and slides of lung tissue; and more samples of more organs than I could keep track of.

Meanwhile, Max had set to work fingerprinting the body. I almost forgot what I was there for. It was time for me to get hands-on. Because the skin on the bodies seemed to have shrunk somewhat from the heat, the hands were clenched into fists and very difficult to open. This made it nearly impossible to fingerprint the individual fingers. And because this was an FBI case, we were required to take major case prints, meaning prints of the palms, the whole hand, each finger, and every fingertip.

But Max had a solution. He had brought along clippers with which to remove fingers at the second knuckle. Oh good. Once the fingers were removed, it was easier to print them. It was also incredibly gross. Because the bodies had been in groundwater that had seeped into the mine, they were somewhat soggy, and therefore when we cut off the fingers, instead of a cracking or snapping sound, they made a squishing sound. Some of the fingers on some of the bodies turned out to be so deteriorated that the skin of the finger detached almost immediately after the finger was cut from the hand.

Max again had a clever solution: he would simply roll the skin off the finger, so it looked much like a rolled-up condom. Then he would take that same rolled-up finger skin and reroll it over his own gloved finger, ink it on the pad, and then roll it on a finger-print card as if he were fingerprinting himself. This was as efficient as it was unpleasant.

Even as the autopsies of the miners continued throughout that day and the days that followed, the regular patrons of the Salt Lake City morgue began to pile up, and Sweeney moved from table to table. For every autopsy of one of my case's victims I witnessed, there were two or three other bodies being processed on the other tables. There was a fascinating array of customers for the morgue. They included a heart attack victim, a man who jumped to his death (impaling himself on a picket fence), a body from a house fire, and an obese man who had died of natural causes in his house in the winter. He was not found, however, for two weeks, and his house thermostat was set on eighty-five degrees. He was bloated like those inflatable sumo wrestler outfits. And forest green.

These brought home to me the suddenness and the unpredictability of death. Minutes before their death, each of these individuals was in all likelihood comfortable and relaxed, never thinking that death waited *that day*. It is impossible to spend much time in the coroner's office without thinking about death and dying—and God. My fear was not related to what happens after death—I believe there is a loving God, and I know he has made a provision for me—but the suddenness with which death occurs. This theme replayed over and over in my mind throughout those seven days.

We worked only one miner at a time. Each miner's overall condition was different, depending on his or her location in the mine. Some had self-rescuers on; some did not. Some had final notes to their family in their pockets, clearly indicating they knew they were about to die. This was very difficult to see.

After the first day of autopsies, I went back to my apartment satisfied that I had well exceeded my goals for the day. I was fine. It didn't hurt at all. It was a level of naïve denial that reminds me now of the Black Knight in *Monty Python and the Holy Grail*, who protested—after both his arms had been cut off in a sword fight— "I've had worse!" I had not become ill at the sights or smells at the morgue. I became certain that I was going to get through this entire experience scot-free. That night, however, I did something uncharacteristic of me. I did not drink except on weekends, and rarely if ever alone. But after the autopsies, I picked up a midweek six-pack of beer and ordered a pizza. I started in on the six-pack before the pizza got there and ended up eating half the pizza and drinking the entire six-pack. I could not remember the last time I'd had six beers in a day, much less in one evening. I woke up to the alarm the next morning at 3:00 AM, still in my living room chair with the TV still on. Again, I dressed for the morgue in my decomp clothes (those I intended to dispose of at the end of the week) and headed off.

The next day we completed more bodies than the day before, and I began to feel like an old pro. The coroner's staff worked on people who had not been found for weeks as well as those whose bodies were inflated by the gases that form during decomposition. It was not uncommon for the coroner's assistants simply to "pop" the bodies with a scalpel, releasing the noxious gas. Once, they popped a scrotum that was the size of a cantaloupe.

That night after work, I once again picked up a six-pack. I reasoned that I should allow myself to drink midweek, as this had been fairly stressful. While downing an entire six-pack for the second night in a row, I had an unusual desire to turn on every light in the house and a reluctance to turn off the TV, just because the sound of voices was comforting in a weird way. In a completely uncharacteristic move, I went out and got flowers for the house, which I put in a vase in the middle of the family room. Still, I was naïvely certain that this experience was not affecting me.

The next day we autopsied a miner who was very distinctive in appearance. His height, weight, and facial hair all made him stand out from the others. That night at home, opening the first beer of my third six-pack in three days, I made the mistake of turning on the news. Salt Lake City is actually a somewhat small town. The deaths of twenty-seven miners and their final removal from the mine were big news. Local TV did a special report on the miners who had been lost. I should have turned the show off, but my curiosity got the best of me.

Halfway through the piece, the miner who we had autopsied that very morning appeared in home videos from his last Christmas, two years prior. He was unmistakable. The videos showed him chasing his baby daughter around the room on hands and knees. The daughter was not yet walking and giggled as her father chased her. The films were precious. The reality was hideous. It took an inanimate object from that morning and created a living man with a life and a family who was being mourned. It made me wonder about the inspiration for Mary Shelley's "Modern Prometheus."

Probably I should have realized that while I may have, from a physical standpoint, been well suited to be an autopsy participant, I may not have had the emotional tools to safely do so. But this was 1985, and those types of questions were not asked.

My drinking continued unabated during the week, likely why my sleep began to deteriorate. On Sunday morning I stumbled sleepily into the outer room of the morgue at a little before 4:00 AM. I called out to see if anybody was around, and halfway through the words I saw Angie, the corner's assistant, asleep on one of the gurneys. Just as Steve Sweeney had predicted, it must've been a pretty good party the night before—maybe their winter formal. She was still in her elegant gown. I tiptoed past and went into Steve's office. I found him there—*sitting next to Angie.*

Seeing Angie there startled me. I was confused and felt a little like a cartoon character who was seeing somebody in two places at once.

"Angie," I asked, "weren't you out on the gurney asleep?"

Sweeney looked at her quizzically, and she shook her head, confused for a moment.

Then Sweeney realized what I had asked. "No," he said softly, "that's one of our customers."

"It couldn't have been! There was color in her cheeks," I protested, as if protesting could change the reality.

Angie looked at me as if I was a naïve kid, which in some ways I was, and told me that the dead girl had color in her cheeks because she had been wearing makeup at a dance the night before. Less than eight hours before.

"What happened to her?" I asked, horrified.

"Looks like suicide," Sweeney told me bluntly.

Angie then filled in the blanks. "It was her high school's winter formal, and her boyfriend chose that night to break up with her. She dropped him off and drove up the canyon and apparently took a bottle of pills. There was an empty bottle on the seat next to her."

"She was seventeen," Sweeney added.

These words hit me like a hammer. My ears began ringing, and for some reason I felt a tinge of panic. How could this happen? How could she do this to herself, to her parents? Then I realized that this was none of my business, and I wasn't there for that. I couldn't figure out why I cared.

But I couldn't get it out of my mind. I walked out to the gurney and looked down at her, and indeed she had been at the winter formal. She was a very pretty girl and was still wearing a corsage on her pink formal dress, and one of her high heels was still on her feet. As Angie had said, her makeup was what added rosiness to her face. Her strawberry-blonde hair was done perfectly, and she wore a tiny tiara. I could imagine her mother helping her with her hair and her father taking pictures before their child left for the dance. And I could not imagine where they were or how they were feeling right that second. Somehow, for reasons I couldn't understand, I began to *mourn*.

I tried not to think about it, but I couldn't stop. Something was so wrong with this, so evil, that the horror just wouldn't leave my mind. I kept thinking about her parents and her sister, her brother, if she had them. If this had been a movie, it would have been disturbing, but at least I could say, "It's only a movie." I thought about the boy who broke up with her and became angry. And while we were doing our autopsies of our miners and fingerprinting them on one table, they dissected the winter formal girl on the other. The beautiful hair that had been put up so nicely for the dance was, by necessity, desecrated by the bone saw that removed the top of her cranium so that brain samples could be taken. Even the usually blasé medical examiner was somber and treating this girl gently. Her dress hung in the corner of the autopsy room to return to the parents.

I understood that there is evil in the world. I understood that there is unfathomable pain and tragedy in the world. I understood that people do horrible things to other people and themselves. None of this was an intellectual mystery to me. But I had never had to bathe in those facts. I had never had to see them within inches of my face and deal with the absolute ugliness of it. To this day, the image of that girl lying on the gurney is burned into my mind as completely as if it had been tattooed on my eyes.

Things didn't get better that day. Hours later, a loud commotion started in the anteroom. A woman was screaming. Everyone looked up from what they were doing and froze. Within a couple seconds we realized she was likely the wife of one of the mine victims, and she was arguing with a funeral director. I took a quick look at the body we were working on. As I was manipulating the corpse to fingerprint it, Sweeney and a forensic odontologist were working in the victim's mouth, and the victim's lips had been pulled back to a horrible sneer. That, combined with the completely open torso with organs spilling out and the face and hands scarred with smoke and coal dust, made him look like something from a horror movie. Nobody seemed to be moving as the voices came closer to the door of the exam area. They were looking at me. Oh, I remembered, I'm the FBI guy. I have to do something. I dropped what I was doing and hurried into the anteroom, wearing rubber gloves that were covered in body fluids and jet-black ash.

It was the wife of the miner on the table. Her funeral director had let it slip to her that *all* of the miners were having all their fingers cut off as part of the autopsies. While this was inaccurate, it pushed her over the edge. She was demanding that we stop the autopsy. When I came out of the room, she saw me and immediately started screaming at me. She shrieked, "Butcher!" and lunged toward me.

The funeral director grabbed her, and it took most of his strength to keep her from getting to me and/or the exam room. She sobbed that we were cutting off her husband's fingers and disfiguring her loved one. The funeral director held her fast while she shouted at me, calling me every name she could think of, vomiting her grief and anger verbally at the funeral director and me before she collapsed into sobs. But at least she did not fight anymore to go into the room. The funeral director told her over and over that she needed to remember her husband as he looked alive. He reminded her that it would be unfair to his memory for her to go in there. He handled the situation masterfully and calmed her down within five to ten minutes.

I gained a new admiration for that profession that day. But I increasingly felt emotionally drained and strangely numb. I didn't feel happiness, sadness, horror, fear, or excitement. I was just emotionless. I suspected I had overloaded my emotions, and they had gone to sleep, much like my leg does when I sit in an awkward position. I was sure that after this assignment was finished, I would regain feeling. In all, I witnessed the twenty-seven autopsies for the miners and another twenty-five on the other tables.

In my career in the FBI, I wore just about every piece of protective gear there is. I wore a flight helmet, a SWAT helmet, a construction helmet, climbing helmets for rappelling; I wore earplugs, headphones, and different types of hearing protection; I had four different kinds of goggles to protect my eyes from everything from chemical sprays to the wind in open-cockpit airplanes. I wore fireproof flight suits, SWAT suits, and chemical and biological protective Tyvek suits to protect me from pathogens. I even wore a charcoal-filtered combat uniform to protect against radioactive fallout and biological warfare. And I wore at least five different vests to protect me from everything from a .22-caliber pistol to a .30-caliber bullet from an AK-47. The FBI supplied more protective equipment than I can possibly recount. I did not, however, have any gear that could protect me from what I experienced at the morgue.

In the FBI Academy, firearms instructors discussed with us what we should do with our gun at home. There were special cautions given to those agents who had children, especially small children. We were reminded that the gun we had been issued was essential at work but incredibly dangerous around our families. It was recommended that we put this gun under lock and key as soon as we got home. I now believe that there is a corollary to that warning. Empathy is an essential emotion at home, especially with our families. But if an FBI agent brings it to work, it can be terribly dangerous. In many ways, empathy must be treated just like a gun; it has to be locked away when you are *at* work.

At the end of the seven days, I returned to the office, and life returned to normal. But there was now a ticking time bomb inside of me.

For good or for bad, my time in Salt Lake City was quickly coming to an end. Another winter had started, and each of my good friends had been receiving orders to Top 12 offices within days of their second anniversary in the FBI. Top 12s are, logically, the

FBI's twelve largest offices. But it was a well-known fact at the time that New York was seriously understaffed and begging for agents, so almost all Top 12 transfers were going to New York. First Matt, then Kalb, then Randy, in that order, were all transferred to New York City. With true FBI sensitivity, each New York transfer was announced by the office public-address system playing Sinatra crooning "New York, New York." I didn't want to go to New York; I wanted to be transferred somewhere that would keep me close to family, somewhere I could enjoy more temperate weather for a change. In a way, I felt like I had given the FBI my New York obligation when my dad was an agent, but I knew they wouldn't see it that way.

I began to pray every day, every single time I thought of my transfer, which was a lot. It had been a miracle that I even made it into the FBI; why couldn't there be another miracle to get me to L.A.? These weren't frivolous, cathartic prayers. These were actual pleas to God, knowing he could arrange this if he wanted. Then I heard through friends in the Aviation Program that the Los Angeles FBI office needed pilots (even copilots) in its Aviation Unit at Point Mugu Naval Air Station near Ventura, California. I did all I could to lobby with the guys at Point Mugu to request me. They said they would ask, but these types of transfers were rarely given to first office agents.

At Thanksgiving, I went to San Francisco to spend the holiday with my family. Two days after Thanksgiving, I received a call from ASAC Danny Klaus. My orders had come in. I was breathless. Danny was cruel, as I expected he would be. It's just an FBI thing.

"Steve, I've got your orders here," he opened.

"Wow." I fought the urge to scream *Tell me!*

"I kind of like to play a little game with these things," Danny said. Of course he did. "If you could choose any office to be transferred to, which would it be, Steve?"

"Los Angeles," I said without a pause. He knew that. Big, long pause.

"Do you have a second choice?" He was enjoying this.

"Chicago?" I replied, not sure anymore.

"Damn," he taunted, "did headquarters *know* where you wanted to go?"

"I don't remember." I was too devastated to care anymore.

"Well, let's try it this way; if there was one office in the whole FBI that you *don't* want to go to, what would it be? I mean, let's give you some good news, at least," he said, setting me up.

"The office I would *not* want to go to? That's easy. Newark." Loooong pause, then he sprung it on me.

"Shit. Isn't that always the way?" he said, sounding frustrated. "How do they choose these things?"

I flatlined. "Is it Newark?" I asked, trying not to throw up.

"Naw. It's L.A."

I was unsure that I had heard that. "Huh?"

"Congratulations."

I almost fainted.

In my time in Salt Lake City, I had seen horrible things: I had witnessed the autopsies. I had assisted in the investigation involving the murder of a twenty-three-year-old woman who had been forced to watch her precious nine-month-old girl's throat slashed before she herself was also butchered. I chased a fugitive who had picked up a girl on the way to her twenty-first birthday party when her car broke down on the freeway. After raping her, he stabbed her exactly twenty-one times in honor of her birthday. I had investigated the murder of a man whose wife claimed it was a suicide, but her fingerprint was the only one on the shotgun shell that killed him. And the one fired into his head after that. I worked the murder of a man by his brother during a card game. When the brother (who had been stabbed in the stomach) continued to moan while the card game continued, he was dragged into an outhouse in subzero weather, where he might have frozen to death before he bled to death. I was ready to go flying.

Returning to Salt Lake City that week, I commandeered the PA and boomed Randy Newman's "I Love L.A." throughout the office, loud enough to register complaints, but I didn't care. I was going back to California.

7

Career Number Two

MY TRANSFER TO Los Angeles was the beginning of my next FBI career, it seemed, as well as a new life. Taking an airliner out of Salt Lake City that February morning, we lifted out of the forty-degree semipermanent winter fog that blanketed the Salt Lake Valley and broke out into crystal blue skies. Arriving over the Los Angeles area a couple of hours later, I looked down from the window of the airplane and there, under me, was Point Mugu Naval Air Station, my new FBI "home." If you believe in coincidences, that was a pretty big one. The airliner turned east, and I looked down and saw a beautiful meadow in the Santa Monica Mountains between the San Fernando Valley and the Oxnard Basin. It turned out to be Thousand Oaks, California, and that became the only hometown I have ever really had.

Reporting to Point Mugu on my first day as an FBI pilot, my excitement was hard to contain. It was a dream for a frustrated military pilot. Driving to the FBI hangar, I passed Phantoms, F-14 Tomcats, and F-18 Hornets. Instead of the Cessna 182s that I had flown in Salt Lake City, the FBI flight line at Point Mugu was populated with Cessna O-2As, surplus air force observation aircraft from Vietnam. O-2s have an engine in front and an engine in back. Its nickname is the Mixmaster. The O-2s were beat up by that time of their lives, used-up relics from the 1960s and 1970s.

Looking inside the cockpits, I saw a cluttered black instrument panel with radios and gauges that seemed to be from another era. Instead of plush fittings, the interior was simply painted metal (in those areas where the paint had not been worn off long ago). On the top of the instrument panel was the gunsight mount. On the wings of several were bomb racks designed to hold either small missiles or machine guns. The aircraft was a veritable porcupine of antennas, and the cockpits were liberally surrounded with Plexiglas. There were even metal patches over bullet holes from 'Nam. Though they were only twenty years old, they looked fifty. They were beat up, and oil seeped through just about every opening. They were truly the most beautiful and exciting aircraft I had ever seen.

The rest of the first day was almost a dream. After I went to "flight gear issue" at the base and picked up my flight suits and other gear, Dick Francis, one of the pilots, offered to "take the kid out" in an O-2 to "give him a familiarization ride and see if he knows what the hell he's doing in an airplane." The O-2A is a military airplane based in part on a civilian airplane, but in reality the two have little in common. The O-2A does not handle like, nor have the built-in safety margin of, the civilian version. Even the airfoil of its wing is a different shape. But it handled like a dream, just without the FAA-required built-in training wheels. After a preflight of the aircraft, I was told to sit in the pilot's seat. It just kept getting better. Dick showed me how to start the engines and, cleared to taxi, I nudged the throttles forward. I felt like the baddest pilot in the world. I was having so much fun I was not able to take it all in. At the run-up area next to the runway, Dick went through the pre-takeoff checklist, we set flaps to ten degrees and cinched the harnesses, and Dick got us takeoff clearance.

"Well?" He asked through the intercom.

"What?" I asked back.

"I'm not flying," he said. "You are. Are we going to sit here or take off?"

I am surprised I didn't soil myself I was so excited. "Sure. Let's go. Just throttles to the stops?" Dick nodded. As I did, hundreds of unmuffled horsepower converted 100-octane aviation fuel into noise. Substantial noise. It sounded as if the aircraft were actually blowing up in slow motion. I winced and continued bringing the throttles forward.

"Noisy, aren't they?" Dick laughed.

I nodded. But I didn't care if it deafened me. We rattled down the runway, gathering speed. At eighty knots we were airborne.

Dick reached forward and raised the landing gear and the flaps. Accelerating through 110 knots, the sluggishness went away, and it flew nicer than any airplane I had ever flown. Dick had me take it up to forty-five hundred feet out over the ocean between Point Mugu and the Channel Islands. We did steep turns, unusual attitudes, and all sorts of different maneuvers. I was in heaven. I was having so much fun my face was getting sore from smiling. I can do this! I thought to myself.

"Let's do some stalls," Dick said.

Stalls are few people's favorite maneuvers. Stalls have nothing directly to do with the engine running or not running. Stalls are when, for any one of a variety of reasons, the smooth airflow over the wing (which is essential for lift) is disrupted and the air on top of the wing literally stops following the contour of the wing and breaks off into turbulent confusion. The instant this happens (and it happens in an *instant*) the wing is no longer a wing, it is simply a useless structure sticking out the side of an aluminum anvil, and the aircraft begins to free-fall. It feels somewhat as if you've just driven your car off the roof of a skyscraper.

I slowed the aircraft as Dick talked me through the stall. Recovery from a stall is simple in most aircraft. You lower the nose of the aircraft, which lowers the angle at which the air is hitting the wing, and normal airflow over the top is reestablished. At least that's the way it's supposed to work. I had never even attempted a stall in a military aircraft.

As the O-2A slowed, the mushiness of the controls returned. I could hear the decreasing whistle of the wind on the windscreen. At we slowed through sixty-five knots, I began to feel a buffet in the aircraft. The stall was getting near, and the deck angle was somewhat steep. I wanted this to be over fairly quickly. It was.

After two large "bumps," the airplane stalled sharply. But instead of falling straight ahead, wings level, the left wing began to drop rapidly. Instinctively I rolled the yoke to the right to pick up that wing. This would have worked if I was flying a civilian plane, which the FAA requires to be a little more "tame" than military aircraft. In this aircraft, using the ailerons during a stall only *pisses it off*. It acted like a horse that was tired of us on its back. Immediately after turning the yoke to the right, the airplane snapped from left-wing-low to a right-handed spin in the blink of an eye. It did so with such gusto that my head hit the left side window with some force, partially dislodging my headset. I looked out the windshield and saw not sky, but spinning ocean. In a mere second, we had flipped upside-down and the nose had dropped almost straight down, and we were spinning down at a frightening rate. I really didn't want to die on my first day.

"Hey, kid! What'd ya do?" Dick yelled into the intercom.

I pushed the yoke forward and stomped on the left rudder, desperately trying to recover the aircraft from the spin. We were diving through four thousand feet, and a quick glance at the rate-of-descent indicator showed the needle to be "pegged"—maxed out and leaning against the edges of the gauge. We were less than a minute from the water, I realized. After another half turn, the airplane responded to the input and stopped spinning. The resultant dive was easy to pull out of. Now I was panting, sweating, and frightened. I had never before entered an inadvertent spin this vigorous.

"What happened?" Dick yelled through the intercom.

"I don't know," I gasped, flying with my knees as I tried to put my headset back on right. My eyes were as big as saucers, I'm sure.

"Let's try that again," he instructed. We climbed back to forty-five hundred feet. I was truly shaky at the thought of doing it again, but I was eager to redeem myself.

A few minutes later, at forty-five hundred feet and sixty-five knots, I felt the same two aerodynamic bumps and the airplane rolled *sharply* left, until we were completely upside-down, the nose falling toward a vertical dive. This spin was even more aggressive. I kept the yoke centered this time and stomped on the right rudder to raise the left wing. If anything, this time the aircraft snapped from a left-turning spin to an even harder right-turning spin!

"*Shit!*" I screamed.

Again I pushed and stomped the controls to the "stops," and we pulled out level at about three thousand feet.

"That was worse than the first one!" Dick chided. "I guess you've got a lot of training ahead of you. Let's head back, I don't want to do *that* anymore." I was humiliated. I could feel my face burning. We headed back to Point Mugu, and I entered the pattern. Dick talked me through lowering the flaps, landing gear, turning final, and the touchdown. How could it be that easy to land if it stalled like that? I taxied in wondering if I would make it in a "big-time" unit like this. Shutting down, I realized I was soaking wet. We got out of the aircraft wordlessly, handing the clipboard to the mechanics who came out to the aircraft. My hands were still shaking as we walked into the office. The FBI aviation coordinator, Chuck Stokeley, looked up from his desk.

"How'd it go?" he asked pleasantly.

"Not as well as it could have," I answered.

His smile disappeared and he looked concerned. "What happened?"

Dick answered for me: "Kid had some trouble. Kept spinning the plane." I was humiliated.

Chuck got a wry look on his face. "Did you take thirty-six out?"

The airplane we took out was indeed call sign Idaho 36.

Dick tried to keep a straight face but laughed as he said, "Yeahhhh . . ."

A big smile broke out on Chuck's face. Then he said to Dick, "You're a jerk, you know that?"

Dick laughed and walked back to his desk without giving me a second look. I looked at Chuck, still confused.

"What?" I pleaded.

"It's not your fault. Thirty-six is all tweaked from battle damage, so if you stall it, it's going to spin. Every time. We can't get it rigged right." I heard Dick laughing in back and wondered if Dick was his real name or just what they called him.

Dick and I eventually became friends. He could be a jerk, but he was harder on himself than he was on anyone else. If you listened to him, he'd tell you he could do nothing right. But in actuality, he was a sharp pilot and an even better agent. I also became reacquainted with Norm Kemp, a pilot I had flown with on the Aryan Nations case. "Stormin' Norman" and I began a lifelong friendship. Norm was, as another agent once said, "pathologically nice." His only vice was that he occasionally fell asleep while flying, and he fancied himself a fighter pilot. We never knew when he might turn the airplane on its tail.

Dick may have been messing with me that first day, but he was actually right; I had a lot of training to do. In that first year, I got my O-2 checkout, my instrument rating, my commercial license, and my multi-engine rating and passed my FBI pilot in command

(PIC) check ride (which makes an FAA check ride seem like a joy-ride). In my first ten months at Point Mugu, I flew seven hundred hours. Since that year, I have never since flown seven hundred hours in a single year, much less in ten months. By the end of 1986, I had almost a thousand hours under my belt and felt like Chuck Yeager. I was averaging 3.5 hours of flying every single day of the work week. I was as on top of my game as I would ever be. The next year I began on helicopters.

When I transferred to Point Mugu, the FBI Aviation Program was still young, and the Bureau was far behind in establishing guidelines and rules for their airplanes and pilots. Because they were playing catch-up, coordinators like Ed Nellis in Los Angeles arranged (without FBI permission) for the FBI to obtain dozens of free O-2s from the air force. Not since the purchase of Manhattan Island had so much been bought for so many for so little. We flew not only air force surplus planes but also drug-seized aircraft and helicopters on loan from the army. The benefits were that we flew whenever we wanted, and for whatever reason, and our skills improved quickly. The downside was that we didn't have established safety standards, and pilots began to damage airplanes with some regularity.

The program had a little of the feeling of the wild, wild West, and I am embarrassed to say that in this environment I flourished. One summer afternoon, Ken Bell and I were watching an F-18 carrier squadron practice carrier landings on land. Ken was a former army pilot of Hueys and scout helicopters. He seemed to have little interest in the FBI beyond flying, and that was just fine with the FBI, because few pilots had the skill Ken had; he instructed pilots, gave checkouts throughout the FBI, and flew fixed-wing planes with a skill that few could match. He enjoyed flying immensely, and like me, was easily bored. On this particular gorgeous day, we were fighting boredom by watching the F-18s practice. On most naval air stations, there is a carrier deck painted on at least one runway. This runway has a carrier landing system installed and sometimes even has arrester cables. The procedure is to approach the "carrier deck" as you would an actual ship: slam the aircraft onto the pavement and instantly firewall the throttle and take off again before the end of the carrier. It was fascinating to watch. Ken and I had just come in from a flight and were sitting on an aircraft tug watching the show. While watching, we debated whether an O-2 could land on a carrier and take off again in the space of the deck. When the F-18s were done, we decided to do some empirical research. We climbed into an O-2 and tried it ourselves. The first few tries were miserable failures. It was easy enough to put it on the "deck," but there was no way we could get off again before the carrier deck ended.

Then it occurred to us that if we touched down at a speed that was well above our takeoff speed, say . . . 110 knots (127 mph), then all we would have to do is pull the nose up and it would lift off again with gusto. The trick would be getting the plane on the deck at around 110 knots, which was a slow cruising speed, not a landing speed, for an O-2. After several tries, we discovered that with ten degrees of flaps, gear down, and a low power setting, the O-2 would descend with its nose up. If we crossed the airfield boundary fence at about fifteen feet, we could literally fly the airplane onto the ground at a speed at which it could immediately take off again. It worked. On touchdown, we would ram the throttles to the firewall, rotate, and shoot skyward like a rocket, but it required us to fly the aircraft at the very edge of its performance envelope. It was an absolute riot, and we were laughing like madmen. After about a dozen landings each, we called it a day. When we taxied back past the F-18 squadron area, the F-18 pilots who had been watching us bowed in a mock "not worthy" salute. It was a sight I will not forget. It is a miracle that I survived my early career without a crash.

All the fun was secondary, of course, to the mission. In that first year, I spent four hundred hours on surveillance over kidnappers, drug dealers, and bank robbers, to name just a few. On one case, we spent weeks over a group of violent bank-takeover robbers as they planned their next hit. A difficult decision had been made by FBI bosses and the United States Attorney's Office: If the robbers were arrested before they robbed a bank, the only charge that would be successful against them was conspiracy, and that would be a very light sentence indeed. They were also heavily armed, and intervening *during* the robbery was too risky. So we were going to allow them to rob a bank as we watched, and arrest them afterwards.

We observed them for weeks as they stole and positioned "cold cars"—vehicles with no previous connection to the robbers. These were the getaway cars. They would allow the subjects to escape the robbery in a car that could not be traced back to them and make several car switches before they finally got to their own car. In our case, it was thought that by the time they had switched cars twice, they would have stowed their weapons. We just didn't know when or where they were going to do the robbery. We knew that the cars, however, were stashed near Warner Center in Canoga Park, an upscale business area. Then nothing happened for a week.

One warm morning while we were following the suspects through what appeared to be another boring day of shopping, they drove to the first cold car—a van—and our throats tightened.

"Nine-oh-five to all units," I broadcast using my call sign, "the subjects have driven behind the grocery store and have parked next to the cold car." I had to force myself to relax and to concentrate on what was going on below me. Because of the location where they had stashed the cold car, no ground surveillance could take place without giving up the fact that they were being followed. The ground teams hypothesized that the robbers just might have gone there to make sure the battery hadn't died.

"The trunk on the subjects' car is open, and they are loading bags—long bags—into the back of the van. Guys, it appears to be duffel bags, and they are at least as long as rifles," I said, trying to maintain my composure. From three thousand feet, through stabilized binoculars, I could almost see the outline of rifles. Then I saw something that sent a chill up my spine.

"All right . . . they appear to be pulling on camouflage clothing over their street clothes." This was it. They were going to hit the bank.

"Roll SWAT," came the order from the ground team leader.

We tried desperately to predict which bank they were going to. We knew that the second cold car was on the roof of a parking structure at Warner Center, and the decision was made to allow them to escape as far as the parked vehicle, away from people. The robbers drove through the parking lots of several banks, trying to determine which one "felt right" that day. Each time, we were sure that "it" was about to start, and our nerves were rattled from numerous false alarms. Finally, they drove to a fourth bank and parked in the back of the lot.

This was it.

"All units stand by," I called out. "Subjects have parked the van in the southwest corner of the lot and are exiting the van at this point. . . . Subjects are carrying long rifles—repeat, subjects are carrying long rifles, possibly M16s. They are dressed in camouflage—repeat, camouflage, and their faces are covered with ski masks." It would be impossible to describe the adrenaline going through my veins at that point. It was all I could do to keep my voice under control and let people on the ground know that I was calm.

Within seconds of the robbers entering the bank I watched as four of five other people came sprinting out. A few seconds later came a chilling call from the surveillance van positioned nearest the bank.

"Shots fired! Shots fired!" I could see SWAT cars responding to the bank at a high rate of speed. This was a worst-case scenario.

"All units, maintain your position!" It was from the arrest team leader.

"This is part of their MO!" he shouted. "When they go in, they usually fire several rounds into the ceiling to get everybody's attention and let people know they're serious!" That might've been something we should have known by now! I thought. By now, the tension in the air was thick. Absolute silence reigned for about two minutes.

Then a call from the arrest team leader: "A bank robbery in progress has just been broadcast at this address to all LAPD units, by LAPD dispatch, and we've had them discontinue response." Somebody in the bank had pushed the alarm button. A black-and-white responding to that bank would face impossible odds, and people might die. That very scenario played out a few years later at a robbery known simply as "the North Hollywood Robbery," when two armed and armored suspects held off thirty LAPD officers for an hour before a SWAT team took them out. As I mused over possibilities, I saw the door of the bank swing open.

"They're out! They're out and walking toward the van!" I broadcast. They went directly back to the van and unlocked it as casually as you might when coming out of Home Depot. They got in and drove away slowly. They didn't seem to be in a hurry.

"They're out and moving. They're driving east in an alley behind the bank paralleling Victory Boulevard!" I was concentrating on keeping my voice calm and my reports concise.

"Out onto Owensmouth and north toward Victory. Right turn onto Victory; this is an eastbound in the two-lane." Looking back westward on Victory I could see a string of vehicles following at about a mile behind. They were handling the situation perfectly. As long as the helicopter had an eye on the subject, there was no reason for them to get close as the crooks drove to the next cold car.

"Southbound on Topanga—this will put them in the direction of the cold car on the Warner Center roof." As they drove closer and closer to the parking garage where their second car was stashed, I knew that this was going to come to an end in just a few minutes, one way or the other. It was an extremely tense time. I watched as the first cold car entered the garage from the ground floor, and then I waited for it to emerge on the roof. I could see the SWAT units lining up near the garage, waiting for authorization to enter.

"OK," I transmitted, "they are parked next to the second cold car," which was a windowless van, "and they are throwing bags into the back of it." I advised that they were still wearing their camouflage outfits and still carried their M16s.

"Nine-oh-five from Sam-Ten," Sam 10 radioed to me. (Sam 10 was the SWAT team leader Bill Rathman, "Rat-Man," a good friend of mine.) "What are they doing now?"

"Rat, they're in the van; all doors in both vehicles are closed. They are not visible through the windshield." The unspoken message here was that they might be changing out of their camouflage into street clothes and putting their weapons away. There was a short window in which they could be apprehended on a deserted parking structure roof instead of in a crowded Los Angeles intersection or near a grocery store.

"All SWAT units, this is Sam-Ten: move to the van and execute." With that, the conga line of SWAT Suburbans and cars moved into the bottom of the parking structure, and I watched as they disappeared into the building. My heart was in my throat. I desperately hoped that the robbers would not start to leave before SWAT got to the roof. Within seconds, faster than I thought they could move on a parking ramp, the SWAT vehicles burst onto the roof. They moved to the van, blocking it in against the edge of the parking structure, and I could see operators bailing out of vehicles in their

SWAT gear training dozens of weapons on the van. As Rathman gave instructions on positions, I could hear a bullhorn in the radio background instructing subjects to come out of the van with their hands up. I remember wishing I was down there with SWAT—I could imagine little else that exciting.

I swung the helicopter around in front of the van and hovered, then descended to where I could see through the windshield, about one hundred or two hundred feet above the truck.

"Rat-Man, I don't see anybody in the driver or passenger seat," I warned him.

Rathman then transmitted a warning to the SWAT team: "Stand by; they're in the back with their weapons! All units watch your crossfire!"

Watch your crossfire? They were preparing to open fire on the van! My heart sunk. Almost simultaneously, I saw the rear door of the van crack open slightly and something emerge from the back of the van. I thought, Here we go. But Rathman's voice came on the radio: "Hold your fire!"

Poking out of the back of the van were the subjects' *empty hands* showing that they did not have weapons in them. The tense stand-off had lasted less than three minutes, but I was having trouble catching my breath. Later that day, SWAT hit the house rented by the subjects and found thousands of rounds of ammunition and a concrete firing range built into the basement of a fancy house on a cliff. These people meant business.

Needless to say, the work in the Aviation Unit was demanding, the rewards were high, the risks were also high, and I had never enjoyed life more. But things were about to change.

8

So I Just Met This Girl . . .

ABOUT A MONTH after I transferred to Los Angeles, I had settled in an apartment in Thousand Oaks. I was living the dream. Those first few months, it seemed I spent more time above the ground than on it. I followed extortion victims as they drove to pay ransom money; I watched more drug deals from five thousand feet than I could count, and I spied on bank robbers as they cased upcoming jobs. It was more wonderful than I could imagine. When I wasn't flying surveillance, I was training, sometimes flying a full training mission after a four-hour surveillance. Money wasn't as plentiful as it was in SLC, mainly because my rent had tripled, but I didn't need much, really, and I had enough. What I wanted to do was make some friends. The pilots at Point Mugu were all significantly older than me, so the great gig I had in SLC with agents my age was gone.

I had found a church I liked and discovered that it had a singles group. On my first night there, I knew no one, and in came this girl with a round face and a pretty turned-up nose. She was wearing a rugby shirt with yellow and black horizontal stripes that made her look like a bumblebee. Her jeans were dark blue and did little to hide a beautiful figure. When she glanced my way looking for a seat, the deep blue of her eyes glowed from ten feet away. I don't remember what was talked about that night, or frankly anything else but her. I do remember that this bumblebee girl began to look around at the people in the room, and then back down at a piece of paper, obviously concerned about something. Finally, she tapped the girl next to her and asked her a question, pointed to the paper in her lap, and the girl shook her head. It was obvious to me that she was in the wrong place and she knew it. Within a few seconds, she quietly picked up her things, excused herself down the row of seats, and walked out.

After doing some investigative work, I "accidentally" ran into her at a get-together; I sat down next to her and she looked up.

"I'm Steve," I said. (I came up with that opening line after hours of focus-group studies.)

She nodded and smiled and motioned to her mouth to let me know her mouth was full. When she finished, she looked at me with those ocean-blue eyes and said, "Hi! Ahm Mishaiyall."

For a moment I was confused. What language was that?

"Mish-*ai*-yall," she repeated as if I were hard of hearing.

I stared at her confused for a beat, then it hit me. She was speaking southern. "Michelle?" I asked triumphantly.

"Yes, silly. Mishaiyall."

Without an interpreter, I was able to determine that she was Michelle Celestial Easterly from Baton Rouge, a student at Louisiana State University. I was absolutely captivated. FBI interview techniques rock, and I soon knew enough about her to track her down in the next few days and convince her to go out with me on, as she pronounced it, a "dite."

If there was ever a date where a man and woman's eyes met and they knew instantly that they were meant to be together, if ever two people spending time with each other for the first moment knew that they had found "the one," if ever a date existed where the couple was lost in time and the moments flew by seemingly at the speed of thought, this wasn't it.

Once she learned there was an eight-year difference in our ages, I discovered that dating a man eight years older was apparently a very serious issue for a good southern girl. We tried to continue with small talk for the rest of the evening, but the awkward silences were deafening.

At one point, she nicely asked, "What do you do for a living?"

I answered, "I'm an FBI agent," apparently in a way that appeared smug to Michelle.

"Should we *both* be impressed?" she asked in her sweetest southern drawl. Southern girls could tell you to go to hell and you would thank them for it.

I was certain this was a one-date relationship. But we had mutual friends, I dated some of her girlfriends, and we ended up seeing each other several times a week, it seemed. At the end of the summer, when Michelle was due to go back to Louisiana, she made the decision to stay in California.

On November 7, 1986, I had a group of friends, including Michelle, over for a party at my apartment. We listened to music and drank wine until past midnight. Sometime during the evening, I was asked about my career in the FBI, and eventually I mentioned the Wilberg Mine disaster and the autopsies, not realizing that it was the one-year anniversary of the beginning of that experience. After the party, I cleaned up, went to bed, and forgot the memory—I thought.

At three that morning, I woke up sick to my stomach. Within seconds, I ran to the bathroom and threw up. I hadn't had that much to drink, I was sure. I chalked it up to something I ate. I woke up half an hour later and threw up again, but after that I felt fine. Nobody else at the party had been sick. But the next night, it happened again.

I became deeply concerned when I began waking up *every* morning around 2 or 3 AM and throwing up, sometimes more than once a night. But each morning I felt fine. Finally, I took a day or two off from work and tried to get over whatever bug was bothering me. But it continued. I finally saw a doctor and over the course of several months, endured what I believe to be every gastrointestinal test known to man. At the end of this regimen, the doctor told me that there was nothing physically wrong with me.

"But I'm still getting sick every night," I protested with great frustration. I had lost ten pounds, and while I was relieved that I wasn't dying of cancer or some similar disease, not having an answer was discouraging. His suggestion was even more disturbing.

"I think you may be at the wrong type of doctor. This could be psychological."

I reacted badly to that. I wasn't crazy. I was afraid of how the Bureau would view a psychosomatic illness. But he was actually concerned that there was an outside event that might have triggered some problems. With that I finally told the FBI of the problem, and they sent me to a psychiatrist who worked exclusively with firemen, policemen, and other first responders. I really wasn't concerned who he worked with, because by that point I would have gone to a witch doctor to get well.

It was that doctor who pointed out that the illness began on the one-year anniversary of the beginning of the autopsies. I was, he said, suffering from something of which I had never heard: post-traumatic stress disorder, or PTSD. I learned more about myself in the next few months than I had ever wanted to know. I learned how the event had affected me; I learned strategies for dealing with it; and I learned how to deal with similar events in the future as best I could. Finally, though, I learned that because of my personality, this would likely be a recurring problem throughout my career. Though the nausea and vomiting went away, the pain of the autopsies, and the things I was destined to experience, would never fully leave me.

My complete control of my own life was being threatened. After seeing Michelle in social situations for two years, I was having feelings for her that I did *not* want to have. I had always assumed that I would date and marry a woman with a profession and a college degree. Michelle had neither. She worked very hard as a waitress at two different restaurants to try to make ends meet. She met none of my preconceived criteria for the woman I would eventually marry. But I couldn't stop thinking about her. Part of it, I knew, was that she was one of the most unique women I had ever met. She had a resolve made of some type of tungsten steel/Kevlar/carbon-fiber alloy—only stronger. She hadn't a mean bone in her body but was fiercely loyal to her friends, and her desire to do the right thing was the driving force in her life.

I began to think about her even when I was getting ready to go out with my girlfriend. The miners didn't haunt me anymore, but Michelle did. I did stupid things to get to see her. I took my girlfriend to dinner at the restaurant where Michelle worked, sitting at what I knew to be one of Michelle's tables. I realize now what a creepy thing that was to do to both of the girls, but I didn't think that Michelle knew I was interested in her and was sure Michelle had no interest in me. I was wrong on all counts. In fact, Michelle refused to serve us (without notifying us of that, of course), and that night I found my FBI car covered with silly string from one end to the other. I suppose that was better than Michelle slashing my tires.

Finally, I had to tell my girlfriend that I had developed an interest in another girl and that I needed to follow my heart. She knew who it was and was so understanding that I almost wondered if I had made a mistake breaking up with her. I hadn't; it's just that some other guy got a great girl, too. Michelle agreed to go out with me again, which in and of itself was a surprise. After just a few dates, I knew that if she would have me, I would never marry anybody but her. There was no guile in Michelle. She despised manipulation and falsehood. She loved me—not my career, not what I was professionally, not my money, not my future prospects. Just because of who I was. This thought disoriented and terrified me. My whole future was up in the air. I was completely unnerved.

It was a miracle that in the next few months I didn't crash a plane while I was preoccupied with Michelle. In November, on a foggy beach with the ocean booming on the rocks, she agreed to be my wife. Life was wonderful. Our future looked bright. But I almost didn't live to see the wedding.

With less than three months to go before the ceremony, the invitations were out, the venues secured, and final planning was taking place. My assigned mission for Friday, March 3, 1989, was going to be a milk run. The weather was perfect, the mission easy, and Michelle and I were going to dinner with friends that night.

Just before noon I was climbing out toward Malibu. This was the first FBI mission for my copilot, Neil Harris. It would be a familiarization flight, an ideally easy surveillance to start to get the hang of FBI aviation operations. In Malibu, just twenty miles down the coast, was a trendy restaurant known as the Surf that catered to the rich and famous. It was almost on the sand, had a spectacular ocean view, great food, and an almost limitless supply of cocaine. The Surf was a major supplier of cocaine in Los Angeles. Several principals of the restaurant were under extensive surveillance, and aircraft were part of that.

My first week of rifle practice at the FBI Academy, January 1984. It was thirty degrees Fahrenheit and we were shooting out to two hundred yards. I hadn't learned yet to keep my finger off the trigger when my sights were downrange. Ten months later, I'd be depending on the M16 for my life in the woods of Idaho.

At the FBI Academy in March 1984, the exact moment I found out that I'd been transferred to Salt Lake City. You can see me pronouncing the word "Lake." Notice my delight.

The home of white supremacist Gary Yarbrough, 1984. I took this photo on the afternoon prior to our raid.

The cockpit of a Cessna O-2A, somewhere over Oklahoma in June 1986. I was delivering the worn-out Vietnam-era aircraft to a museum. Three-day trip, only one emergency declared.

In November 1994, I flew my helicopter over to Camarillo Airport to have lunch with Michelle, Meagan, and Stevie. The kids loved to sit in the helicopter.

Minutes after arriving at Point Mugu Naval Air Station in July 1995 with one of the Army OH-58As I had picked up as "spare parts" at Fort Rucker. The FBI still didn't know they owned four new flyable helicopters.

LEFT: This "shoot house" was part of my Los Angeles SWAT assault training in February 1997. I'm closest to the camera. In these training sessions, guns were live and ammo was real. Observers watched from the balconies above to critique.

RIGHT: The US Marine Corps' Mountain Warfare Training Center, in the Sierra Nevada mountain range. I'm the one waist deep in the water—yes, it was cold. We had to fasten ourselves to the rope with carabiners in case the strong current knocked us down and tried to drag us downstream. Like it had just done to me.

Nuclear/chemical/biological weapons combat school at the Nevada Nuclear Test Site. It was one-hundred-plus degrees outside—much hotter in our sealed suits— but we still had to run, shoot, and perform to SWAT minimums. My biggest fear was not passing out, it was throwing up in my mask from heat exhaustion.

Michelle and the kids on January 2, 1998. We had gone to see the Rose Parade floats on display in Pasadena. I was too gaunt and yellow from chemotherapy to want to be in the photo.

Teaching Meagan to shoot my 10mm MP5 (a weapon unique to the FBI) at a SWAT open house in 2000. Notice that her finger is *not* on the trigger. Good form.

A Gulfstream G-V over Iran en route to Karachi, Pakistan, following the US consulate bombing in June 2002 that killed thirteen people. I had lots of time to read the inch-thick briefing book prepared for us before we departed.

The bomb scene at the consulate two days later, one hundred yards from the point of detonation. Body parts had (for the most part) been retrieved and we were beginning to dig out the crater. Vehicles were those on the street when the bomb went off. Note that most of the trees are missing leaves and/or branches.

LEFT: August 2002 in Karachi. Reviewing weapons (grenade launchers, AK-47s, explosives, land mines, and booby traps) seized by Pakistani forces during sweeps following the bombing of the US consulate. FBI and CIA information provided in June was valuable in locating the cells.

BELOW: Another bomb site: the JW Marriott Hotel in Jakarta, Indonesia, in August 2003. I supervised the investigation for the FBI. This is the remains of the hotel's luxury restaurant, in which several of the twelve victims died. A large portion of a victim's body was later found inside the chandelier at the center of the photo. The head of the suicide bomber who drove the bomb truck was found on the pool deck on the fifth floor. You always find surprises at bomb sites.

Aerial surveillance at dusk, May 2006. Notice the bare foot on the instrument panel in the lower right. This plane is identical to the one in which I had my in-flight fire in 1989.

Madison, Meagan, and I dance at a wedding shortly after my retirement. My feelings about these two are obvious.

It was very warm that day, and as was my custom, my flight suit was my summer uniform of a T-shirt, shorts, and flip-flops. In our surplus air force O-2As, we flew in flight suits and occasionally helmets. In the helicopters, flight suits and helmets were the required gear. But with these new "civilian" aircraft in the fleet, fireproof clothing seemed silly (and hot) to me. After boarding the aircraft, I would even slip off the flip-flops and fly barefoot. Completely out of policy, but, boy, was it fun.

I was talking to Eli Tanaka, call sign 907, the pilot of the plane we were replacing. I had just confirmed his altitude for the second time. It is considered bad form to arrive at the surveillance location at the same altitude as the aircraft you are replacing, because you will likely hit it. Our aircraft were elaborately equipped with the latest equipment. In a move that was so enlightened that I still have trouble believing that the US government made it, a decision was made to spend a significant amount of money to make the FBI surveillance aircraft instrumentation roughly the equal of new airliners as far as avionics were concerned. We had advanced autopilots and navigation equipment that was second to none. I could navigate to any point on the Earth long before GPS made that seem easy.

With Point Dume, home of Johnny Carson and Barbra Streisand, among others, in sight, I began searching the sky for Eli in "Rock 32."

"Nine-oh-seven, are you at four [thousand feet]? We're coming in at three and a half," I broadcast.

"We're level at four, Nine-oh-five," Eli answered.

At that second, I caught a glint over the restaurant. It was Rock 32, in a graceful, left-wing-down orbit. Cessnas sometimes look ungainly on the ground, but with the gear retracted, they are simply beautiful in the air; they remind me of seagulls. I passed behind and below Eli, entered a left-hand bank, and slid in behind and below him in a very wide right echelon position. As I maneuvered, I began to hear an unusual, high-pitched, almost dog-whistle-like tone in my headset.

It was loud enough that I winced and turned down my earphone volume, which had almost no effect. A noise like that would almost certainly be related to the electrical system, so I checked the ammeter and saw to my surprise that the gauge was spiked on the full-charge side. This was a serious problem. The alternator on an aircraft can generate much more electricity than it needs to operate but when working properly only provides enough electricity to do the jobs required of it. Excess electricity is a serious problem. On this aircraft, the alternator could generate enough electricity to cause the battery to explode, and right then the alternator was out of control. Our battery was in that slender, waspish part of the tail of the aircraft where the rudder and elevators are attached. If the battery blew up, it could blow the tail off, which is generally considered to be a bad thing, as we did not have parachutes aboard.

I had only a few seconds to act. Instinctively I keyed the mike and transmitted, "Eli, I'm gonna be off the radio for a few seconds."

I didn't have time to listen for his response, tell him what was wrong, or do an orderly shutdown of the radios and systems. I reached down to the master switch just above my left knee on the instrument panel and slapped it to the OFF position—this was like pulling the plug on the whole aircraft. Instantly, the high-pitched squeal stopped, as did all power to the aircraft except the engine. Unlike a car engine, aircraft engines in general are configured to run without electrical power from the alternator or the battery. Cars will die if either is disconnected from the system.

With the electricity off, I had time to take stock, but not too much time. My transponder was off, which meant that my identification codes had disappeared from air traffic control, and I had no means of communicating with anybody. But it was a beautiful day and I was certain that I knew what the problem was. The alternator control unit (ACU) had failed.

This had happened to me before in the O-2s, and I had learned a procedure: reset the ACU, much as you would reboot a computer if it froze. It had always worked like a charm. This would quickly solve the problem and demonstrate my mastery of the aircraft to the new copilot. What I didn't know was that on this aircraft, the ACU could not be reset, and it is not advisable to try. Again, there is a difference between military and civilian aircraft. With the intercom out now due to the loss of the alternator and battery power, I shouted to Neil above the noise.

"The alternator ran away. I'm gonna reset it and then we'll get back to work."

I could imagine how impressed Neil was going to be as I went through the restart procedure from memory. Anytime your ego has more control of the plane than your fear of sudden death, you're in for trouble. The last step on that restart procedure is to turn the alternator back on with the master switch. Before I did so, I took one last scan out the windows to make sure that Eli was still where I had last seen him. He was. I reached down to the master switch above my left knee and clicked it to the ON position.

What happened next occurred in the blink of an eye but seemed to last for minutes. As the switch reached the ON position and I felt that usual click, I also felt and then heard a strong *pop* from behind the instrument panel. There was an immediate shower of sparks from left to right in front of me, like a roman candle. The sparks seemed to fly in slow motion across the cabin, bouncing off the windscreen, the instrument panel, and the right side of the aircraft. They were bright orange even in daylight. I distinctly remember watching as the arcing sparks bounced off the right side of the cockpit and onto Neil's and my laps. Smoke emanated from the cooling vents on top of the instrument panel, and looking down into the foot well, I saw a flickering glow that indicated something under the panel was on fire. Instantly, I slapped the master switch off again, but the damage had been done.

I had not expected this.

We were in serious trouble. We were three-quarters of a mile above the earth, we had a fire in the cockpit, we had no parachutes, and I was wearing shorts. Of equal concern were the fuel lines from the wing tanks, which went through the very area where the fire seemed to be centered. If those fuel lines ignited, I was going to miss my own wedding.

I thought, Somebody had better do something about this. Then I realized that if anything was going to be fixed, I would be the one to do it. For maybe an entire second—an eternity—I sat there confused, not knowing what to do, panic knocking at the door. Then I gave myself the best advice I could think of: Do just *one* thing. The rest will come to you.

Small bits of melted plastic were falling from under the instrument panel onto my aforementioned bare legs. We needed to get on the ground. I rolled the aircraft into a very steep right bank, simultaneously pulling the power to idle and dropping the landing-gear handle so that the aircraft would not gain too much speed in the resulting dive. The fact that the gear was inoperative now did not occur to me until I blew through the aircraft redline airspeed in just a few moments on the way down from thirty-five hundred feet. Loading a couple of *g*s onto the aircraft, we started to slow down as I looked for an empty space to put the aircraft. But the only empty space I could find was the Pacific Ocean. The beaches on this beautiful day were elbow to elbow with tanned hardbodies. The roads were jammed, and there were surfers in the breakers. However, beyond the surf there was nobody. I angled out offshore about a quarter of a mile and paralleled the shoreline as I descended.

I screamed at Neil over the aircraft noise: "Get the in-flight fire checklist!"

"I can't hear you!" Neil shouted. "My intercom isn't working!"

"I know!" I said, wondering if he thought I had missed anything that had recently occurred. One needs to remember that this was Neil's first operational mission, so I grabbed the checklist myself. I opened my window and told Neil to do the same so that we could clear a bit of the smoke out of the cockpit. The checklist for "Electrical Fire" was fairly simple and involved removing all electrical power to the aircraft, which I had achieved when I turned off the master switch. Within a second or two I complied with every instruction and flipped over to the "Ditching" checklist. Neil looked over and saw what I was reading.

"*Really?*" He asked.

"*Really!*" I answered, in shock just as he was.

Per the checklist, Neil and I opened our doors, took off one shoe (or flip-flop, in my case), and wedged it between the door and the frame to keep the doors from jamming closed when we hit the water. I pointed out to Neil that there were life vests in the seatbacks, and he started pulling them out. I would have to put mine on in the water. I looked down and saw that the landing-gear handle was down and realized I couldn't land in the water with my gear down. I looked out the window and realized that the gear had—of course—not come down, and I had a moment to chuckle at myself.

We were now below a thousand feet, and the smoke was still emanating from the panel. I needed to advise somebody of my predicament. The radios were burned up, but I remembered that we always kept a spare Handie-Talkie in our flight bags. I reached for the HT, grabbed it, and turned it on. I was delighted to see that the battery was charged perfectly. I selected channel C-6, the frequency on which the surveillance was operating, and I called for Eli.

"Eli, can you hear me?"

Nothing. I switched the radio to C-7, which was a repeater frequency and would broadcast to all surveillance team units in the L.A. area. Once again I transmitted, and once again I got no response. Finally, I decided to go all in. I clicked the radio dials to channel A-1, the main channel for the FBI in the Los Angeles region, which is heard everywhere from Palm Springs to Santa Barbara. Eli would *have* to hear this.

"Eli!" I called over the engine roar. "This is Steve!" I had given up on fancy radio call signs.

Again, nothing. But then I felt a tiny vibration in the radio. I realized that Eli had heard me and was responding, but I couldn't hear him over the din of the open-windowed aircraft. So I placed the HT in contact with my headphone ear cup, and the vibrations from the radio speaker transmitted perfectly into the ear cup. I could hear him almost as well as I could with the regular radio.

Then, to my immense relief, I heard him ask, "Steve? Where did you go?"

"Eli, I'm on fire! There are sparks flying all over the cockpit. I'm going to put it in the ocean off of Zuma!"

Eli's calm response was stunning. "Roger."

"Zuma" is Zuma Beach, one of the most popular beaches in Los Angeles. It is where I had courted Michelle. With that last call, every FBI agent between Bakersfield and San Diego, Palm Springs and Santa Barbara, within earshot of a radio, heard me say that I was on fire and that I was putting the aircraft in the ocean. In hindsight, I would rather not have done that. That call became the stuff of legend.

But then I began to realize that the smoke was clearing, and the glow under the panel was gone. Could the checklist have worked? With a glimmer of hope, I stopped my approach to the water at four hundred feet, added enough power to maintain altitude over the waves, and reassessed my situation. The engine was running perfectly. I had communication with Eli, and he could communicate with air traffic control. If the fire was truly out, I had a great chance of making it back to Point Mugu, even if I had to belly-in. I decided to continue west toward the base, but I was not going to climb above five hundred feet; I needed to be ready to get into the water if the fire kicked back up.

"I think the fire may be out. I'm thinking I might try to make it to Mugu," I told Eli.

Eli had me in sight and was descending rapidly toward me. "I let them know you're coming."

At five hundred feet and about one hundred knots, with the situation calmed down somewhat, I felt a weird sense of betrayal. I had never abused an airplane, and I somehow felt wronged, almost as if a woman I loved had robbed me at gunpoint. I had never seen this side of "her." Obviously, no pilot can fly for very long without knowing intellectually that this kind of thing could happen, and I understood that my actions had contributed to the problem, but on such a beautiful day, on such a beautiful flight? It didn't seem right. I looked at the instrument panel of the airplane that I'd come to love so much and realized that I had trusted her *too* much. I will always love flying, but after that day, I could never love it in the same way. Never again would I trust my aircraft so completely. It was an odd feeling.

"Steve, Mugu is ready for you, and there's a SAR"—search and rescue—"helicopter headed our way." This was reassuring, but not as reassuring as seeing the outline of Mugu Rock in the distance. The Rock is a hundred-foot promontory on the southeastern-most point of naval air station Point Mugu.

"Steve, the tower says cleared to land, Runway two-seven."

"Roger that, Eli, cleared to land, two-seven."

That was good news and bad news. I was happy to be cleared to land, but we still didn't have wheels down. The Cessna 182RG has an emergency hydraulic landing-gear pump between the pilot and copilot seats on the floor. When the landing gear, for whatever reason, will not come down, the pilot or the copilot simply extends the handle of the emergency hydraulic pump and pumps up and down as if working a hydraulic jack. Eventually, when the gear locks down, a green light will come on. Unless, of course, you had recently been on fire or something like that; then the lights won't work. So we had to just guess when the gear was locked down. I told Neil to pump until he could no longer move the lever and then quit. Neil followed the instructions to the letter.

As we passed over Mugu Rock, the runways came into sight, and it was a beautiful thing. At the approach end of Runway 27, I could see the lights of three airport fire trucks. That was very reassuring. With great relief I turned final. We were not going to be able to put down any more than the ten degrees of flaps that I already had down when the problem started, but that wouldn't mean anything more than an unusually fast landing speed, which did not jeopardize the outcome. As I floated over the approach end of the runway at about twenty feet, out of the corner of my eye I saw the fire trucks pulling onto the runway as I passed. Unknown to me, these trucks accelerate pretty aggressively, and they'd almost caught up with me by the halfway point of the runway. The touch-down was surprisingly soft. I applied maximum braking, as I did not want to be in the aircraft any longer. I was out of the aircraft the second after it stopped and walked slowly away, backward, staring at it as the firemen swarmed over it.

I grabbed a ride on an FBI tug back to the hangar. At about that time, people started to arrive at the office. The ground teams that we were working with at the Surf had almost beaten me to Point Mugu in their Camaros and Mustang GTs, blasting down Pacific Coast Highway. They denied being concerned for my safety, of course, and would say only that they had never seen a plane crash and were curious.

It was Lawrence Hatch, the surveillance ground team leader, who coined the moniker "Sparky." And as we began to relax, they began to do impressions of me on the radio, sounding scared. This game did not initially amuse me. With each rendition, however, my voice was portrayed another octave higher. By the final performance, it was up to dog-whistle high. All swore that this was how I actually sounded. I still do not believe that. However, all began calling me Sparky before they left for the day. To this day, there are agents who are my friends who still do not know my real first name.

The Aviation Unit in Washington, DC, came out to investigate the incident, and they were able to determine that the cause of the electrical problem was simply a single important wire from the FBI-installed electronics package that was misrouted and began rubbing on an aluminum part of the aircraft. Over time, this wire wore off its own insulation, and it chose my flight to make metal-to-metal contact with the airframe for the first time.

I did not tell Michelle about the gravity of that flight for several years afterward, even though I knew that was wrong. I did not want her to worry.

9

Don't Lose Him,
Don't Get Burned

MICHELLE AND I were married, and we settled into a life so unpredictable that it became routine. Our first child, Meagan, arrived in 1990, and she scared us to death when it took the doctors five minutes to get her to breathe. She emerged unscathed and due to my strange schedule, I got to spend a lot of time with her as she grew from infant to toddler.

Stevie Jr. arrived ten days before my birthday in 1992. I had a son! I immediately began dressing him in baby flight suits and leather helmets. Life was glorious. My family was growing, and I had the time I needed to spend with them. We had moved to a perfect little suburban ranch home and even bought a minivan. Time seemed to stand still.

There was always something new happening at work. In addition to flying, I had been put in charge of aircraft maintenance at Point Mugu, so I did most of the postmaintenance test flights, which gave me the distinction of being the pilot with the most "declared emergencies" in the Los Angeles FBI. As has been said so many times, flying is hours and hours of boredom interspersed with moments of sheer terror.

It was not just the mechanical problems that proved that; it was the cases.

The call "Return to base" came in on my car radio as I was driving home from Point Mugu on September 16, 1992. A kidnapping had occurred in Santa Barbara, and there was a ransom demand. This didn't happen very often. Sadly, most kidnappings by that point were, as now, for sexual not financial reasons, and the victims were usually dead within hours. This, however, was the classic "rich kid kidnapped by unknown subjects with large ransom demand" scenario. The family lived in an area of Santa Barbara known as Hope Ranch, where homes start in the double-digit millions.

Calls were coming in from the kidnappers through that first night, but they were from pay phones, and the kidnappers were gone before anybody could ever identify the phone and get there. The next day, surveillance teams set up all throughout Santa Barbara at half-mile spacing, ready to go to any location once a call was made. The kidnappers had said that they would call that night and give instructions for the delivery of the ransom. Then they seemed to make a stupid mistake: they made a single phone call from a traceable line that was not a pay phone.

That night, the FBI traced that call to a specific house. The SWAT team made an entry, and we all thought the case was over. But it turned out to be the wrong house. We were dumbfounded. The people were not involved, but the call had come from their house.

The answer to the conundrum came the next day from GTE, the phone company in that area of the world. GTE had what are known as "B-boxes," which is apparently a truncated form of the slang "black box" throughout Southern California. These boxes were probably a familiar sight to most people but were so ubiquitous that they were rarely noticed. A B-box is a three-foot-tall metal cabinet with two handles in the front that are locked or padlocked, and inside are the phone circuits for fifty to a hundred houses. It is essentially a miniature switching station, and if you know how to work a B-box you can use a lineman's phone to tap into any phone number you want. The box for that house was inspected and found to have been broken into, and there were fresh alligator-clip marks on the copper terminals. It was an embarrassing failure. But next time they called from a B-box, the SWAT team would be ready for them. At about noon they began to set up positions around all the known B-boxes in Hope Ranch and surrounding areas. They spent a lot of time getting their positions perfectly camouflaged. From their position, they could see anybody going to any B-box in the area.

That night nothing happened. Not even a phone call. There was only one incident, when a jogger stopped to urinate in the bushes—right on a camouflaged SWAT guy. Not only was that good camouflage, but it took amazing dedication not to stand up and scream.

The next call came on the ninth day of the kidnapping. They assured the family that this was absolutely the last night that they were going to put up with delays. They advised that they would call again at 8:00 in the evening and that the money had better be ready that day. Crawling into the airplane that afternoon with my copilot Marty Chamberlain, I was determined that nothing would go wrong that night. It was entirely likely that I would be (as I had been several times before) the only eyes on the kidnapping suspect at some point or another. If I lost the subject in traffic and the victim died, I would live with that for the rest of my life. I both loved and hated that responsibility. If I were the victim's family, I would want me to fly the mission. Twenty minutes later we were airborne and climbing to eighty-five hundred feet. By 5:00 that afternoon I was over Hope Ranch. The call promised at 8:00 did not occur. No call came at 8:30, no call came at 9:00. We were getting discouraged.

I was getting jittery. We had already been airborne four hours, and all the other crews had used up their allowed flying hours for the day. We were the last airplane the case was going to get that night. It was pitch black outside, the fog was starting to roll in again, and the call had not come in. I knew that once the fog topped Santa Barbara, the airports near our base would be at minimums for an approach, and we would be useless anyway. Three more hours passed and no calls. By midnight Santa Barbara was half covered by fog. I was pulling out approach charts, because I believed that the night was over for us.

"All units standby—we have an incoming call from the kidnapper!" cracked the radio unexpectedly.

My heart jumped a foot. I tossed the approach charts and grabbed my stabilized binoculars, powering them up. Several agonizing minutes went by, and I could only guess what was going on. I later learned that the kidnapper was angry with the parents and was chewing them out over the phone for not following his instructions. The chewing out gave the FBI and GTE the time they needed to identify the phone booth from which he was calling. In his anger, the kidnapper had made a mistake.

"All units! All units! We have a location for the outgoing call. SWAT units stand by. SOG—the address is Carillo and Castillo, southeast corner of Carillo and Castillo." My copilot turned on his red flashlight and started to flip to the appropriate page of the map book to find the location, but I knew the corner: it was just off the 101 freeway. I rolled the airplane into a steep bank, pulled hard, and fed the power to the Turbo 210. "Nine-oh-five is en route. ETA one minute," I transmitted. When still two miles away, I began to scan the intersection with the stabilized binos. I couldn't find a phone booth, and the fog was covering half of the intersection.

The north side was clear, and when on that side, I could look under the fog on the south side. If the kidnapper was under the fog

I could see him only for a minute at a time—airplanes can't hover. As I was scanning the small area, a streetlight-shadow I thought had been that of a sign *moved* on the southeast side of the intersection. I zoomed the binos to that point, and standing at a phone booth was a white male. I took a deep breath and told myself to calm down. It was time to go to work.

In the calmest voice I could muster, I reported, "I've got him. Nine-oh-five has the subject at a booth on the southeast corner of the intersection."

I could hear the elation in the command-post voice. "Excellent! Maintain visual."

"Jay," I transmitted to Jay Rollins, the SOG ground team leader, eschewing the formality of call signs, "I've got a white male on the southeast corner. He is in long dark pants and a light shirt. He's wearing a baseball cap, do you copy?"

Rollins keyed up, and in the background I could hear the engine of his Z28 wailing. Jay had his foot buried in the throttle and was ripping across downtown Santa Barbara as fast as he could.

Jay Rollins was the best they had down there. He was a former SWAT guy and the best ground surveillance guy in L.A. He and I had worked together so long we could finish each other's sentences.

"I copy! Sparky, I'm at least three away; hang on to him!" Three minutes. An eternity. At that moment, it felt like there was only Jay and me in the world, and we were having a very private conversation. All formality went out the window. All bravado and "FBI talk" gave way to the bare facts and fears.

"Jay, if he goes south or west I can't go with him and we'll lose him. Fog is covering the entire south and west portion of the city—if he goes south of that intersection, I'm out of it! Do you copy?"

"Copy," Jay shouted over the roar of the Camaro's engine. He was moving as fast as he could possibly go, not helped by traffic in

Santa Barbara, even at midnight. Then the shadow began to move. The subject was leaving. My calm façade began to crumble.

"Dammit. Jay, he's walking away from the booth. What's your twenty?" I transmitted as calmly as I could. Panic would ruin what little hope we had left.

Then from the command post: "All units. The call ended. The call ended."

"No shit, Sherlock," I deadpanned in the intercom to my copilot.

The command post continued, "The kidnapper is angry and has broken off communications." Shit. Things were going south. Then I got a break. I saw the guy from the phone booth approach a car and appear to go through the motions of putting a key in the door. It was close enough to a streetlight that I could see some detail.

"All units," I broadcast, "I may lose him. Subject is at a gray compact vehicle. Four door. It's not all the way in the light; I can't tell you what it is. OK, now he's getting in the driver's seat . . . Jay, how far out are you?"

"I'm almost there, Sparky. Stand by!" Jay sounded pissed. At himself? At the situation? At me? It didn't matter; I couldn't stand by. If he went south we lost and that was it, and then it was over.

"Brake lights on!" I called out. "Backup lights on. . . . Pulling out of a parallel-park spot north. . . . This might be good, he's heading north. . . . No! He's doing a one-eighty in the middle of the street and he's going to be heading . . . *south*, and I can't go with him!"

It was over. I watched helplessly as he disappeared under the fog. Just before he completely vanished, I saw him turn onto the on-ramp for the southbound 101 freeway. But the 101 south was under the fog.

"One-oh-one south!" I shouted. But then he was gone. My nerves gave way to shock. We had lost him. Rollins's car streaked through the intersection seconds later, and he called out, "Are you sure he took the 101? I've got taillights ahead on Carillo!" Jay shouted. He was arriving at the intersection.

"Yes," I said, disheartened.

"I'm jumping on the freeway. Trailing units head south!" Jay said, directing his team.

But on the freeway, what were the chances of him picking him out of all the cars between him and the kidnapper? The guy could take the next exit and Jay would never know it. I sat there for thirty seconds wondering what we could do, when my headphones crackled to life.

"Does he have a burned-out brake light, Steve?" Rollins's voice came out of nowhere.

"Yes!" I had noticed that when he put his foot on the brake to shift into reverse, only one side of the lights went on. "Right side brake light burned out!"

Then Jay said in the most wonderfully serene, matter-of-fact voice, "Forty has an eye on him." We were back to radio call signs. Jay had him. Jay was in his element.

"You owe me a big, fat kiss, Sparky," Jay said.

"You'll get it," I promised. "No tongue this time."

Jay immediately began marshaling his six-car team, having each car parallel or drive ahead of the subject, or trail. That way, the subject never saw a car behind him for more than a block. Jay was a pro.

"He's southbound on the 101. It's a light gray Honda Accord with primer on the right rear fender. Copy all units? I'll be getting a plate at the next ramp." And with those words, I turned to Jell-O. With the sudden relief, I found myself physically exhausted by the stress. I looked at the aircraft clock and realized that we had been in the air for well over seven hours. A look at our fuel gauges got my attention. This airplane really wasn't supposed to be able to fly seven hours. It was only the super-low power settings that the FBI used during surveillances that let these planes stay up that long.

Reluctantly, I turned the radios to air traffic control just after I heard that SOG had followed the guy to a residence. This time it was the right residence. My excitement was tempered by the fact that we were facing another serious problem. The airports where we had fuel to get to were at or near approach minimums. Just a few minutes before, they had all been fairly open, but the fog had moved faster than we estimated. There were four airports we could make: Santa Barbara was now "zero-zero." Point Mugu had closed two hours before, and even if we called the controllers back, I would be out of fuel before they got to the airport to turn on the approach equipment. Camarillo Airport, the farthest from the ocean at ten miles, had a 660-foot minimum descent altitude on the approach. But the fog was at four hundred feet there, and visibility was reported as half a mile. The last option was Oxnard, but they were reporting ceiling indefinite, visibility at a quarter mile, which basically made the approach futile. "Ceiling indefinite" meant the fog was to the ground, and I could only descend to two hundred feet on Oxnard's approach.

I had flown thirty-two hours in the last four days (about the maximum flight time the FBI allowed) and was on my seventh hour that day. Now, at 1 AM, exhausted, I was having to make critical decisions. Minutes before, I was dealing with a life-or-death situation regarding someone I did not know. Suddenly I was dealing with a life-or-death situation regarding my copilot and me.

Calling what was then "Los Angeles Approach," the air traffic control facility for the area, I advised them of my predicament. They asked if I could make it to Van Nuys Airport about seventy-five miles away, and I just couldn't be sure. At 1 AM in pitch-black weather in fog is not the time to run out of gas. I asked for the approach to Camarillo. Though it appeared that the fog was too low there, I had sometimes seen Camarillo have moments where the airport was under a fog "seam," and for a few minutes the ceiling was much higher.

L.A. Approach vectored us to the final approach course. I felt very much alone. The air was so calm, we could have been in a simulator—a simulator inside an unlit closet, inside a dark room, inside a cave, during an eclipse. Camarillo's approach would allow us to descend to the 660 feet in stair steps, and once we reached 660 feet, all we would need to see were the runway lights or the runway end identifier lights (REILs).

"Intercepting final approach course, gear coming down," I announced to no one in particular. I had started talking to myself.

"Two thousand five hundred," Marty called out.

"Two point five," I confirmed.

Down we went, with Marty calling out the altitudes: "Nine hundred . . . eight hundred feet . . . approaching minimum descent altitude . . .seven hundred."

I began to increase power to level at 660.

"Six-sixty," Marty called out matter-of-factly.

Nothing. Not a light, not a glow, nothing. We flew in total darkness, looking intently for the lights of the airport.

"You got anything?" I asked hopefully.

"Nothing," he said. "But we're still a mile or so out."

For the next minute, we continued on the approach. The needles were centered, the approach was perfect, but the fog was solid. At the missed approach point, I called out, "On the missed! Gear coming up!" As I simultaneously fed in climb power and raised the landing gear and flaps, I switched back to Los Angeles Approach: "L.A. Approach, Rock Nine-eight back with you on the missed."

"Rock Nine-eight, roger, say intentions."

"Gimme the ILS two-six Oxnard." I gave up on Camarillo. Oxnard, though reporting fog to the ground, would let me descend to two hundred feet.

"Rock Nine-eight, expect vectors Oxnard ILS."

I climbed back up, leaning the engine until it ran slightly rough to save fuel. We broke into the clear at twenty-five hundred feet, and the stars were beautiful. As we leveled at four thousand feet, Marty picked up a signal from the SWAT operation. The SWAT team had hit the house. The victim was found. Alive.

"Turn off the Bureau radio," I instructed. I was elated, but I didn't need the distraction. I thought we might have fuel for one more approach after that, but I really wasn't sure. I was leaning aggressively, keeping the engine at minimum power on the approaches. The ILS is an approach where you are in a constant descent right to two hundred feet. If you don't see the airport (or its lights) at two hundred feet, you must abandon the approach.

Marty called out the altitudes as I kept the needles centered. I entered the clouds at twenty-five hundred feet. Three minutes later we were approaching minimums. "Three hundred . . . two-fifty . . ." Marty called out. Just below 250 feet, I thought I saw a glow. At 200 feet I saw what looked like a flashbulb in a paper bag. I had a visual on the approach strobes! Only one light, just a glow, but that was all I needed. That allowed me to descend below 200 feet.

"I've got a light!" I shouted to Marty, "I'm continuing . . ."

Holding the rate of descent, I saw another dim strobe and then another. By 150 feet, I could see two strobes in a row. Then, at 100 feet, about the time I should have been thinking about getting ready to level out for touchdown, we began to see runway lights on either side. They didn't go very far before they disappeared in the mist, but I knew we were in the center. Within seconds, the landing light on our plane reflected off the runway, and just that quickly, we flared and were down, rolling out the length of the runway. I didn't apply the brakes right away. My legs seemed to have lost all strength. I opened my window and the moist, cool air entered the cockpit, refreshing me like smelling salts. I didn't realize how stuffy the cockpit had become. I looked at the time; we had been in the air for more than eight hours.

After parking the plane and tying it down, we made our way to a pay phone to call for a cab. Then, I called the SOG supervisor at the command post to tell him we were safely down. It was a short call.

"This is Steve. We missed at Camarillo and we just barely made it into Oxnard. I'm wiped. I'm going home and getting drunk. Then I'm taking the next two days off." And I hung up. My logbook for that night showed eight hours of flight time: seven hours of night flight and a solid hour of hand-flying the airplane on instruments. True to what I told the supervisor, I did not fly again for two days, and then only to retrieve the airplane I had left at Oxnard.

When SWAT hit the kidnappers' location that night, they discovered that the suspects were high school friends of the victim who had written out an entire kidnapping plan. They had kept the victim for a while in a truck-bed toolbox, the type that sits crosswise behind the back of a pickup truck. Later, he was simply chained to a bed. Their written plan indicated that they were going to kill him the next day. As horrible as his ordeal was, the gratitude I have for being allowed to be part of his release in a small way is something that I will always treasure.

Soon after the kidnapping in Santa Barbara, a decision was made to swap out the Cessna T210 we had used on the case for a different aircraft. That particular T210 was a "dog." It was rare that it made two flights in a row without a mechanical failure of some type. A Bureau plane awaited the swap in Lexington, Kentucky. As I prepared to fly to Lexington to make the exchange, I was told that I would be bringing along a copilot: Special Agent Austin McAllister Dodge III, or simply "Dodger."

Dodger was a SWAT team member and pilot who was trying to build flight time to become a pilot in command, and the near cross-country round trip would give him valuable experience. Dodger was a graduate of the University of Southern California and a die-hard USC fan. Our only time constraint on the trip was his absolute need to be back before the following Saturday, because he had fifty-yard-line tickets to the USC-UCLA football game. I told him that should be no problem. Dodger and I hit it off well, and it was an unexpectedly pleasant trip. I learned about SWAT, and I hoped he learned about flying. En route to Lexington, we even had some "fun." Cruising along at ten thousand feet in clouds, we were beginning to pick up ice, and I was working out a deviation with air traffic control, when our navigation instruments chose that moment to quit. Dodger, a former Army Ranger officer, was ready for that. He pulled out a handheld, battery-operated aviation GPS unit, and we navigated with that little Garmin until we were clear of the clouds, beating the dying batteries by only minutes. Experiences like that bond people.

Returning with the replacement plane a day later, we were on schedule for an arrival just in time for Dodger to get a night's sleep and make the big game. On the ground for fuel in Joplin, Missouri, on Thursday afternoon, I powered up my pager while Dodger borrowed an airport car for us to get some food. I immediately received an urgent page to call home. The news was grim: Michelle's grandfather, a man I loved and admired, had suffered a stroke in Baton Rouge and might not live more than twenty-four hours. Michelle was extremely close to her grandpa and had packed up nine-month-old Stevie Jr. and headed for LAX to get the next available plane to Baton Rouge, leaving three-year-old Meagan with her cousin. I was crushed. Richard Ketchum was an idol to me. He had been a B-24 bomber pilot in Europe in World War II, who parachuted out of a tumbling, burning bomber only to spend the rest of the war in a POW camp. After the war, he was the commander of a US Air Force facility in Alaska, flying DC-3s on skis, bush planes, and float planes. I lived for his stories. I loved the guy.

I told Dodger of the news and asked if we could fly all the way back through the night without stopping so I could get to Baton Rouge in time.

"You realize that we're just six hundred miles north of Baton Rouge right now?" he asked quietly.

"Dodger, you're a copilot. If we landed at Baton Rouge, you couldn't drop me off and keep going. You'd be stuck there. You'll miss the game," I explained.

"You might not get there in time if we go all the way to California," he said grimly. You know," he pointed out, "they have those games every year." I argued some more, but my heart wasn't in it. We headed south to Baton Rouge, explaining it to the FBI as "deviation for storms." Dodger did the flying so I could be alone with my thoughts. Arriving at Baton Rouge Metropolitan Airport just before 8 PM, I found out that we had somehow beaten Michelle's flight to Baton Rouge. Dodger and I used our FBI credentials to be at the gate when Michelle deplaned after two connections and six hours of flying alone with a fussy nine-month-old baby, to say good-bye to someone she dearly loved. She was spent.

I could hear Stevie crying in the Jetway before I could see Michelle. I will never forget the look on Michelle's face when she saw me at the end of the tunnel. She was stunned. She began to sob and ran to me with Stevie in her arms. Dodger, a bachelor, gently took little Stevie from her, and as Michelle cried, Dodger played with him and within seconds had him not only calm but laughing. As we got luggage and met Michelle's family at the airport, Dodger carried Stevie and took care of him as if he were his own.

When we had loaded up the car, Dodger simply shook my hand and said, "I'll get a rental car and find a hotel." He told me to call him when I felt it was the right time to leave. Since that day, Dodger's friendship has been one of the most important things I possess. That weekend, I got to say good-bye to a hero of mine, and got Michelle situated with her family. Dodger and I were westbound very early Saturday morning. An hour before game time, we had gotten as far west as San Angelo, Texas. Landing there, Dodger and I watched the big game in a sports bar near the airport. We had the best seats in the house.

A little more than a year later, on January 17, 1994, at almost exactly 1:00 AM, I was forty-five hundred feet over Long Beach, California, following a group of gangsters who we believed were doing a bunch of drive-by shootings. Again, Jay Rollins was on the ground heading things up, when he transmitted an unusual message.

"Nine-oh-five, I just received a call from Nine-oh-five and a half." Any "half" added to an agent's call sign meant "spouse." The airplanes didn't have phones, so the spouses knew that to get in touch with us they needed to call our ground team leader. In my entire flying career, I received two of these calls: one when Michelle caught the kitchen on fire trying to dry a wet towel, and this one. This time, I thought I knew what the call was about. She was nine months pregnant with our third child.

"Go ahead, Jay," I said nervously.

"The contractions are five minutes apart; you might want to head west," Jay said with obvious glee.

Head west—return to base—I did. Turning for home like a fighter jet, I heard congratulations from all the ground team members. I flew that plane home faster than it knew it could fly. Out of the plane and into the car, red lights and siren (I know, I know, that's not right and it's not ethical. But if you could, wouldn't *you*?) A call on the way told me that Michelle was at her aunt's house and to go there.

Michelle's uncle was her doctor, conveniently enough. I arrived just before 3 AM and found her on the couch. Contractions were stalled at five minutes apart, so Uncle Paul suggested we get a few hours sleep. We lay down and turned off the lights but couldn't sleep. We chatted like little kids. At 4:30 the contractions began to quicken.

At 4:31, the 6.7 magnitude Northridge Earthquake struck, centered twenty miles from us. We were showered with broken glass and books from nearby shelves. There was widespread damage in our area, power was out, the hospital was on emergency power, and our garage back at home began to flood. But everyone in our family was uninjured, and Michelle's contractions stopped. For two days!

But on the nineteenth, in a hospital that was red-tagged due to earthquake damage but operational, Madison Michelle Moore was born during aftershocks, in a delivery room covered in clear plastic to keep plaster from the cracked walls from falling on the patient during the delivery. It was like a war zone. The family was complete.

Even with high points like the Santa Barbara kidnapping case, the routine of flying had become, well, routine. If you take anything you love and do it too much or in the wrong way, it ceases to be that same thing.

On the upside, I had become a helicopter pilot in command, and I love flying helicopters as much as anybody can love anything. But I had this badge in my pocket, and it seemed that it had been too long since I had been a street agent. As much as I loved flying, I had decided that what I wanted more was to be an FBI agent. I was also getting frustrated with the aviation bureaucracy. As an example, we had two army helicopters, OH-6As, but both were approaching engine overhauls, and neither the army nor the FBI would pay for the work, and the military had run out of surplus engines. It was incredibly frustrating, as it appeared that both would be grounded indefinitely when they were so crucial to the mission. Helicopters gave us capabilities we could get no other way. They allowed the FBI to drop off Park Rangers on nearby islands and set up cameras to identify seal poachers. Helicopters could fly surveillance in weather that would ground fixed-wing aircraft. Helicopters allowed us to fly to major crime scenes such as airline disasters and ferry evidence, personnel, and SWAT teams into remote areas. They were crucial.

For the FBI Aviation Unit in Washington, DC, to allow these aircraft to be grounded was unacceptable to me. In my frustration, I had begun communicating with the army about their plans to surplus an army observation helicopter type known as the OH-58A. The 58A was far superior for our mission to the older OH-6s we were flying, and they were going to be releasing hundreds of them for free to law enforcement. I had made friends with some of the army officers in the surplus program, and they wanted very much to get their surplus aircraft to the FBI, where they could continue to have an important mission. I reported this to headquarters, but they inexplicably had no interest.

When an aircraft was declared surplus by any military organization, federal agencies had a right to claim, or "screen," this surplus equipment for no cost, according to a priority list. At the top of that list was the FBI, which meant simply that the FBI had first pick of any and all surplus aircraft. Because of that, when the 58A was declared surplus, the FBI could have had the "pick of the litter." But FBIHQ repeatedly turned down L.A.'s request for the aircraft and finally stated in no uncertain terms to *stop asking*. They had no interest in the OH-58, because if they got them for us, "every office would want one, and we can't afford to support one for every office." It was stunning, Hoover-esque logic. It was unbelievable. It was unacceptable. I decided that if they wouldn't get the aircraft, I would. I made plans to obtain them without headquarters knowing.

But as I waited for the OH-58 surplus to begin, a horrible thing happened: Attorney General Janet Reno, as part of President Clinton's initiative to use federal funds to assist state and local police departments, changed the priorities for surplus aircraft to favor city and state agencies over federal agencies. When I saw the FBI's new priority number, I was crestfallen. The FBI's priority had gone from #1 to #241. That put us just behind the Cherokee Nation Police for screening for aircraft. It was not enough that the FBI did not have budget for helicopters, but at that point Attorney General Reno had made it impossible to remedy our problem.

In discussing this demoralizing situation with the army, one of their officers saw a flaw in Reno's plan. The Justice Department had indeed, in cooperation with the military, changed the priorities for aircraft. *But only for complete, flying aircraft.* They had neglected to change the screening priority for *spare parts.* The FBI still had #1 priority for aircraft *parts.* It was a huge oversight but not unheard of with the government. We then very carefully looked up the definition of "aircraft part." An aircraft part, it turns out, can be any *conglomeration* of parts, as long as the conglomeration is not a flyable aircraft. It was there that we hatched our plan.

At Fort Rucker, Alabama, there were four of the most pristine OH-58 aircraft in army inventory. They had the latest engines and avionics and were "clean, one-owners." They were "cream puffs." I wanted those four. In conjunction with some very committed army officials, we arranged to have the tail rotors taken off each of these aircraft—which made them non-airworthy. Then, the army department controlling them immediately declared them "non-flyable," which meant that they were now no longer aircraft but a conglomeration of "parts." At that very second, the aircraft were transferred to the FBI, pursuant to my preexisting request, as "spare parts."

Obviously, FBIHQ was not aware of this plan. Nor were they aware that I flew an FBI plane to the Bell Helicopter factory in

Texas, where I took a weeklong course to learn how to fly the OH-58. They were also not aware that I then brought four new OH-58 tail rotors (which I had obtained using the FBI #1 priority for parts) and flew on to Fort Rucker, where an army mechanic installed the tail rotors, converting the now-FBI helicopters into flying machines once again. I reported to headquarters in a routine communication only that Los Angeles had "obtained a supply of helicopter parts from an army depot," which was absolutely true. Flying them home also saved shipping costs.

The whole transaction happened so quickly that the aircraft were still in their army parking areas in army markings when I and three other FBI pilots arrived at Fort Rucker to fly them home, cross-country, still bearing US Army markings. The trip back to California together was exhilarating and memorable. I do not believe that in the entire two-thousand-mile trip home, we ever were more than five hundred feet above the ground. The weather was beautiful, and we took the doors off the ships, stuck them in the cargo compartment, and flew back in loose formation. I am sure the army got many complaints about a squadron of helicopters buzzing beaches in the Gulf of Mexico that week, and for that I feel almost guilty. Almost.

I am not sure how long it took the FBI to figure out we had those helicopters. By the time they had, I had finally decided it was time for Peter Pan to grow up and become an FBI agent again. My old buddy Larry Page (who had almost gotten thrown out of the FBI Academy along with me for shooting at Patty Muller's target) was now the squad supervisor of the Aryan Nations squad in L.A., and it was a perfect fit. My third "career" in the FBI had begun.

10

SWAT and Other Bad Habits

I HAVE LONG believed that the FBI should not be considered a single career but rather multiple careers sharing the same retirement system. In January 1996 I began what I consider to be my third FBI career. Without a shadow of a doubt, it was the most rewarding, most difficult, and most challenging time of my life. But I said that during each of my FBI careers. Either way, I was in heaven. But this time, heaven almost cost me everything I valued. And it did so in the most insidious ways.

Returning to the office, though, was a series of pleasant surprises. First, I had a predictable schedule, which had been completely absent in the Aviation Unit. It's funny how the mind works; you always seem to want what you don't have. Somebody who has commuted to work and back during rush hour for a decade despises his "rut," wishing for variety. Someone who has had variety for nine years prays for predictability.

Arriving at the office that first day in my crisp new suit and tie, wearing my gun on my hip for the first time in years, I noted that the Bureau had changed significantly. There were multiline phones on each desk, as well as a computer. Wow, I didn't expect that. The FBI had gotten into the computer world, and my learning curve was going to be steep. But I was surprised at how quickly I got back into the swing of things. The time I had spent at Point Mugu turned out to be unexpectedly valuable. Because of the high priority of the cases I had worked at Point Mugu, I had learned what made the Bureau tick, how to improvise to overcome bureaucracy, and how to get things done in spite of headquarters. Though I hadn't been "in the office" for years, I found that I hadn't missed a beat and in some ways had learned more than I would have at a desk.

For the first time, I was routinely assigned great cases. Better cases than I had ever had. I reveled in the simple tasks that I had so long ago tried to learn. I seemed to have boundless energy for my cases. But what I *really* wanted to do was join SWAT.

In the Bureau, there are opportunities for secondary "team" assignments—SWAT, the Evidence Response Team (think *CSI*), the Hostage Negotiation Team, etc. It gives the job variety and makes each participant more capable. Most agents take advantage of the opportunity, but some agents, including full-time pilots, are not allowed to participate in these programs, because it takes away from essential duties. Now that I was out of the Aviation Unit, I was finally going to get a chance to at least try out for the team. For several months I had been working out, lifting weights and running every day, preparing for the SWAT tryouts. When the day came, I was ready. I had to be—I was almost a decade older than the rest of the candidates. The tryouts were an all-day affair that only gave you (if you were selected) the right to go to New Operator Training School (NOTS), which was a two-week basic training course that would further weed out the candidates.

The morning of the tryouts was taken up with strength and endurance tests. No breaks or rest periods were given, except when you were standing in line waiting for your turn at the event. Each event was pass-fail. The "dead-hang" pull-up was chosen as the first event, because it usually eliminated the most people and therefore made the rest of the events quicker. The name dead-hang pull-up is deceptively accurate: You jump up on a bar, palms away from your body, and hang there until your body is absolutely motionless. On the command "Go!" you complete a single pull-up; your legs must hang limp below you. Then you return to a dead hang until your body stops swaying and wait for the next "Go!" command. While this may sound simple, and you might wonder how this would eliminate FBI agents in shape for a SWAT tryout, I forgot to mention something: all pull-ups are performed wearing full SWAT gear, including helmet, forty-pound ballistic protective vest, submachine gun, pistol, about a hundred rounds of ammunition, radio, boots, full gear belt with handcuffs, knife, etc. This is between sixty and seventy pounds of gear hanging off your body during the pull-ups. Completion of two was required to go through to the next event. This was the event I was most worried about. But I managed to eke out two. I held my own during the rest of the strength and endurance tests and the tactical testing. The final event was shooting, and that was where I hoped to separate myself from the pack.

To qualify to be a SWAT operator, one must shoot a 90 percent on a standard FBI shooting course. To put that in perspective; standard agents must score 75 percent to qualify as an agent. I usually shot in the high 90s and expected to shoot mid-90s even with the nerves of a tryout. The way the test works is simple. You have a timed course to fire and are given fifty rounds, which are kept in magazines and in the pistol—not one round more. Extra rounds are not allowed on your person. The course starts at twenty-five yards, moves in to fifteen yards, then in to ten and seven yards, etc. During the course, magazine changes are part of the timed shooting, and your final score is calculated by doubling the number of rounds placed in the scored area of the target, for a possible 100 points. Each bullet counts for 2 percent.

On the whistle, I began the course along with the eight others. My hits were good, and I was flying through the course. We shot the fifteen-yard segment and then went up to the ten-yard line. I only had two rounds outside of the scored area by this time, which gave me a possible 96, and I certainly wasn't going to miss either from the ten-yard line or the seven. I had it made. I relaxed. The course at the ten-yard line was very simple: twelve rounds in ten seconds with a magazine change. Easy. The whistle blew, and I drew the pistol, picking up the front "blade" sight as the Sig Sauer 226 came up. Once on target, I put six quick rounds in the center of the target and reached down with my left hand for a fresh magazine. Simultaneously, with practiced fluidity, I released the magazine in the weapon with my right thumb. As my left hand came up to the gun with the fresh magazine, the used, falling magazine hit the thumb of my left hand in mid-air, dislodging the fresh magazine from my grasp. Because my left hand was coming up at a good rate, the magazine did not so much *fall* out of my hand as it *flew* up into the air in an upward arc. I instinctively grabbed at it with my left hand but only managed to bump it, increasing its rate of speed and the height of its arc. Soon, in slow motion, it came into my field of view, and I watched helplessly as it arced downrange toward my target. I had, for all intents and purposes, tossed it like I was pitching horseshoes. As it reached the top of its arc, it continued straight and true, and before hitting the ground, it impacted the target dead center. As I stood looking in dumbfounded amazement, the whistle blew, ending that segment of the test.

I had not fired the last six rounds. This left me with a possible score of 90. For a moment I was relieved. Then, when I asked to retrieve my magazine, I was told that I was not allowed to go forward of a firing position for a lost magazine or bullets. There were twelve rounds in that magazine. Without those, I was short twelve bullets. Without it, my highest possible score would be 72. I was dead.

As I looked woefully at my completed target, (a 72, true to my prediction), I was crushed. I blew the one event I was sure of. As I began to dejectedly pack my gear, knowing that I would have to wait another year for the next tryout, I learned that each candidate was given two attempts to shoot a 90! Three others had not achieved the required score, so a second relay was to be given. I quickly unpacked my gear, strapped my holster back on, and raced for the line.

On the next relay, I fell into a rhythm and relaxed. The 94 I shot was not as high as I had hoped, but it was enough. A week later, after interviews and evaluations, I got a phone message from SWAT team commander Dan Kurtz; "Congratulations, you made the team. Gear issue for NOTS is Thursday in the SWAT room. Don't get your stuff dirty, you may not be keeping it." As qualified as it was, it remains one of the greatest messages I've ever heard.

Only six of us were chosen to go to NOTS, though the team was short nine operators. Five made it to the end. As Kurtz would later say, "It doesn't matter how you shoot, or if you're tactically sound; we can teach you to do that. We can't teach you to be a team member." Besides me, my class graduated Ryan March, who ultimately became one of my best friends and someone who taught me more about SWAT and tactics than anyone else. I grew to admire him greatly. Billy Kim, born in Korea, grew up next to a US Marine base and made it his life's goal to be a US Marine and an American. He achieved both. Jack Hale was an Olympics-quality wrestler who could effortlessly whip out fifty to a hundred pull-ups. Finally, Josh Cohn rounded out the class. Like me, he was one of the few in SWAT who had no military background, but he was just unstoppable. (Our SWAT team had only two operators who were Jewish, Cohn and Daniel "Pigpen" Fischer. On an operation years later, Cohn was scaling a fence to access a backyard during an arrest, assisted by Fischer. Somehow, Cohn's MP5 snagged on the fence, shooting Pigpen in the foot with a 10mm hollow-point round, seriously injuring him. Recovering in the hospital, Pigpen famously called for an end to the team's "Jew on Jew" violence.)

At NOTS, we shot till our fingertips were blistered. We wrestled, we fought, we ran, we went sleepless for nights. It was not, however, without its lighter moments. At one point, we were running yet another "grinder," an event where you run a mile, drop and do push-ups or sit-ups to exhaustion, then get up immediately and run another mile and do, say, pull-ups to exhaustion. This goes on for an hour or so. When we stopped for push-ups on the military base where we were training, March, Kim, and I found that the ground next to a nearby building gently sloped up toward the foundation. This made push-ups exponentially easier, because you didn't have to go down as far. But we got caught. The SWAT team leader walked over to our group of three push-up artists and blew a whistle. Ryan, Billy, and I stopped and rolled over, exhausted, Billy cursing in Korean. We knew we were going to get chewed out, but at least that meant a short rest. The physical training instructor was *not* amused and began his tirade with sarcasm. Pointing at the slight rise behind Kim, he screamed, "This, gentlemen, is a *slope!*"

At this point, I guess Ryan just couldn't help it. "Damn it, Jack!" he shouted back. "He is *not* a slope! He is a *Korean American*, and I will not have you denigrating a fellow operator!" And with that, everybody but Ryan lost it. I laughed for a good two minutes and chuckled for the next hour. Ryan was like that. He had no fear of authority or of getting in trouble of any kind. We bonded immediately.

We made it through NOTS, but once on the SWAT team, we still spent approximately fifty days a year in regular training of some type or another: airliner assaults, maritime (ship) assaults, winter and summer training at the US Marine Corps' Mountain Warfare Training Center, shooting at the Navy SEAL ranges—it ran the gamut. A year after our NOTS training, the team was at Fort Ord, near Monterey, California, for a week of training at its Military Operations on Urban Terrain (MOUT) facility, a simulated combat environment. Ryan and I had each lived in Monterey growing up, so the evening after our first rigorous day, we did a little sightseeing, then went out for beers at a favorite watering hole on Fisherman's Wharf. Each had our own pitcher of beer, and that, combined with our exertion that day, lit us up just a little. Maybe more than a little. I called it an early night, falling asleep as my head hit the pillow. But Ryan, who was my roommate on that trip, and Jack Hale, another operator from the Thirties, continued to drink. A lot.

I woke in my pitch-black hotel room to the beep of the electronic door key-card. Ryan was finally getting in. I squinted at the clock: 1:20. I had been asleep for an hour. Disturbingly, the door opened only one inch and stayed there. Oh no. He was up to something. As I started to sit up in bed, I saw a boot kick the door open the rest of the way, and as it flew open, an arm reached around the doorframe, and in perfect SWAT form, tossed something cylindrical toward my bed. It was the classic delivery of a "flash-bang" stun grenade. From outside the room I heard Jack Hale scream the warning given before a flash-bang goes off: "Fire in the hole!" I started to cover up, then realized that it didn't look like a flash-bang. In the beam of light coming from the open door to the lit hallway, it almost looked like a plastic cup full of beer. It was. It hit my bed and splashed all over me.

"Boom!" Ryan screamed, simulating the flash-bang going off. Ryan and Hale entered in classic tactical form, quickly clearing the room with invisible guns as if on a high-risk entry. Hale pointed his invisible MP5 at me and screamed, "I've got the subject! I've got the subject!" Oh, crap, they were "arresting" me.

"Cuff him!" Ryan yelled.

With that, Hale reached under the covers and grabbed me by the ankle. As I said, he was an Olympic wrestler; resistance was futile. As he dragged me out of the bed, I was able to snag my can of pepper spray from my nightstand before my butt impacted the carpet-covered concrete floor. Hale tried to cuff me, but he was drunk and I was able to slide away momentarily, him holding on to my right hand. Snap! He got one cuff on. Ryan screamed, "Drag him out into the hall!" I was in no position to be dragged outside, as I was only in my boxers. Fighting for control, I was at a disadvantage because Hale had one arm. In my other arm, however, I had the pepper spray.

"Take the cuff off or I will pepper spray you, Hale!"

"Go ahead!" he dared.

"Hale! He *will* pepper spray you!" Ryan warned. He knew I would. At that moment I was very much in the mood to pepper spray the both of them. Hale hemmed and hawed and threatened for another twenty seconds, but I was aiming. Finally, he said to Ryan, "Do you have a key?" Then, of course, the overused joke of faking like they didn't have a key to the cuffs, as if I didn't have one on my key chain on the nightstand. Within minutes they had produced a key and I was back in bed, sleeping with the swing-bolt latched on the door and Ryan banished for the night.

After the Fort Ord training, I finally earned my way onto the "first string" for the first time, but only for a short time. On a team like the Thirties (more like a squad of the larger team), there are eight to ten operators. Only the first four are part of the primary entry team, which I liked to call the "starters." I was made part of the starting team on one operation for two reasons, I think:

because an operator was out of town, and partially to evaluate me. I flubbed the evaluation.

It was an op to arrest a murder suspect in a gang-infested part of Los Angeles. Because we knew the suspect to be armed and willing to shoot, we utilized flash-bang diversion devices. Flash-bang grenades work by creating explosive sound that is almost incomprehensible. It is more than simply sound, it is a pressure wave that can blow out windows. It can be heard a half-mile away. It also creates a flash of light brighter than hundreds of flash bulbs, temporary blinding anybody looking at it. Finally, it leaves a large smoke-screen cloud that provides cover for the movement of the team. On this particular op, the plan was for me to deploy a bang near the window of the suspect's bedroom as I lined up as #4 on the entry team. Then, the door would be breached with a ram, and the team would enter. *Never* does it go exactly to plan.

We heard the command to execute at approximately 5 AM, and everything went fine until the door was breached—it came off its hinges and flew into the entrance hall, ricocheting back into the doorway, leaning at a crazy angle and temporarily blocking the team's entry. Simultaneously, a large, vicious pit bull ran to the entranceway and tried to get the first operator. Ryan, #2 in line, deployed a flash-bang directly at the dog, but it bounced off the dog before detonating and ended up in the living room, where I could clearly see it for just a moment on the other side of the plate glass window next to me—which I realized would very soon be blowing out. I turned away just in time, and the window disintegrated and blew past us. By that time, March had cleared the doorway and we made tactical entry. The dog was nowhere. The house was pitch black, and the beams of our gun lights made laser-like white shafts through the smoke as we looked for the subject. I was standing next to the hallway that led to the bedrooms when I saw a door fly open. I pointed my MP5 down the hall just as two pajama-clad kids, about four and five years old, sprinted down the hall, hysterical. I didn't blame them. But they were barefoot and running toward a carpeted living room covered with a frosting of glass shards. Instinctively, I put my MP5 on SAFE, dropped it, and let it hang from its sling, scooping up the kids, one in each arm like people used to carry paper bags of groceries. I ran out of the house with them, dropped them on the lawn, and returned to the living room, and we completed the op. But in the debrief, I was eviscerated for leaving my post.

The team leader pointed out bluntly, "We can stitch up kids' feet. If Ryan took a round to the brain because he didn't know you weren't there guarding the hall like it was briefed, how you gonna stitch that up?" He was right, of course. Sometimes, the most difficult part of SWAT was not what you had to learn but what you had to "unlearn."

Investigations continued when SWAT didn't beckon. I arranged a large undercover weapons buy in Las Vegas and decided to bend the rules a little bit. I had been gone a lot with SWAT, and I was really not looking forward to being away from my kids and especially from Michelle for another four days. I came up with a perfect plan. I would have them drive out to Vegas on the same day, and they could stay with me. I'd be gone all day and part of the evenings, but they could bask by the pools, and I could spend some of the evenings with them. It was a perfect plan. I thought.

It worked just fine at first. The meetings went without a hitch, and we were able to arrange the buy. One morning as I said goodbye to the family at the exotic pool, my daughter Madison, for reasons we will never know, thought she was supposed to follow Daddy. Daddy didn't know she was following, and she couldn't keep up. Within a few seconds, a precious toddler in a bathing suit with a tutu was walking into a casino barefoot.

Within minutes Madi was picked up by casino security and a frantic Michelle was found at the pool and brought to security. They needed to verify that Michelle was actually a guest in the hotel. Standard procedure. She told them that she was checked in under "Steve Moore." Too late, she remembered that I had checked in under my UC identification, and it didn't hit her until she had already said my name. She didn't know my undercover identity, but she knew I always used the first name "Steve." They became suspicious of her and asked if she really was a guest of the hotel.

Michelle looked at them and said, "Just check room 1017. I'm staying with a guy named Steve. I don't know his last name," she said, kind of truthfully.

They looked at her quizzically. "We thought you said you were married."

"We are. I didn't say to *each other*. This is still Las Vegas, isn't it?"

With that, they bid her a good trip and took her back to the pool. *That's* an FBI wife!

11

It Was Nice
While It Lasted

AT THIS POINT in my life, I can honestly say that I had never been happier. I was, in FBI parlance, living the dream. I had a beautiful wife, three healthy children whom I adored, and a home in a nice neighborhood, and I was on a good squad at the office. More important than the squad was being on the SWAT team. It was a dream come true. It was better than I had even imagined it would be.

I enjoyed my FBI friends immensely, even their sometimes treacherous sense of humor. For instance, I learned the hard way to never, never, never walk away from an FBI computer without logging off, even if you're just going to be gone a minute or two. It's an official rule, of course, because anybody walking by could access highly sensitive information. But more than that, it's an open invitation for other agents to play a prank. One fateful afternoon, I returned to the computer from the bathroom, and nothing seemed to have changed. However, I soon found out that "I" had sent an e-mail twenty minutes earlier, resigning from the FBI because I was "sexually attracted" to my latest supervisor,

Vince "Lumpy" Monroe, and could not work anymore in an office with him, "unable to tell him of my love." It took me half a day to straighten that one out. I eventually identified the perpetrator and had the opportunity to send an e-mail for him when he made a similar error. He had a desperate crush on an attractive female agent in the office, and she seemed to be uninterested in him. "His" e-mail accused her of not going out with him due to his STDs and chastised her for not being more open minded.

About that time, I had been selected for an undercover assignment that was giving me a lot of satisfaction. I was regularly meeting with a wealthy individual who was looking to smuggle a certain item out of the United States. I was posing as a pilot for a major freight airline and representing that I could smuggle the item out of the country for him. This assignment provided me with a very nice "cold car" (in this context, an undercover vehicle) to match my role as a smuggler.

In every undercover assignment, you must assume a complete pedigree, not just a name and an objective. For instance, if you are working undercover against a mob group, and you tell them that you are single, as likely as not there will eventually be a hooker sent to your room at some time or another as a gift. I explained to Michelle that I had no control over something like that and blowing my cover could endanger the security of the United States.

She simply told me, "We'll find another country."

Apparently, she is not very patriotic.

In order to not be single in the undercover assignments, I told her that I would have the FBI cast a female agent as my wife or girlfriend. But that might require me to act romantic or even kiss the agent from time to time (something I had even practiced at the academy, I pointed out). Michelle was not OK with that plan either. I complained that she was enforcing a double standard. Michelle was an actress. She did small day-player parts on TV shows and was at that very time cast as the lead in a community play, a role in which she had a boyfriend whom she kissed romantically several times during each performance. Several performances on some days. I pointed this out and asked her what made that different from my undercover.

"The difference is that you would enjoy it." End of discussion.

Between the undercovers, the SWAT ops, and the cases, I still flew part time. One day I might be at the firing range for SWAT; the next I might have an undercover dinner planned, or I could be scheduled to fly a surveillance. It was a fabulous life. When I was in the office, I worked out every day. The usual was a run from the FBI office on Wilshire Boulevard about a mile up to Drake Stadium at UCLA. I would run every stair in the stadium twice; grab a set of push-ups, a set of pull-ups, and a set of sit-ups; then head back to the gym at the FBI office. I was in the best shape of my life. But as Thanksgiving of 1996 rolled around, the flu made its rounds in our house, and I was the last one to get it. And once I did, it just hung on. At Christmas, I was still weak and having stomach problems.

Four months later, in April 1997, the Los Angeles FBI SWAT team conducted a maritime antiterrorism training exercise. For this scenario, there were to be several groups of "terrorists" (FBI agents) on Santa Catalina Island just twenty-six miles across the ocean from Long Beach. One group of terrorists would be on a boat in Avalon harbor, one group would be at the airport, and another one would be at a third remote site on the island. The plan was for the SWAT team to leave Long Beach at approximately 6 PM on two Coast Guard cutters. We would then arrive at dusk, when we would put ashore in zodiac inflatable boats. Our orders were to then get to the airport, subdue the terrorists there, and prepare for a long patrol throughout the night to locate the terrorist camp somewhere on the island. It was going to be grueling, but it was going to be a blast. I had been looking forward to it for a long time.

The night before the Catalina op, I started feeling suddenly ill. One minute I was fine, and then two minutes later, I felt like I had contracted a sudden case of dysentery and had to *run* to the bathroom. The whole episode came without warning. Then again, I thought, doesn't it always? But to my horror, I saw that the only thing in the toilet was dark red blood. I was stunned. I felt dizzy. I can remember thinking, with colossal understatement, *OK, that's not good.* I stood there staring at my face in the mirror wondering what I should do. Of course, I suppose this would not be a question at all for many. But for me it was more than a question—it was a dilemma. I did not want to miss the Catalina operation. I did not want to scare Michelle, because I believed that she would see the worst possible prognosis from that one symptom. I assured myself that I had just somehow injured myself in my training regimen. However, the nagging doubt in the back of my mind caused me to remember that I had not felt completely well since the previous fall. When I combined these two facts in my mind, I became afraid. Then I remembered that in my flight physical the previous May, the lab had found signs of occult intestinal blood, but I had decided against further testing, because I was only thirty-eight. This concerned me even more. But I decided to continue with the Catalina training and get medical help afterwards.

The operation at Catalina was as good as I had hoped it would be, but at times it was challenging for me. By about three hours in, I began hemorrhaging again, but I told nobody. My energy was gone. I couldn't keep up with the rest of the team without panting. I was exhausted. I had packed candy bars and sugary sodas in my pack so that I could keep my energy up, and they were the only thing that kept me going that night. At 2 AM, the exercise ended, and we made our scheduled rendezvous with the Coast Guard cutters at the dock at 3. By 3:30 the gangway was up, the ships were heading for home, and boisterous post-training laughter was giving way to fatigue.

Within minutes, all aboard sprawled about looking for an unoccupied space below decks on which to sleep. Red-lit passageways were covered with sleeping SWAT team members, as was every flat space inside the 110-foot cutter. The steady vibration and drone of twin diesels combined with the late hour, the warm inside temperatures, and the rhythmic rocking of the boat to create an almost hypnotic environment. Outside, the bow of the fast ship carved a fluorescent wake from the ocean as a cool, steel breeze blew spray down her flanks. All doors to the outside were dogged down as the passengers slept in the warm bowels of the ship. Except me.

Wandering through the galley, stepping over bodies, I was wide awake and preoccupied with an uncharacteristic endeavor for an FBI agent: I was rationalizing away evidence that pointed to an obvious conclusion. Unable to sleep, I donned a Gore-Tex parka over my three other layers of clothes and climbed the galley ladder to the hatch to the deck outside. Wrenching the latch, I leaned into the heavy door, prying it open against the prevailing deck wind. My next inhale was stopped cold by a blast of freezing wind and spray whipping my face. My eyes struggled to adjust from the red-lit interior to the pitch blackness of the fog-shrouded ocean. Securing the door, I balanced aft and climbed a ladder toward an exterior bridge, searching for a solitary place out of the wind, enjoying the isolation of the deck at night.

I found a sheltered area above and behind the bridge. Sitting on the wet deck facing aft, I could see only the wake of the ship floating in the empty blackness. I was alone in the world. The roar of the ocean and the whistling of the wind passing my shelter gave the only life to my location. As I cocooned myself completely into my parka, the nagging pain returned to my gut as if mocking my efforts to ignore it. With it came the final surrender to the realization that something was seriously wrong inside of me. The evidence could no longer be ignored. Feeling defeated, I drifted off into a cold, fitful sleep.

The colonoscopy I had the next day revealed a large malignant tumor in my colon. It had broken out of the colon into my gut and was all over the other organs. The prognosis was not good. The only good news was that it had not metastasized to my liver, which would have been game over.

It was difficult to go back into the office and clean out my desk. I went to see Dan Kurtz, my SWAT leader. In Dan's office, I told him of the cancer and that I was going to "turn in my gear," SWAT language for quitting the team. Dan gave me my first and one of the few votes of confidence I got that day: "Keep the damn gear. You're going to need it when you get back." I knew that Dan had no control over my physical health, but for some reason that gave me a shred of hope to hang on to.

It's funny how the mind works. It was a weird feeling to be clearing out my desk knowing that I would be gone for at least several months. I didn't know whether to take everything or leave some of my stuff behind to prove that I thought I would be back. I wondered if I should just go ahead and clean the desk out completely to save other people from having to do it in case I didn't survive to go back to work. These were scary thoughts for a thirty-nine-year-old man.

Surgery was called for, and the doctors removed a foot and a half of my colon. After surgery, the news could hardly have been worse. I got an update at my bedside from the surgeon, Patrick Reiten, a good friend. The tumor had turned out to be about the size of a grapefruit. It was an aggressive form of cancer, and they had not gotten it particularly early. The nurse started to cry and left the room. That news hit me pretty hard. But I could tell that it absolutely rocked Michelle. I had another question I wanted to ask but was almost too afraid to utter it. But I knew that I would hate myself until I did ask.

"Pat, how many lymph nodes were involved?"

In talking with the doctors and researching my particular type of cancer in the days before the surgery, I had learned that one predictor that oncologists use to judge prognosis is the number of lymph nodes involved with the cancer. As a matter of course, ten or twelve lymph nodes surrounding the tumor are removed with the tumor, and they are sent to a lab to check for cancer cells in them. The success rate of keeping the tumors from recurring is directly tied to the number of lymph nodes involved. In 1998, any more than three lymph nodes out of ten indicated a very poor rate of survival over a five-year period, with the prognosis becoming poorer as the number of lymph nodes increased. So I had to know how many lymph nodes of mine were involved.

Pat took a deep breath and exhaled his answer: "We removed twelve lymph nodes, and there was cancer in ten of them."

With this news, Michelle had to sit down. I myself was in shock. I felt like I had just heard my death sentence. My only ray of hope at that point was Dr. Michael Masterson, my oncologist. I will never forget the day he came into my room after I was out of intensive care and, with Michelle and my parents in the room, said that he thought we had a good chance. But I wasn't persuaded. We were in the oncology ward of the hospital, and as Dr. Masterson spoke, we could hear sobs coming from another room.

Dr. Masterson, like most oncologists, was as much psychiatrist as he was oncologist, and when he looked me in the eyes, I knew immediately that he knew that I thought he was blowing smoke.

"You don't believe me, Steve?"

"I just need to be realistic," I said

"Do you think that I'm afraid to tell people bad news?" he asked. I shrugged.

"I don't believe in lying to patients. Do you hear the sounds from the other room?" I nodded yes.

"That's the room I just came from," he said. "Their results were different than yours. Does it sound like I sugarcoated it with them?" I immediately began to like Dr. Masterson. In all my life, I had never met a doctor who was so completely perfect for his one demanding specialty in medicine. I will forever be indebted to him.

Regardless, there was a lot of soul-searching to do. I was in the best shape of my life. I had small children. I was doing good things for the world, I thought. I had a beautiful wife and everything to live for. But for whatever reason I could never bring myself to ask God, "Why me?" The reason is simple and not noble. The fact was that I had seen worse tragedies every week, every day of my life. Maybe that was one benefit of being in the FBI. Were the deaths of the children at the Murrah Federal Building less of a tragedy than me getting cancer?

I remember a man whose books I used to read. His name was Paul Little. He wrote about God; he inspired me, and I knew that he had a relationship with God that I could only wish for. One of his most fascinating books was *Affirming the Will of God*, which was designed to help us understand why God does what he does, why he allows what he allows, and how to deal with the hard things in life. One day when he was in his forties and I was seventeen, Paul Little was hit by a car and killed walking across the street. Inconceivable! So pointless and tragic! *Why?* I could not understand how God allowed that to happen. But it drove me back to Paul's book on understanding God's will, and the realization that we may not understand everything that happens—at least while we're in this life.

And then, when confronted with something so seemingly senseless more than twenty years later, I remembered. Paul Little had affected more lives and done more good for this world than I ever will. The question after all those things is not "Why me" but "Why *not* me?"

I never had really bad symptoms from cancer. I wasn't sick until the medical community "treated me" for cancer. I'm not denigrating them; I'm grateful for the science, but chemotherapy in 1997 was like pulling a tooth without anesthesia. First they had to cut me open and drag a foot and a half of my insides out. Then for a year, I was "blasted" with an unusually high dose of chemo, which is another way of saying "poison." Within days of the first treatment, I was an old man. Walking across the room was something I actually thought about and planned. Nausea didn't leave me for fifty-two weeks. I could never be more than a good three minutes away from a restroom. I took chemo once a week, but I was in bed for the next two days after each treatment.

If my health was deteriorating, my relationship with God was growing daily. I spent hours each day praying, and I will admit that 90 percent of it was for my family and me. I did not want to die. So I prayed groaning, agonizing prayers about not dying. At the same time I prayed until I was exhausted for the well-being of my family after I was gone, if God decided to allow me to die from this.

During this time, I could not have been at a better place than the FBI. Regardless of what you might think about the FBI, they take care of their own. At the academy I had been told that the FBI is a family. Now I was seeing it put into practice. After three months, I had decided to return to work a couple of days a week to save sick leave, as I didn't know how much I would eventually need. Most of the days that I was not at work, my supervisor would stop by my house on the way home to say hi, bring mail, and check on me. I got daily calls and weekly visits from my friends.

One day, I was sitting in the squad bay, typing on my computer, feeling pretty queasy; and out of the corner of my eye I saw somebody standing in the aisle looking at me. It was "the boss," the special agent in charge of the Los Angeles field office. He knew me and what I was going through. He walked up to my desk with a thoughtful look on his face and said, "How do you feel, Steve?"

"I feel pretty good," I lied.

"Well, you look like shit," he said bluntly. I didn't know whether to thank him or not, so I just stared dumbly at him.

"What the hell are you doing here?" he said in a way that intimidated me. I tried to explain to him my need to save sick leave because there was a good chance of a recurrence and by that time I would be out of sick leave. After listening until I was finished, he pointed to something on my desk.

"What's that?" I followed his pointing finger to my desk.

"It's a laptop," I answered.

He then said, with a stern face, "Pick it up and come with me."

For the life of me I was sure I was in some kind of trouble. We marched straight into my supervisor's office, and then I *knew* I was in trouble.

"Lumpy," he said to my supervisor, "I'm sending one of your employees home."

Why? What had I done?

"He's got a laptop; there's no damn reason he can't be doing his work from home." He then told Lumpy that my time at home working on the laptop was not to be considered sick leave because I was working. That saved most of my sick leave.

Over that year, I learned the value of spending time with my kids and Michelle. For the entire year, Michelle raised a seven-year-old, a five-year-old, a three-year-old, and a thirty-nine-year-old semi-invalid by herself. We could not have survived without the love, the prayers, and the daily help of our family and friends, but there was no one who could do the things Michelle had to do. I tried, but I was fairly useless. Most evenings when I was well enough to get out of bed, I went to work, came home, and would walk from the front door into the bedroom and flop down on the bed. There were days when Michelle literally took my clothes off and hung them up for me. No matter what, she never complained. It's somewhat unfair that FBI agents can win medals for valor, but there was no medal of valor for Michelle. So while the world doesn't acknowledge her or other people like her for what they do, I believe God saw every single time she summoned the strength to do one more task, to respond to the crying child or respond to the husband who was sick. I learned more about her in that year than in all the years before or since combined.

The woman that I had fallen in love with in 1988 had turned out to be *so* much stronger, so much more resilient than I had ever expected. In that year, Michelle became my hero. I was bonded to her like never before, and I knew that I would never leave her, that I would never ignore the kids again, and that I would never put my career before the family again. I had learned the hard way. If I lived through this I would be a changed man and a better man.

I was kidding myself.

12

Stupid People Tricks

THOUGH I HAD continued to work one or two days a week throughout my chemo and my cancer, it was not until the chemotherapy ended in May 1998 that my life actually restarted. In many ways, it was exciting and wonderful. In many other ways, though, I was ending a time of growth and learning.

In reality, there was great medical danger—and even probability, according to some people—that the cancer, due to its significant involvement in my lymph system, would return at some future point, likely within the first year after chemotherapy stopped. I was aware of this and decided to live the next year as if it would be my last. I used to love the phrase (and later the song title) "Live Like You Were Dying." It's a great philosophy, but it can be taken too far. Not until I had lived like I was dying for about five years would I realize how destructive that can be. You tend not to see things for their long-term implications, only what you can achieve in the next year. So, in essence, regardless of what I had learned or thought I had learned during cancer, I began to invest myself in short-term things and not long-term things like, oh . . . children and family. I went back to my cases with a creative vengeance—but my first priority was to rejoin the SWAT team. I began working out and working back into a physically healthy place, and within two weeks went on my first post-chemotherapy raid.

In August 1998 the US embassies in Dar es Salaam, Tanzania, and Nairobi, Kenya, were bombed. The L.A. SWAT team had built quite a reputation with FBIHQ, and we were to be sent to Nairobi and Dar to provide security for the FBI investigators combing through the wreckage. We all showed up at a nearby air force base to get our shots and prepare for departure on the air force transport, but the day before the C-17 left with the team, the team leader, Dan Kurtz, took my name off the deployment list. I was bitterly disappointed, but he explained, surprisingly perceptively, that because of my recent chemotherapy, I had very little resistance to disease and might still be too weak for the conditions we were going to face. I have to say now, years later, that he was right. Even some of our healthiest team members became terribly ill on that trip.

But Kurtz had a consolation prize: sniper school.

Sniper school is a coveted and competitive training program that is not open for applications. The school sometimes is held only once a year, and some SWAT teams go several years without a slot. Even large teams such as New York and L.A. get precious few slots. In the late summer of 1998, L.A. was given a single slot, and Dan offered it to me. I didn't want pity; I didn't want him to give it to me because I had come back from cancer, and I told him so. But it turned out that L.A. chose its sniper candidates the old-fashioned way: firearms scores. It might not surprise you that just about every single bullet fired by a SWAT team member is scored. To give you an idea of how many rounds we fired, FBI Sig Sauer pistols were retired after 10,000 rounds were fired through them, and my Sig was retired in little more than 18 months on the team. Firearms scores were the basis on which candidates were selected, and then candidates were assessed by Kurtz himself.

Sniper school took place on a military base in the Midwest. The physical training was rigorous, the heat severe, and the humidity oppressive. Each day would begin with films, much like a football team watches themselves after their games and their opponents before a game. Each morning, we were shown a "bad shoot" by a sniper captured on film, usually by news cameras. We watched in quiet horror as police and other snipers killed *hostages*, or missed the target and had to watch as the hostage was murdered, or made other fatal mistakes. The message was blunt: *This isn't a game. You screw up, and people die. Period. If you do your job right, a person still dies. But the right person dies.*

It was a sobered group that went out on the range each morning. The first few days were spent with gunsmiths who were "fitting" our rifles to us. These guns were accurate in the extreme, and each one was tailor-fit to its shooter. You would not trade rifles any more than you could wear someone else's eyeglasses. Most of the rifles had a long history in the FBI, handed down to successive "owners," and they had nicknames known by the gunsmiths: "Excalibur I through Excalibur XI," "Millennium Falcon." Each rifle came with a book that logged every single bullet it had ever fired. The goal was to know how the rifle "behaved" in every temperature, wind, and condition. For instance, my rifle would shoot absolutely dead-on with the first round, known as the cold bore, or cold shot. But with each successive round, the barrel got hotter and the bullets tended to hit lower, bullet by bullet, finally maxing out at half an inch low after five rounds. Other rifles acted differently when hot. So if you were deployed to a scene in, say, fifty-degree temperatures, you would look in the log to find out how the rifle shot at that temperature. There is no room for error when the hostage-taker could be two hundred yards away and head-to-head with the hostage and there are no practice shots.

The first half of the school was dedicated exclusively to shooting. We would shoot all morning and study ballistics in the afternoons. We learned everything there was to know about rifle cartridges. (For instance, what most people call a "bullet," is actually a "cartridge" or "round," which consists of the brass case, a primer, smokeless black powder, and the *bullet*, which is the only part that goes down-range.) Each night before we left, we would shoot one more time, then come in to the classroom to view a "good" shoot on video—a time when a sniper saved a life. It was intended to motivate us, and it served its purpose well.

Just before lunch and just before the end of the day, we would take part in a contest known as the "Tour de Sniper." It was a shooting challenge, usually complicated by physical activity and time limits. For instance, we might have to carry our rifles on a half-mile run and fire five rounds, all in five minutes. It might sound easy, but carrying a rifle and wearing sniper boots made it difficult. Sometimes, the challenge was not even completed by all—or any— of the candidates. The winner of each contest was given custody of the coveted Yellow Shirt, patterned after the yellow shirt worn by the leader of the Tour de France after each stage. My goal was to wear that shirt at least once before I went home. As the days went on, the contest became more and more competitive.

An FBI sniper mission is different from a military sniper mission for one significant reason: military snipers generally fire to take down the enemy. Hitting the enemy in the torso is as effective as hitting him in the head. More so in some ways because, as the old adage says, a dead man just lies there, while a wounded man takes three people out of the battle—himself and the two it takes to carry him. The FBI, on the other hand, shoots only to end a hostage situation or eliminate an immediate threat to another life. To do that, not only must the sniper's shot be a head shot, but it must hit in an area of the head where the reflexive nervous system does not cause the body of the shooter to flinch or clench, which would likely fire the gun he has pointed at the hostage. FBI shooting parameters are rigorous. An FBI sniper candidate can usually put all of his rounds within the outline of a business card at a hundred yards, and the graduating shooting test requires two-hundred-yard head shots in a specific area about the same size. By the end of our training, the Tour de Sniper contest winners were determined by the smallest coin that could cover the holes in the target after five rounds from one hundred yards, and winners usually had targets on which all five rounds could be covered by a nickel or a dime. In fact, targets were not even scored if all five bullet holes were not touching. More than one hole for five rounds was usually an automatic disqualifier.

It was with a huge amount of pride that I won the right to wear the Yellow Shirt one afternoon. We had run a quarter mile with our weapons and were given three minutes to get five rounds on the hundred-yard target, which included loading and setting up. That day, I put five rounds in a single hole that looked almost circular. All five holes could be covered completely by a dime. I still have that target.

The second half of the school was dedicated to "stalking," the covert tracking—hunting—of human beings. Again, we were reminded that we were not playing golf. We were taught to hide our scent, to move through tall grass on our belly without being detected, to navigate and move through any type of terrain without detection, all with the express purpose of putting a human head in our crosshairs and putting a three-quarter-inch-long slug of copper and lead through somebody's brain at eighteen hundred miles per hour.

Our graduation exercise was grueling. We were individually dropped off with our rifles in a steamy forest preserve on a ninety-degree day when the humidity was almost 100 percent with drizzle, with a compass and a map with a target marked on it. Our task? We were to camouflage ourselves with local vegetation, navigate to the target several miles away, and move to within two hundred yards of the target without being detected. The complications were as follows. The target was in a cabin in the middle of a swampy tall-grass meadow where the nearest tree was nearly five hundred yards away. This meant that once we had traveled several miles in the forest, we had to traverse the final three hundred yards on our bellies, cutting our way through switchgrass. The mosquitoes claimed this swamp as their own. The other complication was that the "target" was an instructor at the sniper school, and he knew we were coming, had binoculars, and enjoyed the benefit of knowing how we had been taught. If we were seen before we were within two hundred yards, we had to repeat the exercise.

I wore camouflage long-sleeve clothing with grass, leaves, and bivouac netting insulation. The weather was absolutely equatorial. Wearing insect repellent would have given our position away and slapping the mosquitoes would have made the grass move. That last three hundred yards took me more than three hours and were some of the most miserable hours of my life. If it hadn't been for the occasional rain shower, I believe I would have suffered heat stroke.

The anticlimax? What were we supposed to do once we believed we were inside two hundred yards? Notify our instructor by radio. No shot was to be taken, of course. Not even a practice shot. "How," I asked, "will you know if we hit the target then?"

The answer was pretty simple: "If we didn't think you'd make a two-hundred-yard shot with your eyes closed, you wouldn't be out in the field." I passed, calling in at a measured 179 yards to the target. The mosquito bites made me look like I had the measles. Somehow they had even gotten inside my clothes.

As Jack Webb might say, "It was Friday, December 18, 1998. It was cool in Los Angeles, and I was working domestic terrorism in the

San Fernando Valley . . ." Just after two o'clock in the afternoon, I was on my way to interview a witness. My pager went off, and I was advised that the federal bankruptcy court in Woodland Hills, California, had been evacuated because of an anthrax threat. This is new, I thought.

When I got to the court, it was obvious that the fire department was taking this threat seriously. Dozens of fire engines were in a large parking lot across the street from the bankruptcy court. An LAPD helicopter was on final approach to a baseball field a few hundred yards away, and dozens of police cars lined the streets. The courthouse was surrounded by yellow crime-scene tape. Behind the yellow tape were approximately one hundred building occupants; they were quarantined.

There had been sporadic anthrax threats around the nation over the past few months, and the emergency services people had not yet developed an expedient means of dealing with them. Up to this point, their policy was a full response: police, fire, and medical. This placed an immense burden on fire assets, even in a city as large as Los Angeles. With four or five stations completely out of the mix, parts of the city had skeleton coverage. And with skeleton coverage, it was possible that a critical medical situation might not be covered or would just be delayed, which could cost a life. This was what was going on all across the country. People angry at a specific store or company phoned in an anthrax threat and essentially shut them down for several days. It used to be bomb threats, but by this time police and fire had figured out how to expeditiously work those. Anthrax threats were new territory, and without a protocol for quickly triaging them, a full response was required at every one, regardless of how spurious it might seem.

It took until midnight for the FBI and fire personnel in "bubble suits" to determine that anthrax was not present in the building. The investigation began the next morning when I spoke to law clerks in the office of one of the bankruptcy judges. They told me of a case that was being heard in front of a judge they worked for. A contractor had declared bankruptcy, but in the course of proceedings it became clear from forensic accounting that he was taking in enough money to easily cover his debts. Allegedly, hundreds of thousands of dollars were simply missing from his accounts. He had an accountant who was doing the work for him. The accountant's name was Harvey Spelkin. There were unproven allegations that Spelkin may have been embezzling his money. The judge set a hearing for Spelkin to explain the missing money. The accountant failed to make that hearing. And the next, and the next, each time with an almost grade-school excuse, once saying that his uncle had died. Finally, the judge told Spelkin that he was to appear at a hearing at 2:00 PM on December 18 *without fail* or be held in contempt of court. The purpose of the hearing, of course, was for Spelkin to account for his actions and the money for which he was responsible.

At five minutes until 2:00 on December 18, 1998, an unidentified male caller told the operator at the bankruptcy court that anthrax was in the heating/air-conditioning system. This, in the FBI, is what we call "a clue." In my experience, often it wasn't we in the FBI who solved the cases—it was the people we interviewed.

After what I'd heard, I was sure I had the culprit. All I had to do was prove it to myself and to a jury. The second part was harder, because there was no recording of the phone call, and because of the way the phone system was configured, there was no evidence of where it originated. Frankly, without a confession, there would not be a case.

What followed was possibly the most amusing case I ever worked. I had never seen a more inept liar.

That afternoon, after talking with the clerks in the court, I drove over to this Spelkin's house, just a few miles away from the courthouse. He lived in an upscale neighborhood on the side of a hill in an unassuming single-story ranch house. I knocked on the front door and heard somebody quietly approach the other side. I could see the shadow cover the peephole. "Could we speak in the garage, please?" came the request from inside.

As I walked around to the front of the house, the garage door was already opening, and I met Harvey Spelkin for the first time. He was about forty years of age, with thinning curly hair and a Caspar Milquetoast appearance. He didn't seem to be surprised that the FBI was at his house. Yet he was obviously very nervous. I showed him my badge and credentials and told him that I was there to investigate an anthrax threat at the federal bankruptcy court. He volunteered that he had heard about the threat and lamented how horrible it was.

That was the last sensible thing I ever heard him say.

From that point on in the conversation I might as well have been talking to an eight-year-old, except that eight-year-olds are really better liars.

"Mr. Spelkin," I began, "I understand you had a hearing scheduled for the day of the anthrax threat at two PM."

"Yes," he admitted. "But of course the hearing didn't occur because of the anthrax threat."

"Why weren't you at the courthouse then?"

He looked at me like it was the most obvious answer in the world and was confused by why I didn't understand this. "Well, because of the anthrax threat."

I pointed out that the anthrax threat wasn't reported on the radio until 2:10 PM and asked how he had found out about it, because he was due in court ten minutes before that. Then he changed his story.

"Well, I had an accident on the way there, and that delayed me," he explained. I was almost offended that he thought I was stupid enough to buy that.

"How many cars do you have, Mr. Spelkin?" I could see on his face when he realized the problem. He only had one car registered to his wife and him, and we were standing next to it in the garage. All I had to do was ask him to show me the damage and he was in trouble.

"Oh!" he said. "We only have one, but I wasn't driving it when I had the accident."

"All right, just tell me what vehicle you were driving and I'll check the police report for that day," I said. He didn't have a poker face. I could see when I surprised him, and I could see when he came up with the lie.

"Well, I wasn't driving," he explained.

"Were you in a cab? Just tell me what company and I'll check their records," I offered.

"No, it wasn't a cab. I hitchhiked." At that point I simply looked at him as if he was crazy.

"You mean you hitchhiked from your neighborhood?" I asked incredulously.

"No, my wife drove me down to Ventura Boulevard and I stopped at a Starbucks until it was time for court, because we only have one car and she needed it," he said, digging himself deeper.

"Why didn't she just drive you to the court and drop you off?" I asked. At this point, an innocent man would have been offended by my questions.

His lies became wilder and more stupid. I was having trouble not giggling. How was he saying these things with a straight face? It turned out that he had gotten a ride from Starbucks from a man he had never seen before, whose name he didn't get, who then ran into a pole. Spelkin then claimed that he missed the court date because he was at the hospital because of his injured ankle.

"Which hospital?" I asked, nonchalantly. Once again the wheels were turning in his head. "Northridge, but . . . the emergency room was full, so I left." It's guys like this, I thought, who make the FBI look like geniuses.

"Which ankle?" I asked, pointing at his feet. He had been standing on the concrete garage floor for about twenty minutes without the slightest indication of pain or a limp.

"Which one?" he repeated.

"Did you hurt, I mean?" At that point, he feigned soreness in an ankle. Seriously. He explained that he had been taking some good pain medication.

But as stupid as his story sounded, he still had steadfastly denied any involvement with the anthrax threat. It was one thing to prove that Spelkin was a liar; it was another thing to prove that he had something to do with that anthrax threat. While everything he said was circumstantially strong evidence that he had a motive to make the call and no excuse for not being at the court, it might not have won in a courtroom. After all, he had not shown up for court three times before, so not showing up on the day of the anthrax threat would not have been surprising to a jury. In order to convict him we would still absolutely need a confession. I began to work on him.

I pulled the wallet out of my back pocket, and out of the wallet I produced a twenty-dollar bill and held it up. "Mr. Spelkin, I've got a six-year-old boy who is a better liar than you. If you are not in jail by this Friday, I will take you to lunch with this twenty dollars." He looked at me as if I had accused him of the Kennedy assassination.

"Yes," I said. "You made that anthrax call, and I can prove it." Spelkin just stared at me. I walked out of his garage ecstatic.

One day in and the case was solved. But it still wasn't proven. Meanwhile, an extremely dangerous situation was building in Los Angeles. The press had made a huge deal of the anthrax threat. And not surprisingly, when millions of people in Los Angeles saw that the entire court building was shut down for twelve hours, copycats came out of the woodwork. Before this incident, there had not been a single anthrax threat on record in Los Angeles. In the two days after it, the area was hit by six more. By December 21 we were averaging five to six per day. The fire services were completely overwhelmed. They were going from threat to threat, and each one was taking several hours. This left large areas of the counties of Ventura, Los Angeles, and Orange uncovered by adequate fire services. Something had to be done, because there was a general feeling among the public that this was an unsolvable crime, and pranksters felt that they could make these types of threats with impunity. Time was of the essence.

After discussing my meeting with Spelkin with the United States Attorney's Office, we determined that the sooner we could get him into custody, the better the chance that we could stop the epidemic of anthrax threats. But I needed a lever on him, and I got it from the FBI White Collar Fraud agents. I talked to a good friend of mine on that squad, and he told me that Spelkin's alleged fraud was a very small case by L.A. standards, but if it was important, he would take it on.

The anthrax threat could probably get him only a few days in jail and an immense fine, whereas an embezzlement conviction could cost him his CPA license and as much as a year or two in prison. But at this point, lives were at risk due to the anthrax-threat epidemic that he had caused. I firmly believed, and the United States Attorney's Office agreed, that it was in the public interest to nail him for the anthrax threat instead of the alleged embezzlement. As for the alleged embezzlement victims, they could still sue him civilly for the amount he may have stolen.

I called Spelkin on his cell phone and he picked up, not knowing it was me. I told him that I needed to speak to him about embezzlement allegations. You could almost hear his pulse over the phone. He began to stutter and became very agitated.

"Harvey,"—I addressed him informally—"you and I both know that you embezzled the money from your client, and you made that anthrax call. I am going to nail you for one of the two. You get to choose which."

"What would happen to the person who made that call?" he asked. I had him. There had been ten anthrax threats that day alone. He agreed to meet me at the FBI office the next morning at eight.

The Harvey Spelkin who showed up at the FBI office was not the Harvey Spelkin I had talked to earlier. He was obviously coming to grips with the situation and with the threat of embezzlement charges and prison becoming crystal clear, he seemed to surrender. His shoulders fell; his voice got quiet. There was a long pause.

He looked down at his hands, he looked up at the ceiling, and then he said, "OK."

"OK . . . what?" I prompted.

"OK, I made an anthrax threat to the bankruptcy court." I was overjoyed but didn't want to give any indication of my excitement. I treated it like it was the most normal statement in the world. For the next two hours, we wrote out his entire confession, from the time he woke up on the morning of the threat until the time I showed up at his house.

An hour later, Spelkin signed a full confession.

"What now?" he asked, putting down the pen.

"I think you should call your wife or a friend to come down and get your car," I said, quite matter-of-factly. He didn't understand why somebody else had to drive him home. It occurred to me that he didn't understand that he wasn't going home. He had just confessed to a federal felony in writing. I almost felt sorry for him.

"Mr. Spelkin, you are going to jail," I said as if it was the most obvious thing in the world, because it should have been.

"Why?" he asked incredulously.

I explained about that whole federal felony thing, and wondered how he had missed that part. I called the United States Attorney's Office. They were overjoyed as well. Both the FBI press office and the United States Attorney's press office began to call the media outlets to get coverage on the arrest—it was crucial that we got immediate coverage. There had been seventy-plus anthrax threats in the previous week, and we were approaching the Christmas season, when there would be even fewer emergency services people to divvy up among different threat sites. News coverage for Spelkin's initial appearance—the federal version of an arraignment—was heavy. The next day, there was not a single anthrax threat anywhere in Southern California. In fact, there was only one anthrax threat in any location remotely near Southern California for the rest of the year. Our hunch had proved right: once it got out to the public that the FBI had the ability to find these people, the copycat crimes stopped the very same day.

FBI agents can find humor in the most unlikely situations. Extortion drops, for instance. An extortion drop is just like paying a ransom. It is the delivery of (usually) cash to a specific location in return for a bad guy not carrying out a threat. One summer night, SWAT was assigned to cover an extortion drop in a wooded area near an orchard in Oxnard; the location gave the subject a chance to have some cover for the pickup. An extortionist had threatened that unless he was given a certain amount of money, he would kill the children of a nearby wealthy family. While he didn't have the children, he seemed to know everything about their schedules and routines and where they would be at any given moment. He had done his homework, and the threat might be valid.

The planning for apprehending the subject seemed to be sound. There would be an inner perimeter of SWAT operators "dug in"—this meant that there would be three or four agents within twenty yards of the drop site. These would be sniper/observers completely camouflaged into the environment. These three or four agents would have the closest view of the drop and would be able to identify the suspect later after he was arrested— they would report on his activities but *not* make the arrest. There would be an outer perimeter ready to take down the suspect the second he picked up the money package. These agents would be less than a block away, and they would be in vehicles. In case the subject arrived on a motorcycle, off-road vehicle, or ATV, SWAT had operators deployed on dirt bikes all around the zone.

My team, the Thirties, was not scheduled as the primary duty team that night, so it appeared to us that we were "out of the fun." We were relegated to an outer, outer perimeter. One vehicle was to be stationed a mile or two west of the drop site, another one similarly east. Four of us hopped into Billy Kim's Impala and drove to the west position a little after midnight. In the passenger seat was James Benedict. Behind Billy was Ryan March, and I was next to Ryan. We parked between two warehouse buildings, which made us invisible from the road. We were completely geared up right up to our helmets. We had our MP5s slung over our shoulders so that we would be ready to go. But we were pretty sure we were not going to be doing anything that night. Our struggle would be to stay awake.

Soon, we began to talk about the usual office gossip, then we told jokes, and that led to a discussion of a recent team training session that all of us thought was silly. The training had been on the use of "commands and command presence," the mere mention of which caused everyone to groan. It was in essence instruction on how to control a situation by voice alone, exuding confidence and giving unambiguous commands to a subject. It was also an attempt to standardize the different commands that could be given to a suspect at gunpoint. It was also silly. We had been giggling for about half an hour over all this when the time of night, the coffee, the fatigue, and the need to release tension just took over, and we began a laughing jag that we had little control over.

It started when Ryan suggested that the Thirties come up with "intentionally confusing" commands that we could use if we ever came across a subject who we felt just needed to be shot, like a child-killer. Of course, the thought of doing this in real life was absurd, so the laughter increased.

Ryan pointed out that we could actually give an arrestee a command that he had no possibility of obeying and then shoot him when he failed to comply. "We could say, 'Put your hands up and touch your left heel to your right ear!'" That brought a roar from all of us. "Then, if he doesn't comply, we could shoot him," Ryan explained, trying not to spit out the tobacco juice from the dip behind his lower lip. For the next half hour, we made up nonsensical commands that we could use to confuse a suspect and give us authority to shoot him because of noncompliance. With each, the laughter got louder. By now, all the windows were fogged up, and at times I was afraid I was having trouble catching my breath.

"Driver!" Ryan screamed as if he was arresting a motorist. "Take the keys to your car in your left hand. Put them in your mouth! Swallow them! *Do it now!*"

Then James joined the imaginary scene, "He's not complying! He's not complying!"

"Shoot him! Shoot him!" Ryan yelled.

Now we were laughing stupidly hard. The commands from that point got sillier and sillier. James suggested getting a spinning needle from a Twister game and having another SWAT agent spin it to determine what command we were going to give. "Driver! Left hand green! Do it now! Shoot him!"

We were beside ourselves with laughter, tears running down our cheeks. The last command from Ryan that I heard that night was the winner of the evening: "Driver! Say you love me!" Then Ryan delivered the coup de grace: "He doesn't love me! He doesn't love me! Shoot him! *Shoot him!*"

At that point we completely lost it. I do not know how I kept from peeing my flight suit. Here were a bunch of grown SWAT guys—a lawyer, two marines, an Army Ranger, and me—laughing like little girls at a slumber party. I had *never* laughed that hard. There is a point in situations like this when everybody is laughing so hard that there can be a momentary silence as all are trying to catch their breath. There was just that silence as we all tried to inhale. And in that sudden unexpected silence, we heard an unidentified voice on the FBI radio crackle:

"... I don't know. I think maybe westbound!"

The voice was agitated. That stopped the laughter cold. We were glued to the radio, listening for the next transmission. It was from the airplane.

"No, he's westbound for sure! Where are you guys? Why aren't you trailing him?"

Something appeared to have gone wrong with the extortion drop. It sounded like the subject was out and had gotten through the perimeter. We sat stunned, listening to the radio and wondering what we should do. As Billy picked up the microphone, we all started frantically wiping our fogged-up windows and looking out.

"Is the subject out?" Billy transmitted.

"Ten-four!" came the response from the airplane. We listened breathlessly.

"What direction is he traveling?" Billy asked. But as he finished transmitting, a gray Honda Accord screamed past us, right to left (westbound), at approximately one hundred miles per hour. Question answered. Billy started the car and threw it into gear.

"Gray Honda!" came the redundant answer from a random SWAT voice.

Lights went on, siren went on, and we took chase. The guys who had been so sure they weren't going to see any action had become the closest car in a high-speed chase. We didn't know what had happened, and we didn't know how he had gotten out, but that didn't matter right then. When we pulled out, we were a half mile behind and the gap was increasing.

As we started through a slight bend, which wasn't so slight approaching triple-digit speeds, we were greeted by headlights coming the other way. It was the Honda! We had no idea how he could have gotten that far ahead, braked, and turned around, but there he was, screaming the other way. James broadcast from his shoulder mike that the subject was back eastbound, as Billy stomped on the brakes and started to turn before the car could effectively change direction. We slid partially sideways through a dirt median, striking a couple of reflector sticks. Immediately Billy's foot was on the floor and we were accelerating back up to a hundred. We could see that some of our SWAT compadres, including the other Thirties car, driven by Mark Crichton, were also doing the same move, both in front and behind us as they caught up. But we were proud that the Thirties seemed to be the first two cars in the chase.

Ryan broke the silence with an expectedly absurd statement: "It's one in the morning, we're doing a hundred miles an hour, we have loaded machine guns in our lap and no seatbelts on. And an Asian is driving." And then we started laughing again. Laughter is the best way to get rid of surplus anxiety. *Just* as the Honda started to drift back toward us, signaling that we were catching him, Steve Doolittle, a good friend and pilot of the FBI airplane overhead, transmitted a startling warning:

"All trailing SWAT units, be aware that your teammates have blocked the intersection at Gonzales Road, up ahead." Gonzales was less than a half mile ahead of us, and we were doing a hundred miles per hour in an overloaded car. The brake lights on Crichton's car lit up, and the front of the car dipped dramatically. But Mark had only one other person in his car, and we flew by him. As we crested a rise we saw that the rest of the team had indeed blocked the intersection with their Suburbans. The Honda's driver was stomping on *his* brakes and decelerating faster than we were. I braced for an impact, but Billy swerved to the left as we skidded to a stop almost even with the Honda, about ten yards short of the Suburbans. I saw at least half a dozen SWAT agents begin running from behind the Suburbans toward the Honda. But where we had stopped, my door was no more than ten feet from the driver of the Honda, who was trying to get the car into reverse. I bailed out of the backseat of the Chevy and ran to the driver's window, followed by Ryan and several other agents. From three feet away, I put the "red dot" on the driver's forehead as other agents simultaneously arrived at his car. He put his hands up. The chase was over.

At the debrief an hour later, we found out what had gone wrong. The decision had been made that if the subject did not pick up the package, we were not going to give away our presence but would try to establish a covert surveillance. The extortionist had gone to the ransom package, seen by all, but only the four operators hidden near the package could see if he picked it up or not. When the subject did, in fact, pick up the package, the four agents who were watching were *too close* to say anything without being detected—until he got in his car. All of them decided individually that when he shut his car door they would transmit that he had picked up the package. As he closed his car door, all four agents transmitted at exactly the same millisecond. They couldn't have done that again if they had practiced it. What the rest of the team heard was simply a radio squeal for several seconds and then silence. And none of the transmitting agents had any idea that their call hadn't gone through.

When he came out of the area, the hidden perimeter cars let him go, because they believed he had not picked up the package. It was not until he was half a mile from the drop site that the airplane finally noted that the car was disappearing at high speed. This was the first time that the agents at the drop site knew that nobody had heard them. That's when the car screamed by our location.

As a postscript, I should tell you what happened after the driver put up his hands. I was the closest SWAT agent to the driver, so as we had been taught at the recent training, I loudly ordered: "Driver! Take the keys out of the ignition!" He did so, and held them up so I could see them, his left hand still touching the headliner. I then started to tell him to drop the keys outside the car.

"Driver!" I said. But as I inhaled to say the next phrase, Ryan spoke quietly into my ear:

"*Say you love me!*"

13

Big Guns, Small Children

ONE YEAR AFTER my chemotherapy ended, my family and I celebrated quietly. We had no idea what the future held, and it would be four more years before I would know whether I would ultimately survive this cancer or not. There was no activity in my life, no thought in my head, no pleasure or sorrow, that wasn't filtered through the sieve of the possibility of my death. Every little cold, every fever, raised the specter of a fatal recurrence.

At about the same time I was celebrating a year in remission, June 1999, a man who I didn't know yet was also celebrating a new lease on life, but he also suspected that his could be short. One of us would be right.

A civil engineer by degree, he had actually committed himself voluntarily to a mental facility when he felt that he was experiencing homicidal tendencies that he could not control. For nine months, he told doctors during his sessions several times weekly that, regardless of any apparent progress or the effects of any medication, he still had an overwhelming urge to kill. His first targets, he said, would be his estranged wife and his stepson. But his normal appearance and behavior apparently confused the doctors. In June 1999, against his own warnings, this man was released on the public.

The man was Buford O'Neal Furrow. He had been an engineer with Northrop in Palmdale, California, working on a menial part of the B-2 Stealth Bomber program. He collected guns, cars, and motorcycles and vastly overspent his income. Just as he began to lose his treasures to repossession and foreclosure, he was laid off by Northrop. With his world collapsing, he stumbled upon the shortwave broadcasts of the Aryan Nations from Hayden Lake, Idaho, and their founder, "Pastor" Richard Butler. Their anti-Jewish, anti-bank rhetoric struck a chord with the man who was about to lose everything to banks. When his world finally hit bottom, he went to the only people he felt would understand his plight: the Aryan Nations.

Coming into the AN with an actual college degree and the ability to speak in complete sentences and in possession of all of his teeth, he immediately won their admiration. Almost immediately, he became one of their leaders and likely heir to the throne of Richard Butler, had he played his cards right. Almost inevitable was his marriage to Debbie Matthews, the widow of Bob Matthews, the founder of the Order, the group I had surveilled in 1984. Besides Butler, she was likely the most influential person in the AN. Within a short time, Furrow, in his new AN uniform with the Sam Brown belt, was wed to Debbie Matthews in a charming Nazi ceremony in the gun-turreted chapel of the Aryan Nations. The bride wore white. Of course.

But the widow of the anarchist and the White Power Ingénue did not live happily ever after. Counterintuitively, Debbie appeared to have a mean and sarcastic temper. Who would have seen that coming? Her years in the AN and the KKK had inexplicably failed to smooth any of her rough edges. She began to belittle her younger husband, calling him a loser, and berate him for everything from failing to support them to falling short of the "Aryan ideal." She famously taunted him, "You'll never be the man Bob Matthews was."

Eventually, Furrow left the AN, humiliated, and returned to Olympia, Washington, to live with his elderly mother and father in a "single-wide." However, he could only find menial work and gradually became seriously depressed, and developed (or perfected) an addiction to violence-based pornography. He would spend hours at night—sometimes until sunrise—surfing for pornography and obscenely violent images, including videos of actual executions and car crashes and snuff films.

But his violent fantasies had begun to morph into a strong desire to carry out his own violence. After actually planning and starting to execute a plan to kill Debbie Matthews, Furrow instead turned himself in at the mental institution. When he explained his fantasy of machine-gunning mall shoppers at Christmas, the nurse decided to hold him, and she obtained his car keys. Furrow then may have changed his mind and demanded his keys back. When the nurse refused, he drew a Bowie knife and put it under her chin. She gave him the keys. He went out to his truck, and the nurse called the sheriff. When the sheriff's deputies arrived, Furrow still had the Bowie knife in his hand and balked momentarily when ordered to put it down. He later said that he wanted to die but "didn't have the guts."

Nine months later, still professing a strong desire to kill and warning the doctors not to let him go, Furrow was released. He began to amass an arsenal that would stagger the imagination. He had obtained a Chinese-made copy of an Uzi semiautomatic pistol, and he converted it into a submachine gun. On the morning of August 7 he went into his father's safe, the combination of which he knew. He took $4,000 cash out of the safe, along with a Glock 9mm pistol that his father owned.

Driving his pickup truck to a nearby used-car dealership, he traded it and some cash for a Chevrolet van. He then loaded thousands of rounds of machine gun, submachine gun, and pistol ammunition into the truck, along with an M16, the Uzi, flares, the Glock, and dozens of other partial and complete guns. He then set out for Los Angeles to prove that he was every bit the Aryan that Bob Matthews was.

His intent was to attack the Museum of Tolerance in Los Angeles, a museum dedicated to remembering the Holocaust. He arrived in Los Angeles on August 9 and drove to the museum. Realizing that the museum had extremely heavy security, he determined that he would not be able to complete his attack, and if he did, he certainly wouldn't escape alive. He therefore looked for other targets. Driving around Los Angeles, he saw the Skirball Cultural Center, a Jewish cultural institution, and the American Jewish University. He noted with disappointment that the Skirball seemed to be nearly devoid of people ("targets"), and because it was summer, the American Jewish University was a ghost town. He continued driving north toward the San Fernando Valley and after approximately ten miles, pulled off the freeway at a random exit for gas. After a few miles he lucked out: it wasn't a gas station he found but his target. He had randomly passed the Jewish Community Center (JCC) of Granada Hills.

At seven the next morning, Furrow awoke, drove back to the San Fernando Valley, ate, got a haircut, and killed time until approximately ten thirty, when he headed for the Jewish Community Center.

Thirty miles away at the Los Angeles FBI field office, it was a slow day. Sadly, my boss on the Domestic Terrorism Squad had lost his mother the previous week. The funeral was that day in Riverside, approximately two and a half hours away from the office in Westwood. As the second in command, I remained at the office while the entire squad joined the boss at the funeral.

At 11:00 exactly, FBI analyst Bill Fife entered my office.

"Hey Steve." I looked up at Bill, wordlessly asking him to continue.

"News is reporting a mass shooting in Granada Hills."

"Where?"

"At a Jewish Community Center."

If it was a JCC, there was a strong possibility that this could be a hate crime and not a random shooting. I grabbed my car keys and had Bill take down a list of notifications to make; the special agent in charge of the office, the assistant director of the Los Angeles field office, and FBIHQ all had to be made aware that FBILA was responding. Three minutes later, I was northbound on the 405 freeway, code 3: lights flashing and siren blaring.

I arrived at the JCC as LAPD SWAT was still clearing the parking lot. Apparently, the suspect was not in custody yet, and his whereabouts were unknown. Inside the Methodist church next door, LAPD had established a command post, and I went over there for a quick briefing.

An unknown assailant or assailants had entered the Jewish Community Center at approximately 10:50 that morning as a class of five-year-olds were returning to their classroom from the soccer field. The shooter opened up on them with a machine gun, hitting three five-year-old boys, a seventeen-year-old camp counselor, and a sixty-year-old receptionist. The suspect was last seen escaping in a red van. Because there were reports that there may have been more than one assailant, LAPD SWAT was carefully clearing the entire Jewish Community Center and its environs. LAPD reported "no suspects and no motive." No motive? Well, I was fairly certain that I knew the motive. And I had only been there for five minutes.

"It could be," the lieutenant explained, "that it was a disgruntled employee, an angry or jealous spouse, or it could simply be a case of workplace violence." That hypothesis ignored certain important things, the most important of which was that in each of the scenarios mentioned, someone would have almost certainly recognized the shooter.

I went back into the church and started to make a list of priorities for the investigation. I went into what I thought would be the quietest place in the church, the sanctuary, but was wrong. Inside the church were several dozen uninjured preschoolers from the Jewish Community Center. In one of the more startling incongruities that day, they did not seem to understand the gravity of anything that had happened. The firefighters from a nearby station were "babysitting," which was heartwarming to watch. I heard something shuffling next to me in the aisle, and I looked down to see a yellow fireman's turnout coat with a helmet on top of it apparently moving under its own power down the aisle. Only when it got to the end of the aisle and turned around did I realized that it was a four-year-old girl who was completely encased in the helmet and coat. Her eyes were covered, but her ear-to-ear grin was visible. The adults in the room were not as serene. I guess ignorance really is bliss. Some of the staffers had blood on their clothes, and they were quietly crying, trying to hide their emotions from the kids.

Outside, parents had gathered to try and find out if their kids were safe. The police could not let them in to see the kids until the lists of the childrens' and the parents' identities were compiled and the parents of the wounded were identified. The parents were frantic, and at least one had to be handcuffed when he would not take no for an answer. Finally, the parents of the uninjured children were allowed into the sanctuary to find their children, and I had not previously seen a more emotional scene. Both mothers and fathers were holding their kids, sobbing, to the complete confusion of their children.

Within an hour, both the FBI and the LAPD mobile command posts had arrived and were parked in the center median of Rinaldi

Boulevard. The mayor of Los Angeles had come and gone, and FBI management was arriving. A shadow command post was set up at the Westwood FBI office staffed by about half the Domestic Terrorism Squad, who had returned from the funeral. The other half came to Rinaldi. A BOLO (Be On the LOokout) bulletin was sent out to every law enforcement entity in Southern California.

LAPD had control of the crime scene, but it was obvious to me that this was a crime over which the FBI had jurisdiction, and one that would garner enough notoriety that the Justice Department would certainly want control. But for the moment, I was between a rock and a hard place. This was the one place I swore I would never be if I were an FBI agent. I would *never* go up to a police detective, badge him from behind sunglasses and a dark suit with a red tie, and utter those clichéd words, *FBI. We'll take it from here.* Yet that's what FBIHQ and the Justice Department would ultimately require, I was sure. But until then, rivalry would slow the flow of information, and that could not happen. I went over to the LAPD command post, about two feet from ours. It was a Winnebago motor home crowded with uniforms and detectives. I found LAPD Homicide Detective III Brian Carr surrounded by other cops in the back of the vehicle. He exuded competence and control. It was obvious to me why he would have been the first guy LAPD chose to run a case this size. I introduced myself to Brian, who looked at me with a suspicion that was palpable.

"Brian, I'm Steve Moore. I'm with the FBI, and I'm the case agent for whatever part of this case the FBI has."

"Brian Carr. What can I do for you?" he asked, which could roughly be translated as, "What the hell are *you* doing here?"

"Brian, this has all the appearances of a domestic terrorism attack, and you know that something as big as this will grab the attention of Washington." Blame it on Washington. I liked that. "We just need to be kept apprised of what's going on, and we can use our intel branch to provide you with anything you need from the feds."

"Like what?" he asked.

"Like if this guy is not from L.A.—and he's probably not—we probably have FBI agents who know who he is and have a dossier on him already. We can access federal records faster than you can."

"OK," Brian ceded, "I'll give you every bit of information we have, but I'm going to ask you one thing."

"What?" I asked, waiting for a punch line.

"Don't go into the crime scene until we've processed it."

That was it? LAPD would do a great job on the crime scene, and I didn't have to use FBI manpower to do it. I had no intention of breaking that agreement.

"Done."

I left Brian to his monumental task and went over to my monumental task. Leaving the LAPD command post, I saw yet another command post being set up. It was the Bureau of Alcohol, Tobacco and Firearms (ATF). FBI agents, in general, do not have high regard for the ATF. In February 1993 the ATF had botched a (likely unnecessary) raid of the Branch Davidian compound in Waco, Texas, to a degree that boggled the mind. Every "best practice" of tactics and movement seemed to have been ignored. It was a raid that had SWAT people all over the United States simply shaking their heads in disbelief. Tragically, four brave ATF Agents were killed during the raid. Fifty days later, the FBI, in an attempt to end the siege, introduced gas into the compound in an attempt to get the occupants to leave. This was a tragic miscalculation of the Branch Davidians. Members of the cult at that point set fires throughout the compound in an act of mass murder-suicide. There had been little love between the ATF and the FBI since then. Since the Waco debacle, the ATF was, in the eyes of most FBI agents, doing anything they could to raise their stature in the public and congressional eye to get funding and essentially survive. They would go to any length to appear viable and useful. Now here was a case over which they really had no effective jurisdiction, yet they were present.

The first break in the case came while the ATF was still setting up. Just five miles away, a white man in a red van had carjacked a Toyota, and the woman driving it had escaped. He had thrown armloads of ammunition and weapons into the carjacked Toyota but had left a substantial amount behind in the van. I sent Jack O'Brian down to the location. Jack, one of my best friends, was a former prosecutor and the son of a Boston cop. He wasn't arrogant or overly ambitious, but he was fearless; he just wanted to do the right thing and do it well, no matter what it took. Upon arriving at the carjack scene, Jack almost immediately radioed back the first news: much of the ammunition remnants in the van were 9mm "hand-loads." Hand-loads are cartridges that have been reloaded after being fired. It's roughly analogous to refilling printer cartridges yourself with ink to save money: spent brass casings are collected; new black powder, new primer, and new bullets are added, and new cartridges are made. It is generally cents on the dollar to hand-load ammunition compared to buying additional rounds. It also meant that the shooter likely went through a lot of bullets practicing.

The next bit of info moved the ball forward a long way. The van was licensed in Washington State. The Aryan Nations was based within a few miles of Washington State, and many of its members were Washington residents. Things were falling into place. A quick run of the plates and we had a suspect in the Seattle area. But when agents were sent to the residence, they found a couple who had recently traded in their red van at a dealership in Tacoma. Agents in Tacoma contacted the dealership and found that it had recently been purchased by one Buford O'Neal Furrow a few days before.

The Washington state driver's license photo of Furrow that was sent down showed a thirtyish, balding, mustachioed man with a menacing face. The Seattle and Salt Lake City offices knew a lot about Furrow. They had watched him and his rise within the Aryan Nations throughout the years. They had witnessed his on-again, off-again relationship with Debbie Matthews. But when Furrow left the organization, Department of Justice rules of investigation, in the form of the "Attorney General's Guidelines," required that they cease all investigation of him, because the approved investigation was of the *organization* and its members. If an individual was not a member of that organization, he or she could not be watched.

Showing the photo to witnesses confirmed that Furrow was likely the shooter. We now had a suspect, and we knew what car he might still be driving, but L.A. is a big place. Carr also confirmed for me that the rounds fired in the JCC were likely hand-loads. Few of the brass casings ejected by the machine gun were from the same manufacturer. When you load a gun with bullets from a new box, all of the casings ejected will be of the same brand. When all are different brands, it indicates hand-loads.

An hour later, we were still tracing leads, possible sightings, and possible associates of Furrow's in L.A. Nothing was being left to chance. Anybody he ever spoke to in L.A. was being contacted. Then, a news report was picked up by the command post about a shooting about ten miles from our location, on the west side of L.A.'s San Fernando Valley. I went to the LAPD command post to find out about the shooting and ask why I hadn't been advised. Carr was aware of the shooting but didn't notify me because he was convinced that it was unrelated. As he said, "There's a shooting almost every day in L.A. Just because it happened on the same day as this shooting doesn't mean that it's related." But I pressed for details.

The victim was a US Postal Service letter carrier on his route in upscale Chatsworth. He was, according to Carr, Hispanic, and

LAPD believed that it was gang related. Also, the shooter in this attack used a pistol, not a machine gun. I sent Jack O'Brian over to that scene anyway, and what he found changed the game. The victim was *not* Hispanic; he was Filipino. There had been allegations of gang involvement in the family, but nobody could find out where those allegations came from. Also, the shooter used a 9mm pistol, which, though a different type of gun, used the same bullets and left casings on the ground.

"Only two rounds were fired," Jack reported from the crime scene, "and both casings were from different manufacturers." Hand-loaded rounds. While Jack was there, a witness to the shooting was located. Her description of the shooter matched Furrow, and she said that he was driving "a white Toyota." Furrow had carjacked a white Toyota.

The good news was that we had identified the shooter. The very bad news was that he wasn't finished. He was on a spree. And he was just one light-colored Toyota in a city of 5.5 million cars. Helicopters were out all over the valley and the Los Angeles basin, but the chances of them or a street cop stumbling on the car were astronomically slim. But it happened. At 3:00 PM an LAPD black-and-white was cruising about halfway between the Chatsworth and the JCC when the officer noticed a Toyota matching the description in a hotel parking lot. He drove in and checked the car out, and it had the right license plate. He checked the interior of the car and it was full of ammunition and guns. The FBI SWAT team leader got the news first and ran by me at the command post toward his car.

"They've got his car! Follow me!"

The next twelve hours were agony. It took SWAT twelve hours to completely clear every room of the hotel looking for Furrow. He had left the car in the lot but had not entered the hotel. Now the trail had gone cold. It was 3:00 AM, and I had been up for twenty-one stressful hours. I was shell-shocked and exhausted. I was so tired I could feel little emotion. A new command-post crew came on duty, and I designated an agent to run the case in my absence. It was determined that we had to hit it hard the next day. I drove home from Chatsworth wondering what we could have done differently. I got home around 4 AM and found Michelle waiting and awake. She could see the disappointment in my eyes and hugged me. She said she had seen me on TV a lot.

I smiled. Then, I had an unexpected need to see my children. Maybe it was the sight of the blood on the floor in the JCC or the parents rushing to find out whether their kids had been shot or not, or maybe it was just the uncertainty of the whole thing. But I had to go in and wake them up and hold them. I gathered them all on one bed in the girls' room and just held them all. I thought that life was funny; usually the kids got scared and needed to be with Daddy to feel secure and make the pain go away. That night, Daddy needed to be with the kids to feel safe and just ease a little of the pain. I actually felt guilty that I could still hug my children and that they were safe and warm in their beds. Eventually, Michelle forced me to go to sleep. The last time I remember seeing the time on the clock was 4:30 AM.

Less than four hours later, the phone next to my bed rang. It was the command post in L.A. The report was short.

"Furrow turned himself in at the Las Vegas FBI office."

Certainly I was dreaming. I shook my head, opened my eyes wide, and did my best to shake the stupor out of my head, and I ask the caller to repeat what he had just said.

"Furrow turned himself in at the Vegas office."

"Of the FBI," I said.

"Of the FBI," the caller quoted back.

I started to get dressed but was having trouble finding something to wear. In truth, I was so fatigued and shocked and had so much going on in my head that I couldn't concentrate on something as simple as getting dressed. Michelle then showed why she was the

FBI spouse that the FBI hopes comes with every agent. She got me coffee and forced me to drink it. Then, as the calls started to come in, she took notes for me as I dictated from the phone. She pulled out a suit, a shirt, a tie, shoes, and a belt and started to dress me as I stood taking call after call after call. Michelle and wives like her are the unsung backbone of the FBI, and once again, her character, the thing that caused me to fall in love with her, was shining.

I was advised that the ATF had gotten a US Customs Black Hawk helicopter to fly the investigators to Las Vegas. At first, I was angry that the ATF was even going, but if they were providing the transportation, I could deal with that later. I repeated the phone number of the ATF to Michelle so she could write it down. Then she repeated it back to me as I dialed.

"This is Steve Moore, I'm the FBI case agent for the Furrow case. I hear you're running a Black Hawk out to Las Vegas. That's great, I need a seat on that bird."

"Standby, let me check," he said and put me on hold. Check what? I wondered. Besides the pilot, I should be the number-one-priority passenger.

"Steve, could you lift your left foot up, I've got to put your sock on," Michelle said from below. I lifted my left foot. The ATF supervisor came back on the line.

"I'm sorry, but we've filled the seats on the chopper." What the hell?

"What are you talking about?" I asked angrily.

"Well, we've filled all the seats," he repeated back to me.

It became obvious that the ATF was intentionally obstructing an FBI domestic terrorism/murder investigation in order to advance the ATF case. It would take five hours to drive to Vegas, maybe four if I went code 3. I thought for a second about how short a flight it used to be when I flew out of Point Mugu. And then it hit me: Point Mugu. I picked up the phone and dialed Steve Doolittle, the aviation coordinator there.

"Steve, this is Sparky!"

"Hey, Spark . . ."

I explained the situation, and he loaned me an airplane. Forty-five minutes later, I was piloting a freshly fueled FBI aircraft that Doolittle had prepared for me. He didn't have pilots available, but I was still an authorized FBI PIC. In the plane with me was the Assistant United States Attorney (AUSA) who was going to prosecute the case, Ethan Gardella, as well as Jack O'Brian. We were cruising at an easy 175 mph, so a little over an hour later, we would be on the ground at Vegas. I wondered how far behind the Black Hawk we were. Not much, as it turned out.

Entering into Las Vegas airspace, I heard the Black Hawk talking to approach a few thousand feet below us. Keeping the throttle to the wall, I passed him around Primm, Nevada. We were tying the airplane down when the Black Hawk finally came in, blowing sand and paper everywhere. The crew bus that the FBI had sent to pick everyone up went to the Black Hawk first. Six people got out of the Black Hawk—which left six empty seats. They piled into the crew bus, and it drove over to our airplane. The AUSA, Jack O'Brian, and then I climbed aboard. On the bus were ATF people we had been working with the day before and Brian Carr. They were stunned to see us.

One ATF agent couldn't help himself. "How did you get here?" he asked.

I pointed to the plane. "FBI plane," I said.

"Oh," he said, but he didn't look like his question had been answered.

"Where is your pilot?"

"My pilot?" I asked, intentionally acting confused. "What do you mean?"

"I mean, who flew you here?" he asked.

"I flew me here," I said, as if it was the most obvious thing in the world. Then, acting confused, I added, "You didn't learn to fly at the academ—? Oh! I forgot, you're not FBI." I don't think they even picked up that I was joking. As satisfying as beating the ATF at their own game was, the fact that they had lied about the seats on the helo stuck deep in my craw, and I was not going to let this *lie* lie.

While we were extremely fortunate that the FBI had custody of Furrow, small but significant technicalities could play themselves out at any moment. As long as Furrow was in federal custody, the case remained ours. But he couldn't spend the night in the FBI office; we had to send him to a jail, and there was no federal jail in Las Vegas. Federal prisoners were housed for trial at the Clark County Jail, a county entity. So the minute that Furrow was booked into county jail, Brian would be standing there with a California murder warrant and take custody of the prisoner, because the FBI did not have a warrant at that time to hold him. This was not lost on Ethan Gardella. He had the United States Attorney's Office in Los Angeles begin the process of obtaining a warrant, but this wasn't going to happen before nightfall.

My job was to interview Furrow and create a document that outlined his culpability for the crime. Upon arrival at the Las Vegas office I met an old friend, Stan Bennett. Bennett was a former L.A. agent and had found greener pastures in Las Vegas. He had taken Furrow into custody and done a fabulous job putting him at ease and getting incriminating statements during the time it took me to get to Vegas. We went into the room together, and Stan told Furrow, "Neal, this is Special Agent Moore. He's from the Los Angeles FBI office, and he'd like to talk to you."

"You're the guy who's gonna fry me," were Furrow's first words.

It turned out that Furrow hated the name "Buford," and asked us to call him "Neal," a truncated form of his middle name, "O'Neal." My first surprise was that this depraved killer was as polite and obsequious as a priest. He was not a hardened criminal, regardless of how disgusting his recent acts had been. There was a strong desire in a part of me to take revenge for what he had done. But ultimately that would have been the most selfish thing that I could have done. My job was not to impose my revenge on him at that moment; my job was to elicit from him statements that would condemn him. So in a manipulative, backhanded way, I was getting my revenge, but Furrow didn't know it. If he said something offensive or outrageous, I would swallow twice and pretend it was the most normal thing in the world to hear and continue on, eliciting more incriminating statements.

In the federal system, it is not enough simply to have a confession in your hands. Because of the surplus of false confessions that many people don't realize are out there, you have to have not only the confession but also the ability to corroborate it by proving that the circumstances surrounding the confession are demonstrably true.

Early in the interview, Furrow said that when he had cased the JCC the night before the shooting, he had not seen any children. He was there around 7:30 or 8:00 in the evening and saw only elderly people. I later found out that the reason for this was that in the evenings, the JCC Scrabble Club met at the facility. Furrow assumed that it was some type of Jewish home for the elderly. So I had to ask, "Neal, you thought that the building was an old folks' home?"

"Yes, sir."

"So you walked into the building with an Uzi, and instead of seeing elderly people, you saw four- and five-year-olds children. How did that change things?" I pushed.

"Well, for one thing, I needed to aim lower."

I felt a white-hot rage building inside of me. I thought of my five-, seven-, and eight-year-old children at home. I wanted to jump across the table and strangle him. I looked over at Bennett and his face was red, but he was showing no emotion. I looked down and pretended I was writing. I gave myself a stern lecture. I told myself that if I lost it at that point, Furrow wouldn't get what he deserved. So I simply looked at him and said, "Makes sense."

Next I engaged him in conversation on how he learned to shoot as well as he did. He told me that in an average month, he fired a thousand rounds of ammunition. As a member of SWAT and a sniper, I was lucky if I shot five hundred rounds in a month. I commented on his shooting skill displayed in the murder in Chatsworth. He seemed sincerely proud of the shots.

Every sentence was putting him closer and closer to his own end. We had already determined that the Uzi that he had used was actually made by Norinco, a company in China that manufactured junky but operational copies of firearms from all over the world. To be sold legally in the United States, the Uzi had to have a particularly long barrel and a fixed stock. This made it legal. The Uzis most often seen in the United States were those used by the Israelis and the US Secret Service. He explained in detail how he had cut off the stock and shortened the barrel in his father's shed and dumped the remains in a trash barrel.

Bennett excused himself, saying that he had to grab a Coke. But I knew the reason for his departure: he was going to call Seattle and have the agents go to that shed and pull the cutoff barrel out of the garbage can. Agents were already at the Furrow residence serving a search warrant. Bennett was gone for ten minutes, and when he came back, he handed me a small note. It read, "Found the barrel right where he said it would be."

The only thing he wouldn't discuss honestly was why—with his shooting ability, as demonstrated with the Glock, not an easy gun to fire accurately—he had just sprayed the kids at the JCC.

"After the first shots," he said, "most of the kids ran. But some of them were kind of frozen, staring at me. They put their hands over their ears because of the noise, and they didn't run. Kids with their hands over their ears didn't run. They were easy to pick off." I had to fight the urge to vomit or, once again, to strangle him. He just looked at me writing like he thought I was taking his order at a Denny's. No remorse, no anger, no bravado; it just was what it was.

But then I realized that he was lying about that. If that statement were true, at least one of the kids would have had an entry wound in the front. He was facing them, and by his description they were facing him. Not a single child had an entry wound in the front. He was making that part up. The brave Aryan had shot all of the kids in the back as they ran away. But why? Why did he simply spray that room, missing (as it turned out) 90 percent of the shots he fired? I never got a satisfactory answer to that, though I asked him the same question several times over the next two years.

"Why did you attack the postal worker?"

"Because he was nonwhite and he was working for the federal government." This "nonwhite" man working for the government was Joseph Ileto, a man who worked hard enough to help support his mother, who also lived in Southern California. By all indications he was a man of rare character. Especially if he was anything like his family, whom I met several times during the case.

Those five hours or so in the room with Furrow were a shock to my system. Had I not known what had happened and seen it with my own eyes, I would not possibly have been able to believe that this soft-spoken man had committed those horrible crimes. I would also not have believed that the polite engineer in front of me was capable of claiming the horrible acts and the ideas that drove them. It was as if I had fallen down the rabbit hole with Alice. It was surreal. He was spewing the most vile Nazi garbage, yet doing it while calling me "sir," saying "please," and being unfailingly deferential.

The "why" of the attack was less palatable. "It was a wake-up call to kill Jews," he said.

We discovered that after Furrow ditched the Toyota, he walked to a nearby bar, had a couple of drinks, and took a cab to Hollywood. Then he changed his mind and paid a cabbie $800 to take him to Vegas. But why, we wondered, did he turn himself in?

"I had accomplished what I set out to do," he said. I personally think that like someone waking up from a one-night stand, the desire was gone with the new light. The desire had turned to satiation and the glamour to remorse. He got what he wanted. He had experienced the violent fantasy that he set out to live, and whatever sexual gratification came with that. And now he didn't feel like dying. Going to the FBI office was a way to ensure that he wasn't killed in an arrest. It was the easy way out. It was very apparent that Furrow had planned that this attack would end in his death. But each time it could have come to that, he chickened out.

We talked with him for an hour or so about his right to fight extradition; waiving that right would keep us from having to put him into the Clark County Jail. Finally, wanting to remain in federal custody, he agreed to waive extradition and be flown to Los Angeles.

We found a magistrate, and Furrow's initial appearance before the court went off without a hitch. The magistrate remanded Furrow to FBI custody. It was now Wednesday night at 8:30, and I had been up since Tuesday morning at 6:00 AM with four hours of sleep. I was still running on adrenaline and needed to get Furrow to the helicopter. I went downstairs to the lockup, took custody of Furrow, and walked him to the rear loading dock of the courthouse, where we thought we would have some cover. As we stepped out of the dock into what I thought was darkness, we saw cameras and a crowd at the fence. Someone screamed at Furrow: "Coward!"

Furrow, for inexplicable reasons, then attempted to give a Nazi salute with his handcuffed and shackled hands. He screamed back, "Yeah!"

As we started out in a caravan toward the airport, I turned around from the front seat to talk to Furrow, who was in the backseat with Jack O'Brian. "Neal, why did you shout 'yeah' to that guy?"

Furrow looked at me and said, "He said, 'White power!'"

"No, Neal, he said, 'Coward!'"

Neal's shoulders fell. "Oh, that's different."

Within an hour and a half we had bundled Furrow up into the Black Hawk helicopter with Jack O'Brian, and I watched the helicopter depart. It had been a successful day after a very unsuccessful previous day. I returned to the FBI office at about 10:30 that night and called the airport, requesting to have my aircraft fueled for the flight back. As I talked on the phone, Bennett was nearby. At that point the special agent in charge of the Las Vegas field office approached and sat nearby informally. I finished ordering my fuel and filing a flight plan for Los Angeles and hung up. The SAC looked directly at me and said, "Where do you think you're going?"

"Furrow's got an initial appearance at 6:00 AM, and I need to be in L.A. for that. I was getting my plane fueled so that I can get there tonight."

"You're not going anywhere," he said. I began to protest, but there are times when you realize that your boss is not going to be moved. He knew, he said, how little I had slept, and if I tried to go to that plane, he would call the FAA. I guess in hindsight I should thank him for that.

One of the hardest points in the investigation was when the decision was later made to not seek the death penalty for Furrow. This was unpopular in many quarters. However, Furrow himself had warned the state of Washington that he was a danger to society and admitted before he was even released that he was unable to control his homicidal desires. This does not excuse his actions, but it does go to show that had the state of Washington taken his warnings seriously, the crime may not have occurred. The families were gracious in their acceptance of the decision.

Furrow was eventually sentenced to six hundred years in federal prison, one hundred years for each person he shot. He was sentenced to an additional one hundred years for various other ancillary charges having to do with the crime. This sentence was to be served consecutively and without chance of parole. So he had a total of seven hundred years in prison ahead of him.

14

My, How Time Flies . . .

IN EARLY NOVEMBER 2000, I received an unusual call from Ethan Gardella, the chief of the Hate Crimes Unit at the Los Angeles United States Attorney's Office. Ethan was the prosecutor on the Furrow case, but he had something else to talk about and he sounded concerned.

"Steve, I got a call from Park Dietz, and he's got a client who's being threatened by someone. And he thinks the guy really is dangerous." Calls that started like that usually got my attention.

Dr. Park Dietz had been a forensic psychology expert for us in the Buford Furrow case. A graduate of Cornell and Johns Hopkins, he was an assistant professor of psychology at Harvard, the chief fellow of forensic psychology at the University of Pennsylvania, and a professor of behavioral sciences at UCLA. He had testified in the John Hinckley assassination attempt on President Reagan and the Jeffrey Dahmer case and would go on to testify in the Unabomber and DC Sniper cases. He was president of Park Dietz and Associates, a firm that assessed threats for corporations, celebrities, and governments. If *he* felt that the guy was that dangerous, there was a problem.

"Who and what?" were the only questions I could think of.

"I think you need to call Park and get a full briefing; I'm not in a place where I can talk. But call him now; he's about to get on a plane."

"It's that urgent?"

"Park says this guy's an extreme danger, Steve." If Park Dietz thought that, I had reason to be worried.

"How are you involved, Ethan? Is this a hate crime?"

"No, Steve, it has nothing to do with my side of the house. Park just didn't know who else to call."

"Then why did you call me?"

"Getting federal jurisdiction won't be easy, but this really needs the FBI. You're creative. You can figure out how to do something with this."

Talking to Dietz, Ethan turned out to be right on two counts: the bad guy was truly a ticking time bomb, and I was having trouble seeing any FBI jurisdiction. Dr. Dietz could not at that time identify the suspect or even his client. But knowing that Dietz got as much as four figures per hour, I could predict that the client was a celeb, or at least a Fortune 500 corporation. It wasn't until the next day that Dietz had permission from the people writing the checks. The subject making the threats was Ronald Mike Denton, and the corporation was Chevron Oil. Oh good, I thought, Chevron is generally flammable. As I listened to Dietz describe the situation, I became more and more uneasy, a feeling that would not leave me for several months.

Mike Denton had been operations supervisor at Chevron's oil refinery in El Segundo, California. He was known as a hothead and was not well liked by his peers. According to personnel records, he was repeatedly in conflict with coworkers and incited fistfights with fellow employees. In 1999 Denton applied for a promotion at the refinery, but it was given to a Hispanic supervisor. In Denton's mind, this could not have had anything to do with fistfights at work; it had to be due to the job-winner's race. This became so bothersome to him that he left Chevron on a "temporary" stress leave, blaming the company. As part of the stress leave, he was required to see a psychiatrist to help him get back to work.

The psychiatrist, Manny Letterman, had recently contacted Chevron to warn them that Denton was violent and suggested that Chevron (as was their prerogative) order an independent medical examination (IME) from another psychiatrist to see whether Letterman could be mistaken. In actuality, Dr. Letterman was scared and trying anything he could do to get a legal way to let Chevron know what was going on. As a requirement of his continued benefits and pay, Denton was sent to Dr. Patrick Maloney, a forensic psychiatrist of some renown who had worked with law enforcement in Los Angeles for thirty years. Maloney subsequently warned the company not to let Denton back on Chevron property for any reason.

Drs. Letterman, Maloney, and Dietz had been spooked by something that Denton was telling them, but I did not have access to his statements. As psychiatrists, they were severely limited in what they could reveal about clients' disclosures. Mental health professionals may only break doctor-patient confidentiality to issue a "Tarasoff warning"—which is actually a legal obligation. This exception is the result of a 1976 California Supreme Court case in which a psychiatric patient was violently fixated on and stalking a former girlfriend; his psychiatrist knew but did not warn her because of his fear of losing his license for breaching confidentiality. The girlfriend, Tatiana Tarasoff, was subsequently murdered by the doctor's patient. The court found that if a mental health professional believes his or her patient/client has the intent, capability, and opportunity to harm a specific person or entity, he or she is required to warn the potential victim.

The Tarasoff rule is a good thing as far as it goes, but it is extremely limited. It says only that mental health professionals must provide a warning to potential victims and to law enforcement. That is all. They are still not allowed to reveal all of the patient's medical information. Overstepping this rule can result in the loss of their medical license. So we now had three very credible psychiatrists, two of whom were famous for their threat assessment work, all saying that Mike Denton was extremely dangerous but "we're not allowed to tell you why." The one thing they did tell me, though, was "Hurry."

I began by calling Chevron's legal department. They told me that they could only legally divulge that the threat Denton was making was to the Chevron El Segundo Refinery itself. The El Segundo refinery was Chevron's second-largest oil refinery. As bad as this news was, it at least gave me an angle to get into the case. In my early research on the refinery, I had learned that it supplied, via underground pipeline, *40 percent* of the jet fuel used at Los Angeles International Airport (LAX), which was less than a mile from the refinery. Airliners used that jet fuel, and airliners were engaged in "interstate commerce." Title 18, United States Code (USC) Section 844 makes the "Destruction of Property Used in Interstate Commerce" a federal crime and gave the FBI jurisdiction. I had my opening. I immediately began a full-field investigation on Mike Denton.

At the same time, Denton was in the process of making a critical and timely mistake. He filed suit against Chevron for "infliction of mental distress," asking for millions of dollars in damages. How does one prove infliction of mental distress? One has to provide one's psychiatric records. Apparently Denton did not think this through. Seeing their opening, Chevron's attorneys immediately subpoenaed Denton's psychiatric records, and Denton's psychiatrists immediately complied with the subpoena. Chevron then forwarded the records to me. What I read in those psychiatric records was worse than I had feared.

Specifically, in his therapy sessions, Denton was demanding that Chevron pay him $2 million or he would "blow Chevron away," saying, "I'm gonna cause a billion dollars in damage, take out Chevron in thirty-five minutes, then escape to East Texas." What he was doing was in a disturbing way very cunning. Denton was extorting Chevron. He wanted $2 million or he would blow the refinery up. But by telling only his psychiatrist, he believed that he was protected from prosecution by doctor-patient privilege, yet could be assured that his demands would still be passed on to the company. We called it "extortion by proxy." If prosecuted, he could simply claim that he could not extort someone when his "privilege" prohibited his statements from going to the person he was allegedly extorting. Also, he could claim the statements were simply the bluster of someone needing psychiatric care.

I tried to get traction with my FBI supervisor on the case, Supervisory Special Agent (SSA) Aaron Dodds, but he felt that the statements were simply that: big talk from a small man. To bolster the case, I interviewed Dr. Patrick Maloney, the forensic psychologist who had conducted the IME on Denton, and who could now legally discuss the subpoenaed records.

Maloney told me, "Denton is waiting, but anything could trigger him. Just about anything could set him off. If nothing happens before April 1, he will be triggered soon after that, because [Denton's] disability payments and his employment end on that day."

As I was leaving, Dr. Maloney left me with this chilling assessment: "If this isn't the most dangerous person I have ever evaluated in my thirty years in practice, then he certainly stands out above all the others because of his potential danger."

George Duran was a Secret Service agent who worked on the Los Angeles Joint Terrorist Task Force with me. I had immense respect for his work, his insight, and his rational thought. The Secret Service also knows its way around threat cases. I asked him to assist me on the Denton case.

After reading the file, George was astounded that my supervisor, Aaron Dodds, had not assigned half a dozen agents to the case immediately. But, again, Dodds was not convinced that Denton was a real threat. I began to get contemporaneous reports from the psychiatrists after sessions.

Mike Denton, therapy session, December 12, 2000: "My determination to even the score with Chevron is stronger than my will to live."

In mid-December, we began to build our dossier on Denton, and what we read became more and more disturbing. We obtained information from his medical records, his coworkers, and other law enforcement. Ronald Mike Denton came from East Texas, where he had worked a series of menial industrial jobs. According to Dr. Maloney, Denton told him he hunted because "I like killing." He admitted to a fondness for starting fires and torturing animals, finally combining the two by burning animals to death.

He married fairly young, but the marriage broke up just as quickly. He was brutally abusive to his first wife, Paula. At one point, she related to us a frightening insight into Mike: "I had to have dinner ready for him when he got home, and then I had to make sure of things like getting the toothpaste on his toothbrush for him." His wife was several months pregnant when she "made a mistake."

"One day, I did the toothpaste wrong and he just went off." Denton punched his pregnant wife in the face and knocked her flat, stepping on her long hair so that she couldn't get off the floor. He then kicked her in the ribs with his work boots until his anger subsided.

"After that, he told me to get up and serve dinner. He wouldn't let me out of the house until my bruises healed, but I still had to make the meals." It wasn't until she delivered her baby that she found out that Denton had broken three of her ribs that night. When Patrick Maloney asked Denton in an examination whether he had ever been violent with his wife, he said, "No," then added, "Oh, I busted her lip a couple of times, but she needed it."

Mike Denton, therapy session, December 17, 2000: "In April, I will prepare for the end of my life. When I get through with my retaliation, I will destroy the refinery."

A coworker shed the first light on what Denton's actual attack plans might be. Denton had bragged to him that he had enough knowledge to destroy the refinery. None of the other operations supervisors doubted that, as all had received training that told them exactly what the vulnerabilities of the plant were. Denton expressed interest in seven liquefied petroleum gas (LPG) spheres. LPG is the primary component of both propane and lighter fluid. It is highly flammable and heavier than air. These spheres were up to five stories in diameter and filled with as much as 6,272,792 pounds of LPG. Denton had bragged to the coworker that he had purchased a Russian SKS rifle and 200 rounds of 7.62mm armor-piercing ammunition. The coworker felt that Denton might have plans to shoot holes in the spheres containing the highly flammable gas. Within seconds, he said, the tanks could all be engulfed in a massive fire that could easily spread to the rest of the plant. Ominously, Denton told this coworker that he knew that the tanks were one inch thick. The coworker was surprised that Denton appeared to know that, as the employees were never told details like the thickness of the steel in the tanks and spheres.

With this information, I added an extra charge: "threat to use a weapon of mass destruction." It was time to call in Washington, DC. We brought in the Behavioral Sciences Unit (BSU), colloquially known as "the profilers." They asked for a dossier of Denton's medical and personnel records so that they could analyze his personality and his intentions. I let them know that I had put him under surveillance and was contemplating "stiffing-in" (introducing) an informant into the situation. Denton went to the gym every day and might have been a steroid user. That could provide us with a good opportunity. Two days later, the profilers got back to me by phone.

"Steve, congratulations, you rang the bell. That is the most dangerous man we've seen this year."

Our conversation continued to our options. I brought up the undercover agent idea again, and the answer was both succinct and firm: "If you put an undercover agent into this situation, Denton will kill him. And if he doesn't, he'll just move up the timetable for his attack."

Mike Denton, therapy session, January 5, 2001: "I will make my decision regarding violence on April 1. I have days when it's all I can do not to go through with it. Once I start, there is no turning back."

Arrest was still not an option, because if we did, and our evidence did not convince a court to hold him without bail, then he would be freed, and all experts said that he would attack the refinery as soon as he felt he could do so successfully. The case against him had to be flawless before he was arrested. So far, we had the psychiatric reports of three psychiatrists, which would make good evidence, but even their opinions would not be foolproof evidence against skilled defense attorneys. The only evidence we had at that point was the fact that he had accessed plant records to determine the thickness of the metal of a piece of equipment that he was responsible for. Not much to go on. We had to show intent, and that meant we had to show specific planning, which meant that we had to show that he had the instrumentalities of the crime—the things he would need to destroy the refinery. Tick . . . tick . . . tick . . .

If I didn't believe in profiling before, I became a believer on this case. The psychiatrists and the profilers agreed on actions that would indicate that Denton was about to attack:

1. Denton would stop seeing his psychiatrist. He was only going there to relay threats and demands anyway.

2. He would sell off his Chevron stock. All of Denton's investments were in Chevron stock, which he got through company plans. He knew that an attack on Chevron's second-largest refinery would cause stock values to plummet.

These actions could take place any time after he received his final check on April 1. However, if there was a precipitating event, Denton could attack at any time. Examples of precipitating events would be a provocative step by Chevron, a court reversal in one of his suits, an early exhaustion of his money, his arrest and bail, or even a search warrant executed on him.

Therapist's notes, Mike Denton session, January 8, 2001: "Patient says: 'There is a score to settle. That idiot in Massachusetts [workplace violence shooting] killed only seven people.'"

"Patient states that he does not want to come to therapy anymore."

"Denton would stop seeing his psychiatrist." The first sign of an imminent attack.

I established round-the-clock surveillance on Denton. L.A. had four Special Operations Group surveillance teams, and I needed at least one on him every minute, both to warn us if he headed for the refinery and to help us find any storage facilities or weapons caches he might have hidden. But that couldn't go on indefinitely. It was now mid-February, and I was using up the entire SOG, which meant that the office of eight-hundred-plus agents was using all its surveillance resources on a single case.

We began records checks around the country on Denton, and had a hit. We found that he had purchased an SKS 7.62mm rifle just two weeks before in Texas while on Christmas vacation with his brother. (As additional insight into Denton and his family, several years before this incident, Denton's brother had been shot in the neck by his own stepson.) Denton told his therapist that the trip to Texas was for hunting. We couldn't prove he brought the rifle back to California. He also purchased ammunition, but it was not armor-piercing. I purchased duplicates of that ammunition and sent it to the FBI Laboratory in Quantico and asked that they test it against the type of steel used in the LPG spheres. It penetrated only a quarter inch. Not nearly enough. To prove our theory of the crime, we would have to prove possession of the rifle and armor-piercing rounds. Even if he did bring the rifle back to California, his level of paranoia would mitigate against him keeping it at home, so a search warrant would be incredibly risky. Denton had claimed to his psychiatrist that he had *two* SKSs. Meanwhile, he appeared to be destabilizing; he'd begun claiming that Chevron was burglarizing his car.

February 1, 2001: I began to find that I was fixated on this case and having a difficult time thinking about anything else. This was complicated at work, because my supervisor did not feel that the case had any merit. The bigger problem was at home, where I spent an inordinate amount of time silently working through different scenarios as to how I could make a case against Denton before

April 1. I could watch TV for two hours and not know ten minutes later what I had watched. In my mind, I also occasionally went through what would happen if I didn't succeed.

Not a single person in the FBI besides the Behavioral Sciences Unit seemed to think Denton was a problem. I couldn't convince anybody except George Duran. The confidence I had built up with the Furrow case was being put to the test.

Michelle became increasingly impatient with my distraction and pointed out that I might as well be out of town if I didn't talk even when I was at home. This was not the type of case I felt comfortable discussing at home except in the most general terms, and a wedge began to be driven between us. My nerves were frayed, and my tolerance for noise and stress were very low. Bad news in a house with a seven-, an eight-, and a ten-year old.

I frequently stayed late at the office reading and rereading Denton's statements to his psychiatrist for the previous two years. At the beginning, his statements were nonspecific, and he seemed to be searching for what he wanted to do. He mentioned filling a Ryder truck with "fertilizer" (ammonium nitrate, like Oklahoma City) or simply "shooting a room full of lawyers." On the anniversary of the Columbine High School shooting, he had commented on the shooters in that attack: "I give the shooters an 'A' for imagination, an 'F' for execution."

February 12, 2001: I continued to review Denton's old psychiatric statements. Following his Columbine comments, what he said seemed to become very specific. "Either I get a proper settlement, or I blow Chevron away. I'll blow 'em away for less than $250,000."

Maloney had relayed this information to Chevron, which decided that $250,000 would be a bargain given the other possibilities. Maloney then met with Denton and advised that his demand for $250,000 had been met. When he heard this, instead of basking in victory, Denton rejected the offer and became enraged.

Maloney told Chevron that it was no use negotiating, saying, "He doesn't want to settle, he just wants to hurt Chevron." As the year went on, he fell deeper and deeper into a mental abyss.

"I have dehumanized Chevron, I have no problem killing anyone there."

In the second half of 2000, Denton appeared to have decided his and Chevron's fate:

August 7, 2000: "It's about human life and money. And I'll get them."

September 1, 2000: "I was thinking of loading my guns last night . . . it could happen any day."

October 30, 2000: "I'll shut down eight million gallons of gas a day. I'm a pyromaniac. I know how to make explosions—over the past week I've devised the perfect plan, and I dare Chevron to try and make me prove it. I'll do it today if I'm provoked."

My supervisor took these statements to mean that he wasn't serious. "He's said he was going to 'do it' for two years and he's done nothing! The guy is bluffing! Barking dogs don't bite!" Yet the psychiatrists and the profilers were telling me something completely opposite. I went to the United States Attorney's Office with my concerns. They were equally concerned and advised that they would do whatever they could to help, but at that moment, there was not enough evidence for a warrant that would stand up in court.

March 5, 2001: Sometimes even the worst news is a break. But this particular news caused the hair on the back of my neck to stand up. It turned out that Denton *had* told somebody the details of his plan. A coworker thought Denton was just blowing smoke, so he didn't report it to management. Now with the investigation becoming obvious, he went to management. Chevron's technical people reviewed the attack plan Denton had related to him and determined that it was viable and that if it succeeded, it could result in destruction on a cataclysmic scale. The attack was frighteningly simple. Denton told his coworker that he was going to open the gas valves on just one of the seven LPG tanks. Just one. He said that he would have some type of ignition source far enough away that he could get clear before the LPG ignited.

As we listened, I wondered where this was headed. An explosion of that magnitude was significant, but it would not rupture the sphere—it would just burn fiercely and potentially catch the rest of the refinery on fire. And why only one LPG tank? I wondered.

The Chevron supervisor who accompanied me on the interview with the coworker used the word "bleve" (BLEH-vee). I remembered the term from bomb school but could not place it.

BLEVE stands for "Boiling Liquid Expanding Vapor Explosion." A BLEVE is an explosion that occurs when liquid boils inside a closed container until the vapor expands to the point that it violently ruptures said container. BLEVE is the reason you are told not to throw aerosol cans in a fire. By setting the first sphere on fire, with almost a million pounds of LPG to feed the fire, the liquid gas in the rest of the tanks would boil in just a few minutes, and the tanks would BLEVE. The first tank would simply be the igniter for the other six. BLEVEs are remarkably powerful; in 1984, the explosion of several similarly sized LPG tanks in Mexico City killed between five hundred and six hundred people and injured thousands. A BLEVE of a fifty-foot-diameter LPG tank would be catastrophic. The blast wave would travel over a mile and a half. Detonation of all seven of the spheres would be cataclysmic.

"But wouldn't it be fairly easy to put out the fire before the tanks BLEVE'd?" I asked.

"Normally, yes. But not if you shoot the responding firefighters," said the coworker. "That's his plan. That's why he has the SKS."

There was an emergency-response team in the refinery made up of specially trained volunteer refinery workers and supervisors. It was there to respond to events such as a leak in an LPG tank or a fire anywhere in the refinery, and it was to be the first responder until local fire departments could get there. Denton had been a member of El Segundo's team. Denton knew what these teams did, how they would respond, and how to stop them. His plan, he told his acquaintance, was to set his ignition sources, open a single large valve, override the safety devices—not hard if you're trained—and climb a nearby berm, from which he could use his rifles and ammunition to pick off responding firefighters until the fire had grown to the point that the tanks would go off one by one. That's why the ammunition he was purchasing wasn't armor-piercing. It didn't have to be. He was planning on shooting people, not spheres.

George and I worked the weekend trying to find ways to get an arrest that would result in a no-bail hold. Simply arresting him was no good, especially if he wasn't keeping his weapons at his residence. Then, he could just bail out, retrieve the guns, and go to it at his convenience.

March 12, 2001: It was now the second week in March and we had maybe two weeks to go before the attack if the psychiatrists were right—and I believed they were. We got a break. George Duran found a purchase receipt in Long Beach for an SKS semiautomatic rifle. Jackpot! We sped to the gun store, and there was the receipt, signed by Denton and with a copy of his driver's license. It was a huge find. He had purchased the rifle in the past few months, but the purchase hadn't been uploaded before our earlier checks. It proved that he purchased a gun in California.

We drove directly to the United States Attorney's Office. The prosecutor said that he could authorize obtaining arrest and search warrants now that we had evidence of the rifle. However, if we didn't find the rifle at the residence, or other materials that were obviously to be used in the attack—"instrumentalities of the crime"—he couldn't guarantee anything. The problem was that in his last few psychiatric appointments, Denton had begun alluding to the fact that he was "hiding" his SKS rifles. If we dropped a search warrant on him and didn't find the gun, we might simply "initiate launch sequence." We left knowing we had two weeks to go and that it would be a risk to arrest and search now. We were playing a game of brinkmanship that would haunt us forever if we lost. With the rifle as evidence, though, I got the surveillance team back on Denton over the weekend. All I needed from Denton was one trip to the refinery to case the place, or the purchase of ammunition.

Monday, March 19, 2001: Chevron's attorneys called. Denton had been frantically trying to sell his Chevron stock *all the previous weekend.* Our options and our time had just run out. Denton was calling Chevron human resource and benefits people at home and appeared angry and agitated. He had already stopped seeing his psychiatrist, and now he was trying to sell his stock. This was the last action the profilers and the psychiatrists said he would take before he attacked.

"What about the money? Doesn't he still have his check coming on April 1?" I asked.

There was a pause from the Chevron lawyer before he dropped a bomb.

"Steve, we figured the disability payroll numbers wrong. When we said his benefits ended on April 1, we didn't take into account that we pay those in advance. His benefits up through March 30 were paid

on March 1, along with a letter stating that that was his last check."
Shocked, I knew we had to act with what we had, even though it was
a risk. I called the surveillance team. Denton had not left the house
that day. I told them to hold on, that we were going to get warrants.

George Duran and I went to Aaron Dodds with the new information. It was a tense meeting that became confrontational almost
immediately. I had been warned by another supervisor about the
possible reason for Dodds's reluctance. First, he apparently didn't
buy into the psychiatrists' theories. But secondarily, he was desperately trying to get a promotion and move out of L.A. He had
applications in for just about every position available. In order to be
competitive, though, he had to have extremely high performance
appraisals. And in mere weeks, the L.A. office was going to undergo
a regular biennial audit, and it would be a make-or-break for Aaron.
If he did well, a promotion was a possibility. If he did not . . .

FBI supervisors are judged by many different criteria. But an
important one is the use of what are known as "sophisticated investigative techniques." Sophisticated techniques include wiretaps,
undercover operations, technical installation of microphones, etc.
At the time, the FBI believed that the use of sophisticated methods
directly correlated to the importance and difficulty of the cases a
squad was working. If there was no need for wiretaps or undercovers, the squad must be "bottom feeding." Conversely, it was
assumed that those squads with high utilization of these special
methods must be rock stars. What this actually meant was that in
order to look good on paper, some squads were doing undercover
operations on the most menial of cases just to look good at inspec-
tion time. They were killing mosquitoes with hammers.

The belief that important cases always require sophisticated
investigative techniques is obviously naïve, but it is very difficult to measure investigative quality, and the FBI is always trying
something. Dodds had reviewed our squad investigative statistics

and found that we were below average that year on sophisticated methods. My case was not lending itself to those, so it was not going to help his promotion, so therefore, he had little interest in it. He was shifting resources to those cases that were now using wiretaps and undercover operations.

Our meeting ended with an ultimatum from Dodds: "Either put a UC on the case, get a wire up, or do a technical install, and we'll go forward. Absent that, forget it."

"We don't have time, Aaron!"

"We're done here," was the response.

George and I walked back to my desk staring at each other but not saying a word. Fearing just such a reaction, I had thought about creating a document that I believed would have a chance at fixing the problem. It was one of those "I have half a mind to" documents that you'd never really send. The document would either break the logjam or end my career. But I had no choice at this point. The situation was beyond an assignment, beyond a job. I needed to motivate Aaron Dodds, and a supervisor like him fears one thing more than anything else: blame. I had to shift the responsibility for this case off my shoulders and onto Dodds's. In a few minutes, I had written an EC (electronic communication) doing just that. The communication set out all the pertinent facts in the case as well as the immediacy of the threat. It set out the possible consequences if Denton was not interdicted, and it recommended an immediate arrest and search warrant execution on him. It listed each sophisticated investigative technique considered and gave the reason that each was deemed inappropriate for this case.

It concluded with the following: "*Special Agent Moore has exhausted his investigative options and initiatives on this matter. It is requested that Supervisory Special Agent Aaron Dodds, based on his position and experience, provide the necessary guidance on how to successfully resolve this matter and prevent loss of life.*"

The next problem: as supervisor, Aaron had to sign off on the EC or it wouldn't go into the case file, meaning that it might as well have never existed. I was a relief supervisor, however, so I also had the authority to sign off on documents for file—except, of course, my own. Approving your own communications is technically a violation of FBI policy but one that I had never seen enforced or even questioned.

I signed off on the EC myself and walked it to the squad secretary. Meghan Flynn was young, very pretty, as competent as the average agent, and as tough as the average SWAT operator. She knew exactly what I was doing, and she knew she could get in trouble for posting it to the file. She didn't bat an eye when I explained. Her only comment about Dodds was "Screw him, then." Once she'd posted it, George and I took it in to Aaron and handed it to him. Since I had first met Aaron Dodds in 1996 as squad mates, we had been friends. That friendship effectively ended when Aaron took that EC into his hands.

He looked up blank-faced at George and me.

"You've already posted this to file?"

I nodded. I knew what he was asking. If it was "posted to file," it was official. It was a legal FBI record of the case and it was in the computer database. He reread the EC carefully and handed it quietly back to me.

"Arrest him, then." These were some of the last words Aaron and I ever exchanged.

There was no time to waste. This was going to have to be a SWAT operation, and I needed them immediately. My SWAT tour of five years had ended just three months before, so I was dealing with friends on the team. They pulled out all the stops for me and called for an op the following morning.

At four the next morning, I was in the SWAT briefing room. It was one of the first ops for the team after I turned in my gear, and they would be doing an arrest for me. We mapped out the residence, discussed the subject's possible weapons, the threat, and the subject himself. I dearly missed being on the other side of that briefing—gearing up, loading up, and getting ready to hit the location. But this was the kind of case that had made it necessary for me to leave SWAT.

By 5 AM I was three blocks from Denton's house meeting with another close friend, Jay Rollins, the surveillance team pro. Rollins had been on Denton off and on for the last several days. In the previous twenty-four hours, Denton had only gone to the gym. He was definitely at home, and his car was in the driveway. But the lights were on in the house. We had no way of knowing whether he was awake or whether he just hadn't turned off all the inside lights at night.

At 6:01 the SWAT team breached the front door of Denton's house. The *bang* was heard a half block away where I was stationed, as were shouts of "*Get down! Get down!*" Somebody had been awake. I heard the team's radio call that the house was safe, and I entered the living room. Denton was handcuffed in the middle of the room. Behind him on a table was his laptop computer, and the screen was still up. It was a stock-brokerage page, and Chevron's stock was highlighted. He was trying to sell his stock online at 6 AM that morning.

To our immense relief, a search of the house revealed a treasure trove of evidence: *Fourteen hundred rounds* of high-powered 7.62mm rifle ammo were found in his walk-in closet. A small handgun was hanging from a nail above a doorway so that if he was forced to raise his hands while in that room, he could covertly grab the gun as he went through the doorway. An extensive collection of ground-based long-burn fireworks and flares were found in the bedroom on the floor next to his bed, still in their original boxes. This was recently purchased stuff and would be the perfect ignition source he had described to his friend. He would have placed them in a parking lot near the LPG cylinders that is approximately fifty feet lower than the bases of the spheres. Being heavier than air, the released LPG would have made its way to the lower parking lot, giving him time to get to the berm, where he would have his weapons. When the LPG hit the long-burn fireworks and flares, it would have immediately ignited.

In closets, we found manuals on escape and evasion, explosives, living as a fugitive, converting SKS rifles to machine guns, and fighting with knives. Finally, the SKS itself was located, and two full fifty-round magazines were with it. Denton had put a scope on the rifle. Scopes are generally not needed when you're shooting at a fifty-foot-diameter metal sphere. Scopes are antipersonnel devices, which corroborated Denton's plan perfectly. He also had a Glock pistol with hundreds of rounds of hollow-point ammunition.

We found $500 in new, sequential ten-, twenty- and fifty-dollar bills. There were maps and other identifying information. An escape kit. Hanging from the rearview mirror of his car was his Chevron refinery ID and plant placards that would have provided him access to the plant. His blue refinery coveralls were also in the car. Denton hadn't worked at Chevron for two years, but he had his gear in the car. We have no idea how close we might have come. When news got back to the office that the rifle was found and that the instrumentalities for every facet of the plan were located, Aaron Dodds showed up. Denton was held without bail.

In a trial that lasted ten months, Denton was convicted in federal court of interference with commerce by threats or violence as well as threat to use a weapon of mass destruction. It never made the press, really, except in small blurbs, because Chevron didn't want to broadcast what could have happened. But at the time of Denton's conviction, his case was considered the highest-value damage prevention of the use of a "weapon of mass destruction" on record.

15

Drinking Out of a Fire Hose

SEPTEMBER 10, 2001, was the last day for almost eight years that my wife and I would have a functional marriage, that my kids would feel like they had a full-time father, and that I would have my priorities straight. It was also the last day in eight years I would truly know who I was.

There was a general feeling of purposelessness in my head that day. Furrow had been sentenced in April, and Denton had been sentenced in the last week of August. I celebrated by taking the first nine days of September as vacation with my family. The following Monday I went in to the office as usual, but for almost the first time in two years, there was no big case on my desk, and there was no prosecution coming up. I had resigned from the SWAT team to work the cases, and I truly felt like I had nothing to do. That night, Michelle and I went to bed early and slept soundly.

Five minutes before my 6:00 AM alarm was to go off, my cell phone rang. I picked it up and it was Roger Deacon, a friend of

mine from the office who was also the supervisor of an international terrorism (IT) squad.

"Are you watching TV?" he asked

"Roger, my alarm hasn't even gone off yet."

"Turn on the television," he said, grimly.

"What channel?" I croaked, walking to the TV.

"It doesn't matter."

As the TV warmed up, I saw an aerial view of the Twin Towers of
the World Trade Center with the massive black smoke plume coming out of Tower 1. Like everyone else in America I was stunned by
what I saw. Roger and I talked back and forth about the possibility
of an accident, but with the visibility so perfect in New York, that
seemed ridiculous. Then, as we watched, another plane hit. Both
Roger and I knew in large terms what was going on. I looked over
and saw that Michelle had been watching from the bed and was
crying. I went over to her, put my arm around her, and sat on the
bed next to her.

Los Angeles might have been one of the destination cities of
the airliners, but beyond that, we did not immediately know what
our responsibilities would be or how we could help in the short
term. So rather than get in the car and scream off to Westwood
and wait for hours for instructions, I pulled out my packing list
and began filling my bags. I didn't expect to be going to New York,
but I couldn't rule it out.

A couple of hours later, I threw my gear into the car, kissed
Michelle good-bye, and told her that I would try to keep her
apprised of what was going on. I told her that I would be surprised
if I saw her for the next three days. I was wrong—I wouldn't see
her for over a week, even though I was never more than thirty-
five miles from home. Next, I went over to my kids' elementary
school and found each of them in their classes. I hugged and
kissed them and told them I would be gone for a few days.

I got to Westwood and was greeted by an eerie sight. The federal building had been cordoned off, and the parking lot access was being controlled by the SWAT team, wearing ballistic vests and carrying their machine guns. It was chilling. I pulled up and talked to a friend of mine on the team, and he explained that SWAT was there because nobody knew what the next attack was going to be and what mode it would take.

As I predicted, four hundred agents, including my whole squad, were being assigned to different shifts, and I worked through midnight in the command post. I had never worked international counterterrorism before, and so the procedures for the classified material were foreign to me and I didn't have an institutional knowledge of the groups and organizations that were being referenced in many of the communications. But hundreds of calls were coming in from the public about suspicious activities. Those I knew how to handle. It was simply a matter of the right manpower and a quick evaluation of every lead as to whether an agent needed to be sent out, further investigation needed to be done, or we could ignore it. One woman reported a jet diving on Los Angeles. It turned out to be landing at LAX. Other leads were more ominous; there appeared to be more al-Qaeda sympathizers and supporters in Los Angeles than I would have believed.

It seemed that I had just begun looking at these reports and intel briefs when I looked up and saw the next shift arriving for the midnight to 8 AM shift. However, in the time between 4 PM and midnight, a stack of incoming, unaddressed leads and intel briefs almost a foot high had accumulated in the center of our conference table. For the next week or so, most agents worked many more hours than they were off. I spent a lot of time sleeping in my car in the garage of the FBI building.

Sometime on September 12 I was approached by Pete Saunders, counterterrorism ASAC, with Roger Deacon at his side. Roger was the supervisor of the squad that had responsibility for any investigation of the 9/11 attacks in Los Angeles. They asked me to consider being the case agent for the L.A. component of the case. I thought they were joking. I had never worked an international terrorism case in my life, and they wanted me to start with this one? I couldn't figure out whether they were crazy or desperate. I suggested they ask someone else, but they were persistent and I relented. The case was known as "PENTTBOM," and it became the largest single investigation in FBI history. (Only the agents who named the cases really knew the entire significance of the case names, but the smart money said that in this case, PENT referred to the Pentagon and the double "T" stood for Twin Towers. BOM is self explanatory.) There were approximately four hundred agents assigned to the case around the clock in Los Angeles alone. We broke the case down into different components and assigned individual agents to run each of those components.

The entire west end of the fourteenth floor of the federal building became our new command post. For the next several months, I worked out of a large office in the company of Roger Deacon and another supervisor in IT, Todd Prost. Every morning, the director of the FBI would brief President Bush at between 6 AM and 6:30 AM, in Washington, DC, which was 3 and 3:30 AM Los Angeles time. Therefore at about 1 AM, questions on our component of the case began to flood in. We had to have people on board who could answer those questions with authority or at least redirect them to me. It was a rare night that I didn't get a call of some type between 1 and 3 AM asking me about a specific issue. Adding to that, every special agent in charge of every field office in the Bureau with a component of the case had a conference call with the director of the FBI at 9 AM Washington time. That, of course, was 6 AM L.A. time. Therefore, I had to be in the office by 5 AM to review the previous night's investigative results and evaluate them for the briefing to the director at six o'clock. At 5:30 I would go into the office of Assistant Director Paul Eiffel, the overall boss of the Los Angeles FBI field office, and give him a fifteen to twenty-minute briefing on the case. He would then ask questions until the conference call started. I sat through each one of these conference calls for about the first month.

The investigation on the case in Los Angeles began to bear fruit, and what we learned was disturbing. We found that the hijackers had come into the United States through Los Angeles a year before and had been supported by unknown people in Los Angeles for at least a week before they were moved to the San Diego area, where they began flight instruction. Not only was the fact that they had support in Los Angeles disturbing as a philosophical matter, but it also meant we needed to identify and root out that support or al-Qaeda would still have a useful cell in the Los Angeles area.

For the next three months, the agents working on PENTTBOM did some of the most phenomenal investigation I had ever seen. For instance, they went through the handwritten registers of every cheap hotel on the entire west side of Los Angeles to find out where the hijackers had stayed, eventually finding them. They investigated for weeks to determine who it was that visited them in the hotel and set them up there. We made huge progress, but the pressure was immense.

I began to be concerned throughout this investigation that the Los Angeles field office did not have, and had never had, a squad dedicated to the investigation of al-Qaeda in Los Angeles. I bumped into Paul Eiffel in the hallway a day or two after coming to this conclusion and made that very pitch to him. Several days later, Paul called me on my cell phone. This was fairly unusual, as the assistant director generally did not communicate directly to a line agent unless they were in a meeting together.

"I've decided to form an al-Qaeda squad," he said.

"Excellent!" I exclaimed. But Paul's next words stopped me cold. "You're the acting supervisor."

I was sure I couldn't have heard him correctly. "Who did you say was the acting supervisor?" I asked.

"You. And I want you to put in for the permanent supervisor position."

Now my head was spinning. I did not want to be a supervisor. Supervisors looked at cell phone usage, budget, manpower figures, and Bureau car management. These were things that I had no interest in and that caused me to shudder. The pay bump would be almost unnoticeable, and I was afraid of becoming disenfranchised from all of my friends who were street agents. I had no career ambitions in the Bureau—I just wanted to be a street agent and work good cases.

"Steve, I have all the managers I need in IT. What I need are leaders. I will make sure you get administrative help." What, did everybody know that I wasn't an administrative ace?

"Paul I don't want to sit at a desk and hear stories from my agents about how they're working the cases," I pleaded.

"That's exactly what I'm talking about, Steve. I want you to help run the cases. I want you to be out there with the agents, not sitting at a desk. We have too many people like that already." With that, I told him I would give the matter serious thought, but I had already decided I wanted it.

When I came home with the news of the probable promotion and told Michelle I wanted to take it, she did not seem to be as ecstatic as I thought she might be. I had actually hoped that she would be proud of what I had accomplished and understand exactly why I needed to do what I was doing. I was right on both counts, but at the same time, she was deeply distressed that I would be taking a job that would require even more time away from the family and carry more responsibility when we already had zero time together. This was the first time in our entire life together that her first reaction to a positive job move or a new case was not absolute excitement for me and total support. It surprised me and became a source of great stress in my life. In my insular little world, I felt that what I was doing was crucial, and I was stunned when she didn't understand the importance of it.

I spent the next hour or two explaining to her why this was so important. I probably could have done it in less than an hour, but I started getting phone calls. With each phone call she would stare at me with an "I told you so" gaze as I talked on the phone. This was so not like her. I couldn't figure out what was "wrong with her." I was sure that I hadn't changed, so something must have changed in her. Thus began a growing personal myopia about my life and her life and how the two meshed. The busier I got, the more important my work seemed. The more important my work seemed, the busier I stayed. Resistance from the family was futile. I was trying to save the world.

While the time I had spent away from the family during the Furrow and the Denton cases had been supported and even cheered by the family, those cases were cheered with the tacit understanding that eventually there would be an end to those kinds of hours and effort. With 9/11, the end to that kind of life drifted off ahead into the distance and over the horizon. They began to realize something I didn't: I had no intention of scaling back my career. I was loving this. I was getting to do things as an agent few people ever do. It was a dream come true. At the exact time when they expected to get their dad back and for life to go back to normal, it got drastically harder. It was as if I had gotten a running start at ignoring the family. Two years of heavy investigations had already taken their toll. Now, after three months on 9/11, my family wanted me back. But I was going the other direction.

The new position and the new challenges recharged my career batteries. I got to choose my squad from agents in the office, almost like a franchise draft in the NFL. I got to choose some of the best and the brightest, and rarely was I turned down for somebody I wanted. We ended up with a twenty-five-person task force squad made up of the usual FBI agents, plus representatives from the LAPD, the L.A. County Sheriff's Department, the CIA, the Secret Service, INS—we even had a sky marshal. Curiously, we never found a slot for ATF.

The squad hit the ground running. It was an eclectic group, from such disciplines as accounting and white collar crime, to undercover agents, to organized crime, gangs, and violent-crime people. We had lawyers, CPAs, military people, even two PhDs. But we had chosen these people intentionally. We were going to go after al-Qaeda as if it was a gang or an organized crime group, not as if it was some type of political movement. I think that was part of the mistake that had led us to 9/11: the FBI's Counterterrorism Division had been staffed with personnel from the world of counterintelligence, where arrests were rare, there did not seem to be any sense of urgency, and terrorist groups were dealt with through political chess and espionage.

The stress continued. Each day I would walk into my office to find a three- or four-inch stack of incoming leads and paperwork. I would have between 100 and 150 e-mails and more calls than I could count. And the agents were working much harder than I was.

I was amused at the potential threats that would seem to panic Homeland Security or make it big on the news. I'd see a threat that absolutely monopolized the news but knew from our investigation that it had absolutely no validity. Yet politicians delighted in calling up the National Guard or taking other extreme measures to show the populace that they were "doing something." They did this even after the FBI had told them, sometimes to their faces, that the threat they were responding to was not credible. No, at times, threats were political gold. There was not a day that

I didn't have *dozens* of those types of threats, reports, warnings, and "chatter." A person tending toward nervousness could not work the al-Qaeda desk.

It became all I could do just to keep up with the incoming flood of work. It was like drinking out of a fire hose. Todd Prost, who had worked with me on the 9/11 case the year before, had long ago transferred to FBIHQ, where the pressure was, if anything, more intense. He ran one of the dozens of counterterrorism units, so he also had to deal with the 4:00 AM and 5:00 AM calls. Todd was one of the kindest, most quietly intelligent people I had known in the Bureau, and he taught me more about how to work counterterrorism than just about any single person. But if he had a fault at all, it was that he was unable to find a way to release the stress, to build a wall, to avoid carrying it with him 24/7. One morning during a particularly busy threat response, Roger Deacon came into my office to tell me that Todd had killed himself that morning with his service pistol at his home in Washington. He had gotten a call at 5:00 AM, answered the questions posed, and after the call ended, he went into his closet and ended his life. I didn't know who to be angry at.

If a squad's goal is to investigate for a long time and put several people into prison for a long time, that's fine. But if our squad had done that with the al-Qaeda cells, they could have planned another 9/11 during that time without us knowing. Frankly, even if we had put one of them in prison for a long time, someone else would have replaced that person. It became our goal to disrupt the groups from being able to make plans at all.

Deep infiltration of the al-Qaeda cells by the FBI was almost impossible at that early stage, so our squad came up with a unique strategy. We would enforce every federal and state law we could in order to ensure that suspected cell members could not spit on the sidewalk without getting arrested. If a member of a suspected cell had come to the United States on a student visa but was carrying a part-time load instead of a full-time load, his door would be kicked in at 6 AM and he would be dragged out in cuffs. This had a spectacularly chilling effect on the cells we had identified. They began to distrust everybody, even people in their own cells. They did not know whether a person who had been arrested and then deported four days later had spilled his guts about the organization or their plans. They were never sure of what the FBI was doing, and they could not effectively operate. In essence, we were interdicting everything they were doing simply by standing in their way. We needed to use every tool we had in the toolbox.

So I chafed when President Bush's "NSA wiretaps" were mischaracterized in the news and on blogs, but I couldn't say anything then. To me it wasn't a Republican or Democrat issue; it was a national security issue. As a person who dealt with it every day, I could not (and cannot) understand the misconception of the program.

To understand the program, one must first know a few background facts. First, regular courts provide search warrants for ordinary criminal cases, but for counterterrorism cases, to safeguard secrets vital to national security, we had to obtain search warrants and wiretap authorizations from a single court in Washington, DC. It's known as the FISA court, because it was established by the Federal Intelligence Surveillance Act (FISA) of 1978. This created a huge backlog of warrants.

Once a wiretap authorization was obtained from a judge or a FISA court and we began to monitor the conversations of John Q. Suspect, then the FBI was legally authorized to listen to nearly all of Mr. Suspect's conversations, except those patently unrelated to the case. If, for instance, he began to talk about a fight he had with his wife, the FBI would have to "minimize," or turn off the recorder at that point. Every few minutes we could punch back onto the call to see if the subject had changed, but we could not turn the recorder back on until that part of the conversation was over. If *you*, an honest, law-abiding person, were to call Mr. Suspect—say, because he was selling a car—then I could listen to *you*, legally, as long as your discussion pertained or might pertain to the reason for the warrant. I wouldn't need a warrant to listen to what you said if it was related to the alleged crime.

Second, the NSA does not need a warrant to monitor a phone in another country. Nobody disputes this, even if they don't agree with it. Suppose for a minute you had a phone number in Yemen or Somalia that you knew beyond a shadow of a doubt was an al-Qaeda number, used only as an emergency number by terrorist operators—the bomb deliverers. That phone could very legally be monitored by the NSA without a warrant, and one would want it to be monitored. Would it not be very important to see if that number ever called a number in the United States? What if that phone *received* a call from the United States—say, from New York City? Wouldn't that be relevant as well? Not to keep tabs on such calls would be irresponsible.

Finally, the major disconnect between actual operations and allegations in the press was the word "wiretap," which insinuates that *words, conversations* are being listened to. But there are telephone intercepts that do not involve voice or conversations, and these are the types of intercepts the NSA program was going after, using what is known as a "p/n register," or "pin register." A pin register is a device that simply logs the numbers dialed or received by a certain phone.

As the supervisor responsible for all Los Angeles al-Qaeda investigations in the eighteen months after 9/11, I never once saw evidence that the NSA was *listening* to phone calls, rather than simply *logging* them. The investigative direction I received indicated to me that no information beyond the telephone number and the date and time of the communication was known; in other words, all intelligence was in the form of pin register results. When the numbers on these logs were in the Los Angeles area, we would begin a preliminary inquiry to determine if an investigation was warranted. Rarely did these intel nuggets come up empty.

In short, the program was vitally important to counterterrorism efforts in the United States and a major reason that no major terrorist attacks have occurred in this country since 9/11. It made the United States safer than all the ridiculous TSA airport screenings ever have.

I soon became frustrated with the other supervisors on the task force, "legacy" supervisors on whose watch the 9/11 attacks had occurred. They were not responsible for the attacks, obviously, but their "business as usual" attitude baffled me. They seemed to put more value on squad "turf" and their careers than they did the mission. Turf battles are one of the reasons that the World Trade Center is no longer standing. The other supervisors didn't seem to have changed their tactics, strategies, or career aspirations after 9/11, and they weren't even willing to admit that mistakes had been made. They just didn't get it. They were blessed with some of the smartest agents in the FBI and treated them like children. They micromanaged, they frustrated, they obstructed.

As an example: All communications from an agent have to be "signed off" by that agent's supervisor before they are sent out. In exigent circumstances, any supervisor can sign off an agent's communication if his or her supervisor is unavailable. One day, an agent from one of the other squads came to me and asked me to sign off an important electronic communication. I read the EC and realized it was a request for an immediate investigation related to a possible terrorist cell. But it was dated three days before! The agent who brought it to me was not one to sit on such an important lead.

"Why are you bringing this to *me*?" I asked. "And why is it three days old?"

"Because," he said, "Sam"—his supervisor—"has kicked it back to me three times to correct grammar." "Kicking back" is sending a document back for revision. On average, it delays an outbound communication twenty-four hours each time it is done. That Sam was kicking this back on grammar alone was mind-boggling. This was a national safety issue, yet Sam had told the agent, "My reputation goes along with every communication I sign. I don't want people to think I'm illiterate." The grammar errors were minor. The investigation requested was major. I signed it and told him to come to me for that anytime he needed. Of course, Sam would realize within a day or so what I had done.

Needless to say, I began to have heated confrontations with the other supervisors. I thought that maybe I was the only one who was noticing that their methods and sense of urgency had not changed, but within a year, every supervisor who had been "on duty" on 9/11 and before was replaced. My advantage was not that I was smarter or more experienced than them but that I had a knack for recognizing the best agents and getting them to my squad. I couldn't get all of them, but I got most. I was also helped by the fact that I didn't really want to be a supervisor, and if I got in trouble, all they could do was bounce me to street agent, which is where I wanted to go anyway. This led me to take more risks instead of avoiding them.

At the same time, much of our work was taking us overseas. It seemed like every investigation led sooner or later to Pakistan, Indonesia, the Philippines, or Saudi Arabia. There was really no way to effectively investigate if all investigations had to stop where the water started. We needed a squad that could investigate overseas. I talked to Paul Eiffel about this during case reviews and meetings. One day I got a call from him out of the blue that was strangely familiar:

"Steve, I just established an extraterritorial investigations squad to investigate terrorism overseas," he announced proudly. I was amazed.

"How can you do it that fast?" I wondered.

"Did you notice that I'm an assistant director of the FBI? It's good to be king."

I was ecstatic, and said so.

"Oh," Paul continued, "and you're the supervisor."

I felt rescued from a job that was killing me emotionally and physically and doing great damage to my family. I drove home quickly and told Michelle, expecting the relief to be visible.

It wasn't. Michelle was dubious that this would be any better than the al-Qaeda squad. I told her over and over how much easier my new assignment would be on me, because the caseload would be smaller and it wouldn't require that much traveling. I didn't know how wrong I was then, but I would soon find out. I had essentially signed the death warrant for our marriage.

16

Diplomacy, and Other Things Your Mother Warned You About

THE GLEAMING WHITE jet rotated gracefully from the Dulles International Airport runway and climbed out steeply. To anybody watching, it was just another run-of-the-mill (if any $40 million corporate jet can be called run-of-the-mill) Gulfstream G-V ("G-Five") departing on a CEO junket to some world garden spot. But this jet was en route to a hellhole: Karachi, Pakistan. And this jet was not technically a G-V; it was an air force C-37A transport that never wore air force colors. Instead, it received civilian markings and since 2001 had been operated by the FBI.

An hour before, at Dulles Airport just outside of Washington, DC, the faux G-V sat on the ramp at the local fixed-base operation (FBO). An FBO is simply the equivalent of a truck stop for corporate jets. But the ambiance is as superior to a truck stop as a corporate jet is to a semi. The décor is elegant, and for some reason counter personnel all seem to be attractive young females dressed in smart but form-fitting blouses and skirts. It is ultra-plush, as is fitting when a fill-up can run $25,000.

The passengers for this particular plane, however, looked much more appropriate to a truck stop. They all wore the same beige cargo pants, hiking boots, safari shirts, and vests and brought with them not Louis Vuitton bags but distinctly inelegant duffels and watertight, indestructible equipment cases. The passengers looked much more like they were going on an extended hunting trip than a corporate junket. To the initiated, however, they were not unusual; they were absolutely stereotypical. The cargo pants and high-end hiking boots, with either safari shirts or team polo shirts, were by now the de rigueur uniform of FBI special teams. They all spent quite a while stuffing the cargo hold and even part of the cabin with an unlikely amount of supplies and cargo.

In the rear cabin was a literal wall of luggage and investigative gear, guns, ammunition, and personal bags, all piled around a single, precarious aisle that led to the rear lavatory. In the hold below were spare parts for the aircraft, including a landing-gear wheel and tire, because they are awfully hard to find in Karachi. Or Kabul.

The morning before, Friday, June 14, 2002, I was at home taking a comp day. My plans changed when I turned on CNN. Immediately, I saw news feed of that familiar, horrible scene of blood-covered Americans staggering through smoke and debris and collapsed buildings—a scene that is the same each time we see it, whether the bombing occurred in Nairobi, Dar es Salaam, Oklahoma City, Saudi Arabia, or New York City. CNN's briefing beat the phone briefing I received from the FBI by a full two hours. The US consulate in Karachi, Pakistan, had been nearly destroyed by a car bomb almost twelve hours earlier. Thirteen people had died and much of the building had been turned to rubble, but it remained staffed with a skeleton crew. I went to the garage and dragged out my SWAT duffel, brought it to the bedroom, and began going down my "tropical destination" packing list with excited but somber expectation. Twenty-four hours later I was boarding the G-V in Washington, DC.

The plan was simple: go to Karachi, and in the shortest possible time, obtain the most information possible and get out. Karachi is a dangerous place for Americans. After 9/11, Pakistani president Pervez Musharraf had had to make a choice as to whether to side with the United States or be considered an enemy. He chose to side with the United States. This created an immediate sense of betrayal among many in his country who were devout Muslims and idealistically sided with al-Qaeda. Adding to the problem, Operation Enduring Freedom—the war on the Taliban and al-Qaeda in Afghanistan—had resulted in the huge relocation of thousands of trained terrorists in Afghanistan south into Pakistan. Most of those terrorists found homes in the port city of Karachi, far from central government control.

The first stop on the trip was Prestwick, Scotland. Prestwick was briskly cold and rainy when we landed. We arrived sometime after midnight and took a crew bus into the small town of Ayr. Behind the counter at the Ramada was the night manager and his assistant, a Scottish lass of about twenty, obviously sent over from central casting. Redheaded, about five-two, just barely plump, twentyish; had it not been for the rosy cheeks, she would not have had any color at all in her face. I asked her how she pronounced the town name: "Ayr."

"Och, it's simple! Ear!" she grinned.

"'Ear'? Well, that *is* simple," I grinned back.

"Aye, like th' ear ye breathe."

We sat in the lobby early that morning sipping beer as the local high school prom participants returned from their festivities. The long dresses on the girls would have made them seem at home in any small US town. The kilts on some of the guys might have stood out.

After launching the next day, we cruised over Germany, Croatia, Greece, and Egypt and across Saudi Arabia, studying our briefing books and becoming familiar with the details of the attack. Based on what the FBI had already gathered, it appeared that a powerful car or truck bomb had devastated both the consulate and the area surrounding it. The thirteen people killed were all Pakistanis, including two consular employees. About fifty people had been injured. After reviewing the facts of the case, we began to wonder about the obstacles we would face.

Diplomacy is crucial in criminal investigations overseas. The investigation of crime itself overseas is not complicated. Most competent FBI agents would have no problem with the procedures, the technology, or the logic. Bombs are bombs, guns are guns, forensics are forensics, and ballistics are ballistics. It's just like the United States, except the names of the suspects are harder to pronounce. What makes working overseas difficult—and, for many, impossible—is the tact, diplomacy, and "schmoozing" necessary to be allowed to *conduct* the investigation. That's the trick. In many countries in which I worked, my bar bill was huge. I never had a drinking problem; it was because I found out that, for instance, State Department people wouldn't necessarily cooperate with the FBI. But if I bought them a few drinks and showed I wasn't some arrogant, career-centered "hump," they were more likely to help me. Host country police officials rarely wanted to cooperate with America. But after a few drinks, they might cooperate with *me*. Some of the most delicate, crucial work on an investigation—and I mean this with all sincerity—actually takes place at bars after the day's work.

When the US government sends a big team of FBI agents over to a country (especially one not politically or ideologically similar to the

United States, such as Pakistan or Indonesia), two issues arise. The first is that the "host" government—in our case, Pakistan—feels a genuine slight that the United States obviously does not trust them to adequately investigate and solve the crime that occurred on their soil. Additionally, the host governments frequently do not understand the role of the FBI and fear that the agents are there to spy on them. While that would have made the trip more interesting and rewarding for us, that was not our job, and we were never tasked with anything like that. If the host government caught the FBI agents spying on them, of course, there would be immense repercussions: the CIA would be furious.

In this case, however, the most serious obstacle to the investigation of the bombing directed against the US State Department was . . . the US State Department. It really didn't matter what the president of the United States said about bringing "terrorist cowards to justice" if the very people responsible for doing that were stymied by their own State Department. At times, the situation was actually sublime.

For example, if the Karachi attack had occurred in the United States, the crime would have been designated a "special." Compare the Karachi attack to the similar truck bomb at the Murrah Federal Building in Oklahoma City. A cast of thousands investigated that case. No expense was spared. It involved round-the-clock Evidence Response Team (ERT) presence, bomb techs, investigators, and security teams. But other countries don't want hundreds of FBI agents coming to "help" them. I told the FBI that based on what I saw, I would need a minimum of sixty agents in Karachi, but if absolutely necessary, I could do it with forty, but they would be exhausted.

I was told that the State Department would approve *seven agents*. Before I could catch my breath, I was advised that FBIHQ would take three of those slots for bomb technicians.

This was an introduction to the politics we would fight every time we were overseas. Some of the reason was the State Department's responsibility to be attentive to a host country's sensitivities. But a large part of the problem was simply protection of territory. No ambassador I met had real law enforcement experience or knowledge, and his or her only advice usually came from the Diplomatic Security Service (DSS).

DSS is a branch of the State Department that is responsible for the security of embassies and consulates throughout the world. In every embassy and many consulates, there are DSS Regional Security Officers (RSOs) and/or Assistant Regional Security Officers (A/RSOs). They live and work at the embassies and are tasked with keeping personnel and facilities safe. The work is occasionally dangerous, and they do a generally excellent job. The rub is that while the FBI, by presidential directive, has primary jurisdiction over the investigation of terrorist attacks against United States persons and interests both at home and abroad, for years DSS carried that load abroad, and many in DSS appear to believe that they still do.

Happily, however, the CIA never threw any obstacles in our way during my time overseas. In fact, on many occasions, they provided access to information that I would not have believed they would have released. The world changed for both the CIA and the FBI on September 11.

The first agent I chose to accompany me was my trusted friend Austin "Dodger" Dodge, who, besides everything else, was a certified paramedic. Our flight to Baton Rouge nearly a decade earlier seemed like another lifetime. Owen Henderson, a former navy combat pilot in Desert Storm, was next; he was an unbelievably smart, competent investigator in whom I had the utmost confidence. The final position went to Blake Frye, an agent and a lawyer with much counterterrorism experience and a feel for how the Bureau worked.

Taxiing in at Karachi, it was well over a hundred degrees on the ramp, and the humidity was in the 80 to 90 percent range. If you have ever opened a dishwasher during its heated dry cycle, stuck your head in looking for a clean fork, and been repelled by the near-steam, you have an idea of what it felt like. Our sunglasses (yes, FBI agents always wear sunglasses; it's cultural) went opaque and we sweated through our clothes in seconds. Regaining our composure, we deplaned and began unloading. For all intents and purposes, the airport appeared abandoned. We were all alone on the tarmac in front of a fairly modern terminal in a jet with an American registration.

Humping our gear into the semimodern customs hall, we were greeted by no one. The immigration counters were empty, and we could have walked directly into the country without passing through customs, a plan that we evaluated with increasing interest as the room got hotter. The customs hall was not air-conditioned, and we sweltered there for about forty-five minutes waiting for the consulate personnel to negotiate our "official" entrance to the country. This was a little tricky, in that we had not had the time to do small things such as obtain visas prior to our departure. After nearly an hour, a consulate staffer appeared, along with a Pakistani bureaucrat.

"William Bedingfield. I'm the RSO," the staffer said, extending his hand.

"Steve Moore. Thanks for coming and getting us. We don't have visas, by the way."

"Or country clearances," he said, lightly noting our disregard of protocol. Country clearances are pretty important to the State Department and only an irritating formality to the FBI. "Rahim will issue you the visas, and we'll get on over to the consulate."

Bedingfield was a surprisingly soft-spoken man of about fifty. His thinning hair, goatee, well-chosen words, and deliberate speech gave him the air of a professor. But his athletic frame and the way he was constantly scanning his surroundings validated his credentials. On his face were the bandages and scabs of fresh glass cuts he received in the bombing.

Moving outside the terminal, we began looking for our transportation. We didn't have to look long. At the curb were two dark Chevrolet Suburbans with limousine-black tinted windows. Suburbans blend in just fine in America, but in Karachi they might as well have been Sherman tanks, for how they towered over the minuscule Pakistani cars. Behind our trucks was a Pakistani military police vehicle carrying several soldiers sitting face to face in the bed of the truck and one soldier standing in the bed, protecting the caravan with a loaded AK-47.

Frye couldn't help himself. "So we're covert, then?"

In personnel protection, there are two major tactical options, discretion and overwhelming power. This consulate apparently preferred the latter.

Piling into the trucks, we set out, four in one vehicle, three in the next. Riding shotgun in our Suburban was the RSO. This first trip in the Suburbans was itself "a trip." They were "up-armored" trucks, which meant that they were swathed in Kevlar armor, from the floor pan to the doors to the roof, and sported "glass" that appeared to be approximately an inch thick.

Dodge, ever the SWAT guy, had to know his tactical options.

"William," he asked, "if we had to, how do we roll down these windows?"

"They do not roll down. They are fixed," he advised.

"Well, then, can we shoot through them?" Dodge asked.

"Nope, Kevlar. It'll stop an AK-47," he said, scanning the cars around us.

"Well, if we get attacked, how do we defend ourselves? Just open the door and find a tactical position?" asked Dodge in more of a statement than a question.

"The doors are secured with electromagnets. They can't be opened unless they're released with this switch," he said, pointing at his console.

There is a fine line between protection and claustrophobia, and we were straddling that line in those vehicles. I took my comfort in knowing that Bedingfield chose the security, and he was in the car with us. Our little convoy arrived about a half an hour later at a reassuringly familiar Marriott Hotel. The Marriott Karachi is a very modern, Western-looking edifice that sits directly across the street from the US consulate. Unfortunately, its American identity and proximity to the consulate make it an appealing target for terrorists. Pulling into the roundabout in front of the hotel, I spotted a Pakistani military sandbag machine-gun emplacement at the corner of the entrance to the hotel. It looked like something out of a World War II movie. This was a stark reminder that we were no longer in Kansas. So was the fact that the hotel was missing half its windows because of the bomb that week. Every nearby lighted sign and streetlight was shattered, leaving only their metal outlines to give a clue to what the establishment had been. Even the trees were denuded of leaves and branches. The grounds of the Marriott had been scrupulously cleaned up, and it was an island of order in a sea of chaos, as the rest of the area was littered with debris. Before entering the driveway of the hotel, our vehicle chassis were mirrored to ensure that we were bringing no bombs into the Marriott.

Checking in, we were assigned rooms on the front side of the hotel, which was unusual. Agents request rooms on the backsides of hotels, because bombers almost always detonate their explosives in the front. (Terrorists need news shots. Intact hotel façades on

CNN make them look inept.) No amount of arguing with the front desk staff could remedy the situation.

But while unpacking and looking for an outlet to charge my cell phone, I discovered why we had been assigned certain rooms. I found a small pile of white powder on the brand-new blue carpet behind my nightstand. Looking directly above the powder, I found a newly-drilled hole in the wallboard. Through that small new hole ran a shiny new white wire as thick as a phone cord. Intrigued, I followed the new wire to its terminus, which turned out to be my room phone. This was not the phone's cord; it was a *second* cord coming from my phone. The other cord was the same beige color as the phone and terminated at a normal phone outlet on the wall. When it was unplugged, the phone was dead. The white cord that went through the wall did not use the usual plastic phone-cord clip; it was hard-wired to the phone. I always thought that a room bugging would be more elegantly executed. But here it was, as elegant and sophisticated as a caveman's club. Probably as effective, too. This explained why we were unable to switch to the back of the hotel. Our rooms had already been "prepared" for us.

An hour later we were at the decimated consulate, which had a very "Fort Apache" feel to it. Nonessential personnel were gone, leaving only volunteers, and the complex was a ghost town. The offices on the bomb side of the building were in shambles for the most part, with ceiling tiles missing and glass broken. Marines with loaded machine guns patrolled the halls at all hours. Physical damage from the bomb was everywhere, and basic services such as phones, lights, and climate control were intermittent. Everything was on an "adapt, improvise, and overcome" mind-set. The marines bedded down in the basement of the building and made constant armed patrols of the campus. Being marines, they also required exercise and would use the main promenade of the various empty floors as a jogging course at all hours of the day and night. I almost expected morning bugle calls and screams of "Scout arriving on horseback!" After getting our bearings, we went out to the bomb site.

Looking down, I saw something unfamiliar. At first, I thought it was a large caterpillar. It seemed to have a furry coat of black hairs much like the "fuzzy-wuzzies" I used to catch as a kid in New Jersey. This one was larger though, maybe an inch and a half long and oddly shaped. I toed it with my boot, and it didn't move. What kind of weird insects do they have in Pakistan? I wondered. I reached down, pinched it by the hairs, and picked it up for a closer look. Turning it upside down, I saw not legs but congealed blood. I was momentarily confused, so I squinted and looked closer to make sense of what I was seeing. Almost immediately, I recognized skin and hair follicles and realized that what I had picked up was a piece of human scalp, blown from the head of a victim of the bombing. I dropped it back to the ground as if it were on fire, my heart pounding. Looking around, I prayed no one had seen me. I imagined myself looking like a 1950s TV housewife finding a mouse in her kitchen. Taking a 360-degree scan around me at the bomb scene, I saw with relief that nobody was looking in my direction.

Needless to say, everybody deals with carnage and gore in their own way. Some claim that it never bothers them, never intrudes into their thoughts like a rude neighbor barging uninvited into their living room to tell the latest disturbing joke. Maybe some people really aren't bothered. It's all about building "walls." Emotional walls. Impenetrable walls to keep the image of dead, glazed, emotionless eyes from staring at you while you hug your daughter. Walls are essential for law enforcement and emergency-response professionals. It lets a fireman smile and laugh at a family gathering rather than mourn the lifeless toddler he pulled out of a burning home the day before. While walls are crucial, they have as much potential to destroy as they have to preserve. The ideal wall is as strong and as high as the stone walls of Jericho and must be able to come down just as quickly. It is important that you control the walls, or the walls will control you.

The bomb had gone off about 10:00 AM on Abdullah Haroon Road, a busy four-lane thoroughfare fronting the US Consulate General. About fifty feet from where I stood was the remains of a park kiosk, about eight or nine feet in diameter. This small, octagonal, concrete prefab structure had held water jugs inside, which were plumbed to drinking fountains on each of the octagonal kiosk walls. But now, the half of the kiosk that faced the blast was missing, and the concrete roof was teetering precariously on the remaining semicircle of wall. Inside the kiosk, however, was a metal object I could not recognize. Walking closer, I realized it was the chassis of a vehicle. Bedingfield noticed my curiosity and came over.

"It's the chassis of a minivan," he said. It had been blown completely inside the kiosk by the grotesque, unimaginable physics of the explosion. The chassis was bent almost in two, and the car appeared to have been crushed to about one-third of its normal size by the dynamics of the bomb.

"How did it perfectly hit the kiosk?" I wondered.

"Million-to-one shot," William opined.

"Anybody survive?"

"No."

Solemnly, likely in an act of catharsis, William explained: "It was a girl and her father. She was getting ready for her wedding."

"Shit," I barely uttered.

"It's worse. She was supposed to get married a few months ago, but her mom died, and they postponed everything." Without looking away from the kiosk, William finished: "She had finally decided to go ahead with the wedding. Her dad said he would go with her and buy her a wedding dress. That's what they were doing." William walked away and left me with my thoughts.

In this attack, the bomb itself contained several hundred pounds of explosives. It left a deep crater approximately five meters in diameter, roughly in the elongated shape of a vehicle. Inside the oily pit, shards of the shattered car poked out of newly turned dirt. The entire area smelled like stale, dirty motor oil, which reminded me of nothing so much as the smell of a junk-yard where I had spent so much time in high school keeping my cars running. Every bomb scene I have worked has shared this same aroma. It is either the explosives or simply the residue from vaporized automobiles and motor oil. To this day, walking through a junkyard looking for parts with my son to keep *his* cars running, I experience the same strong feeling of melancholy I had at bomb sites.

By the time we began the systematic search of the crime scene, the temperature had risen to 108 degrees and the humidity was more than 90 percent. Each agent was given an hour of searching and cataloging, then a half hour to recover and rehydrate inside the consulate. Clear plastic sheeting had been taped over all the window openings in our area of the consulate so that the air-conditioning would have an effect. Because of the humid heat, our cameras were unusable for a long time after we exited the building: the lenses fogged up until the entire cam-era reached ambient temperature, which made it almost too hot to touch. Finally, it was determined that it was easier not to bring the cameras inside and lose the time at the crime scene.

Inside, we met Mary Smyth, the FBI's assistant legal attaché out of Islamabad. She had come down to meet with us but quickly seemed to feel that we reported to her. We knew we were respon-sible to the legal attaché (LEGAT, Mary's boss) for many things while in-country, but the investigation of the case was managed by Washington, and to a lesser extent, L.A. The legal attaché was there to support the investigation, not manage it. The investigators began to squirm, especially the FBIHQ bomb technicians. The techs were equal in FBI rank to Mary, and they were technically required to take some instruction from her. The reality was, they had enough political cover as FBIHQ personnel to disregard her instructions, but her arrogance was hard to ignore. Thus began a tension that dogged us the entire first trip out to Pakistan.

Later, we discussed it. "She's crazy, Steve. I knew her at the academy," said Dodger. "We have to run the investigation."

"I'm not gonna let her run it," I promised. But I had not yet diagrammed how I was going to achieve that.

Back at the crater thirty minutes later, locals had been engaged to build sifting tables, simple five-foot-square wood frames with quarter-inch-mesh metal hardware cloth stretched between the frames. Three-foot legs elevated them to table level. After grid searches of the street and nearby park, we began digging out the bomb crater. Each shovelful was placed in the sifting table and the dirt agitated. Once the dirt had completely fallen through the screen, anything left on the screen was likely to be evidence. Simple but very effective, and even a little fun in a treasure-hunting kind of way—until you find a finger.

We were looking for parts of the bomb car, certainly, because the chances of finding chemical explosive residue was best on parts of the car closest to the bomb. This residue would increase our chances of being able to chemically identify the type of explosives used. By identifying the type of explosive used, we could then compare that information to the types of explosives particular groups had access to or were known to use. However, just as important were items that were not part of the bomb car. They would likely be part of the bomb itself. We compared wire found in the sifting table to actual automobile wire. If we couldn't identify it as automotive wire, it was segregated for later examination as possible detonation-circuit wire. With any luck, we might be able to draw a schematic of the triggering device.

One of the first items dug from the pit was a set of rear-axle leaf springs. They survived the detonation because they are large hunks of hardened steel. These are the parts that carry the weight of the vehicle. The paramilitary unit that claimed to be the lead Pakistani agency on the bombing, the Sindh Rangers, provided a very competent mechanic and a translator to help us. The mechanic immediately identified the leaf springs as belonging to a Ravi, a Suzuki "truck" made in Pakistan. It's difficult to put the size of this tiny truck into perspective for Americans. The Ravi is *dwarfed* by a Volkswagen Beetle. It is literally *three feet shorter* than the ubiquitous Bug, but it seats six in minivan configuration. It has one-third less horsepower than the VW and one less cylinder. The Ravi sports a Suzuki three-cylinder engine roughly half the size and power of the average American motorcycle. The entire "truck" would fit nicely into the bed of a Ford F-150 pickup.

Ravis obviously do not have a huge cargo capacity. The one used in the bombing, however, was different. We found more suspension leaves in the crater than Ravis are supposed to have. The possible reason for this was quickly apparent. It would not take a lot of weight to make the suspension of a Ravi sag in the back. And the sight of a heavily loaded truck approaching the consulate might have resulted in interdictory measures (read: gunfire) prior to the truck reaching its target. An extra leaf or two would have allowed the diminutive truck to ride level even while carrying a heavy load. By comparing the normal number of leaves in the spring to the number found in the pit, we would be able to determine what weight the vehicle modifiers had set the vehicle up to carry. The catch was that different versions of the Ravi (minivan, pickup, or stake truck) had different leaf-spring setups. We had to know which Ravi we were dealing with.

In the United States or most other first- or second-world countries, investigators would simply dig until they found a car part with
a serial number on it. This would tell them everything they needed
to know on the vehicle: size, color, engine, date of manufacture,
owner ... everything but the last time it was washed. This was not
so in Pakistan. The Pakistani manufacturer of the Suzuki Ravi had
a relaxed attitude toward serial numbers and record-keeping. Even
with a serial number, one could not tell the color of the vehicle, or
whether the chassis was a pickup truck, stake truck, minivan, etc.
And in Pakistan, wrecked cars are almost never junked. They are
simply combined with other wrecked vehicles after accidents, and
two vehicles become one vehicle with two sets of serial numbers.

So it was back to the crater. If we wanted to know what this
truck was, we'd have to dig it out of the hole piece by piece. After
another hour in the heat, going shovel by shovel, one particular
load surrendered what to me could have been a nugget of gold:
a small piece of singed steel that emerged from the dirt on the
screen. I picked it up and examined it, feeling we might have gotten another break. The piece of steel was a rear-gate latch. Rear
gates are found only on the pickup version of the Ravi, and therefore we likely had a pickup. And this latch was painted deep blue,
with chips showing that the deep blue was a repaint over factory
aqua paint. Quickly conferring with the mechanic and comparing the numbers of normal leaf springs and the number pulled
from the crater gave us a ballpark weight figure. Our truck was
configured to carry four hundred pounds in the bed while still
keeping the chassis level.

At the end of day one, with only seven agents, we had identified
the make, model, and color of the vehicle and a ballpark size esti-
mate of the device. A very good day, indeed. But regardless of the
evidence, one fact was obvious to all of us. We would never make
an arrest in this case. We might identify the subject who did the

bombing, but we were never going to bring him to justice, unless by some freak occurrence he was found on US soil. And, frankly, I had doubts about whether the actual perpetrator would ever be publicly identified.

There is a complicated problem with bombers in Pakistan that is an embarrassment to their government: terrorist bombers are almost always trained by the Pakistani government. Since the Russian invasion in Afghanistan, and during the entire dispute with India over Kashmir, Pakistan's version of the CIA, the Inter-Service Intelligence Directorate (ISI for short), had a robust program for training terrorists. The United States certainly hadn't minded Pakistani-trained terrorists attacking Russian assets in Afghanistan or assisting the Mujahedeen. The "freedom fighters" were trained in bomb construction, squad ambush tactics, and planting of mines, just to name a small part of the curriculum.

The walk back to the Marriott from the armored rear entrance of the consulate was only fifty feet, across a narrow street, Brunton Road. Brunton had, for protection, been blocked off at either end near the consulate since a 1995 machine-gun attack against a consulate vehicle killed two staffers, one a CIA technician.

Reaching the other side of the street, we entered the hotel very easily by stepping into what was once a trendy hotel bakery shop, through the place where a plate glass window had been. The bakery was on a corner of the building and until recently had sat behind two floor-to-ceiling plate glass windows that provided its patrons and employees with a beautiful view of the park, the consulate, and the bomb truck as it detonated. Behind a plate glass window was not the place to be at the moment of the explosion. The shock wave of the detonation reached the windows before the sound did. Hypersonic air is different than the breeze blowing on your face, in the same way that jumping into a pool is different from jumping off the Golden Gate Bridge. The shock wave at that distance is, for all intents and purposes, a solid thing moving faster than sound. Too fast for the patrons to even blink, the windows disintegrated into small and large shards, razor-edge shrapnel blasting at them at the speed of rifle bullets, blowing into and through the patrons before the visible debris from the bomb even reached the café.

Walking through this unrepaired section of the Marriott was the closest distance between two points and provided us with the least street exposure. But coming or going, we were confronted by beautiful marble floors covered nearly completely in some areas with thick dried blood. People had died here. Food and plates were on the floor, the furniture moved haphazardly around by emergency personnel. Soiled bandages and medical equipment were visible in corners in this area of the hotel, which was cordoned off to the public. Walking deeper into the hotel, we began to feel air-conditioning and hear the televisions in the restaurant playing cricket highlights. After turning two corners and taking a left past a Ralph Lauren store, we were at the lobby. In those fifty feet, we might as well have left orbit and reentered Earth's atmosphere.

Nearly every day that we were there, I noticed the same man in the lobby of the hotel. He was there when I went for breakfast in the morning and when I came back at the end of the day. The one time I went to the pool with the team, he was there. If we were eating dinner in the hotel on a particular night, he would walk by. I even saw him nearby when I was shopping. We didn't know who he was or who he worked for, but he was a constant reminder that we were making somebody uneasy. I called him Barney, after the Mayberry deputy sheriff.

Back at the consulate, we had a lone refrigerator in which we kept food and chilled our water bottles to get us through the day. However, every day we were continually cataloging, classifying, and storing significant body parts recovered at the bomb scene. Everything from rib fragments to skull pieces, jawbones, and fingers were in plastic evidence bags, and there was only one place to store them: in our food refrigerator. This was not an acceptable long-term situation. The body parts started on the bottom of the fridge and our edibles on the top shelf. But the tide of gross stuff was rising inexorably to meet the food shelf. Blake Frye sent an immediate communication to FBIHQ requesting permission for us to purchase a refrigerator "on the economy" (in country with cash or credit cards, rather than through any federal purchase procedure). Blake dutifully transmitted the request, and it was almost as quickly denied.

I asked him to show me his request and discovered that Blake had made a simple but understandable mistake. He had told the truth. In the FBI, truth is essential in investigations, evidence, testimony, and justice. However, when dealing with federal red tape and an administrative structure designed to protect careers, not support operations, truth is the kiss of death. It is important to remember that the *FB* in *FBI* stands for Federal Bureau. Blake's request read in part: "Due to the presence of victim body parts, we are unable to continue to store food and water in the refrigerator. Request is therefore made for authorization to purchase, on the economy, one commercially available refrigerator in which to store food and water."

The comfort of agents is not a high priority, but the Bureau will spend anything to ensure that a case is not compromised. I had Frye resubmit the request with the same verbiage except for the final sentence, which I had changed to read, "Request is therefore made for authorization to purchase, on the economy, one commercially available refrigerator in which to store body parts and evidence." The request was immediately approved.

After obtaining the DNA samples from the relatives of the missing, Dodger and Blake arranged to have the bodies X-rayed. Shrapnel that ends up in victims is of evidentiary value. The parts of the vehicle closest to the explosives are propelled the fastest and therefore frequently the farthest. Simple physics. The shards that kill victims are frequently those pieces of the bomb or bomb vehicle that are closest to the explosives and therefore are likely to be parts of the bomb themselves. In the X-rays, investigators have found wire, battery components, switches, and even bone fragments of the bombers. As gruesome as it seems, these are all helpful. Sometimes, the shrapnel will also yield a chemical "fingerprint" for the explosives used.

About a week into the investigation, news came to me that a source had information that he wished to give the FBI that would shed light on the attack. But the source could not come to us; we would have to go to the source, but not in our vehicles. He proposed that I walk over to the Metropol hotel and wait for "his people" to pick us up. This sounded vaguely familiar. Then it hit me. That's what American journalist Daniel Pearl had done just a few months earlier to meet a source: "Wait in front of the Metropol hotel and 'our people' will pick you up." He did, and they did, and he was never seen again.

But I went, too. I was picked up a half mile from the consulate by two men in traditional Pakistani clothes who carried AK-47s and spoke no English. I was sure I had made a huge mistake—nobody had said anything about guns. The drive seemed to go on forever. I spent the time trying to figure out how to get my Glock in a position to shoot the two guys with AK-47s without it being seen. I finally unzipped the side of the fanny pack in which I concealed the pistol and managed to keep my hand on it, pointing at the goon next to me as we drove.

I kept hoping I was overreacting, but I was sure that's what Daniel Pearl thought, too. I knew that if something went wrong, Michelle would be angry at me for making such a foolish decision. After half an hour, I considered trying to get out of the car at a stop, but at that point, we began to accelerate into an area of town where I had never been before. We came to a compound, likely a

British colonial estate of some kind; it was certainly not of traditional or modern Pakistani design. As we stopped in front of large iron gates, they were immediately opened by two men in uniform. I knew this was my last chance to bail out, but I decided not to take it—I still believed there was a good chance this trip was legitimate and I thought the risk was at least reasonable. As soon as we crept forward, the gates closed behind us, and I knew I was "all in."

We continued down a long entry road and stopped in front of the colonial mansion, and they motioned for me to get out of the car. As I did so, I noticed a familiar face: it was Barney, the guy who had been shadowing me since I got to Karachi.

I likely went pale. I was sure I had screwed up. Immediately, another man, wearing western clothing, exited the mansion in bare feet, ordering a servant to bring me tea and greeting me in very passable English. I began to relax. I didn't think they would bring me tea if they planned to cut my head off on the Internet. The visit lasted an hour and was very cordial, and it provided me with vital information for our investigation. My hosts never discussed having followed me, and when I brought it up, they claimed not to know what I was talking about. Barney was suddenly nowhere to be seen. After the meeting, I was chauffeured back to the area around the Metropol the same way I had come. I went back to my room and called Michelle just to hear her voice.

I learned much that day. It turns out that not all parts of the Pakistani government are on the same side. And some who seem not to like you might help you, and some who you think are friendly are not to be trusted. I learned that with the biggest risks come the biggest rewards. But most importantly, I learned why the American Club in the consular district is so vital.

Ahhhh, the Club . . . In the midst of the body parts, tensions, homesickness, and tattered nerves, there was one place we could go and get a break. The US Consulate Club, unofficially known as the American Club, was an oasis in the truest sense. It was located in the diplomatic zone of Karachi, less than a mile from the consulate, behind very high walls, and I personally felt safer there than in the hotel. The Club was absolutely the only place I could relax completely. The Club's ambiance reminded me of Rick's Café Américain in *Casablanca*. It was certainly tiny compared to Rick's place, but the patrons were no less interesting and almost as diverse. Diplomats from nearby missions, French, British, and German, frequented the watering hole. Network reporters and producers found it an ideal oasis, and FBI, the State Department, and the CIA found it the only place to drink safely in Karachi. Oh, sure, you could go over to the Sheraton, but it kept getting blown up. An ancient projection-screen TV dominated one wall, and distinctively inelegant round tables and metal chairs filled the meager space around a small bar in the rear of the room.

We drank them out of Budweiser each night we visited, and it was the only relief I felt in Karachi. Alcohol is important, as it helps patch holes in your "walls." An unspoken rule of the Club was that business would not be discussed. This was simply a practical measure, as one could not be sure who was at what table. But even if a ban on work discussions hadn't been necessary, the thought of bringing the case into our only sanctuary was obscene, at least to me.

The work was physically exhausting, the heat was oppressive, the report-writing constant, and the mental strain, both from concerns about safety and the body-part recovery was like a huge weight we could not set down. Tensions grew. One morning, RSO Bedingfield stepped into the office.

"Steve, have you decided on your team's intentions?"

"In regards to what?" I asked, confused.

"The threat information."

Now he had my attention. "What threat information?"

William looked at me as if he thought I was joking with him, then realized I was serious.

"Has Mary talked to you?" he asked. She hadn't.

"Two days ago, we got intel that there is 'significant chatter' in the air about an attack against a US consulate in Pakistan in the next week," he said. "There's only two US consulates in Pakistan— Peshawar and Karachi. Karachi would seem to be the obvious target, because there's eight FBI agents operating out of the consulate, and the timing is certainly right."

"Really. Why am I just hearing this," I stated rather than asked, afraid I already knew the answer.

"Steve, I told Mary the minute we got the information in. She said she would brief you."

When Mary returned that morning, she stepped into a buzz saw.

"Did you know about this?" Henderson challenged, gray-faced.

"Don't take that tone with a supervisor, Owen" Mary retorted. Mary had been in high school when Owen was bombing targets in Iraq. I felt as indignant as he did, I'm sure.

"Mary, did you or did you not know about this?" I pressed.

"Yes! I knew about it!"

"And what? It wasn't important enough to tell us?" Dodge joined.

"It's insignificant!" Mary said.

"How in the hell is that insignificant?" Owen demanded.

"You don't work here! You don't know what it's like in Karachi! A threat? Wow!" she mocked. "There's threats every day! This doesn't raise the threat level one iota! It's always dangerous here. Didn't they tell you that before you left?" Mary was getting toward the thin edge of the ice.

"How about you let us make decisions about our own safety?" I said.

"If everybody who came here to work bugged out at the first sign of a threat, we'd never get anything done!" she yelled back.

"We didn't say we were going to leave, we just have the right to know what we're dealing with," Frye, the lawyer, chimed in.

Then Mary uttered words that would not be forgotten by anybody who heard them.

"Maybe I should call New York or Washington Field and have them come out and replace you. Their agents don't seem to be afraid to work in Karachi."

This was wildly out of bounds. A line had been crossed. No words were spoken for several seconds. I knew what Dodge and Henderson were thinking: How much trouble will I get in for murdering an ALAT? It was apparent that Mary did not understand the gravity of her actions or her statement.

I had no choice. I called Los Angeles and spoke to my management, while the Washington bomb techs called FBIHQ. I then grabbed a plane to Islamabad and spoke with the LEGAT. We talked over drinks in the surprisingly comfortable bar at the embassy. We had a long and sometimes heated conversation, but at the end, we had a meeting of the minds. I flew back to Karachi the next morning.

Mary never intervened again. Within six months, in an unprecedented move, Mary had been reassigned to FBIHQ. It was extremely unusual for an ALAT to be removed from the field. Agents in the know muttered about the reasons, but the most we could get out of them was simply "a stress issue."

After nearly three weeks, the evidence from the bombing had been collected, crated, and shipped to the FBI lab. It filled a half-dozen four-foot-square crates. Interviews had been completed. The feared attack on the consulate had not materialized. Further investigation would be predicated on lab results, and those were several weeks away. There was literally nothing to do at "Fort Apache" until those results came back. The decision was made for us to return to the United States until the evidence results came back rather than wait with little to do at the consulate except make good targets.

I would return to Karachi in three weeks with a larger team and we would narrow the search even further. But we were leaving without achieving our goal of identifying the bombers. That would come on the following trip. Delayed gratification is one of the hazards of counterterrorism investigations; they take time and are not the place for people who need immediate gratification.

Dodger and I were able to walk for the first time out the front door of the hotel, down the street, and into the bomb area. We ambled down the street, pensively, and I wondered silently whether we had done any good and whether we would get usable results from the lab. Just short of the bomb scene, we noticed a couple of the ever-present street mutts arguing loudly over something. We stopped and watched them.

"What are they fighting over?" I asked quietly.

"Looks like a bone," replied Dodge.

It took a full second before the import of what Dodger had said washed over both of us. Wordlessly, Dodger and I made eye contact and walked toward the dogs, shooing them away. It was a bone. A couple of bones, in fact. Dodger the paramedic almost immediately identified them as the lower portion of a human upper femur (the large leg bone) still attached somehow to the patella and a fragment of the upper tibia (shin bone). It still had just a little bit of meat on it. I was able to immediately put up my "wall." It had become instinctive.

"What do you wanna do, boss?" Dodger asked.

"I'm not pickin' it up," I replied.

I didn't have the emotional energy at that point, and we didn't need it for the case. My mind was already on the plane home, and nothing more could be gained, so I closed the subject:

"We're off the clock."

17

"Isn't There Anybody Else Who Could Do Your Job, Daddy?"

IT WAS TUESDAY night, December 2, 2003, Michelle's birthday. I had planned a long time for this. As we pulled out of the driveway that night, however, the car was quiet.

In November, I had come home from a two-week trip to the Philippines that had me ending up in Indonesia for almost a month. I missed plays, football games, and family traditions. When I got home, I promised the whole family that I would not travel again until January or later. Michelle and I were looking forward to celebrating her birthday together.

That afternoon, just before heading home from work to celebrate with my wife, I had gotten disturbing information that one of my agents in Jakarta had made a very serious error in judgment. Jimmy was a brilliant agent when his ideas originated above his belt. But his most recent decision had not. He had shacked up with an Indonesian national in violation of every FBI and State Department rule, and without notifying anybody. It was not a well-kept secret, apparently, because the call I got notifying me of the problem originated in Washington, DC, from a three-letter agency.

I knew who the girl was; I had met her on several occasions, as she was the hostess at an Irish bar in Jakarta (yes, an Irish bar in Jakarta). She was tall, especially for an Indonesian, and strikingly, almost supermodel beautiful. But despite her best efforts, she was unable to hide the row of cutting scars up and down both arms. Her questions about our reasons for being in Jakarta led to concern that she was trying to gain intelligence for an Indonesian agency.

If something wasn't done about Jimmy right away, the Los Angeles Extra-Territorial Squad could be history, and our initiatives would disappear like cigar smoke. My friends in Washington had given me just a short time to rectify the situation. I spoke to my ASAC, characterizing it as a hypothetical situation, and he told me that hypothetically I needed to get to Jakarta right away and "fix it."

So the car was quiet because Michelle and I were not going out to celebrate her birthday. She was taking me to the airport.

The Extra-Territorial Squad was my dream. It was more than I ever hoped to achieve in the FBI, and I felt I was making inroads into terrorism, making a difference. I also enjoyed the travel. Compared with dealing with three preteen children, flying business class to Asia was more vacation than work. It was fourteen hours of free booze, music, movies, and steak and lobster dinners with exotic destinations and duties waiting for me. The hotels in which we stayed were five-star. However, even with all that, I started to wonder about how long I could keep it up. One of two things was going to happen, and I didn't know which it would be:

1. I would either become too exhausted and too distant from my family to continue with the job, or

2. The tenuous thread between my family and me would snap, and I would find all the enjoyment that I was missing at home—on the road.

The second possibility was something I didn't even want to admit to myself. I was also having a nagging thought that would not leave me. It was that maybe, just maybe, I wasn't doing the right thing, even though it was a patriotic, important, and sometimes even dangerous job. The question certainly wasn't whether the job needed to be done; it was who needed to do it. I had confidence that I was doing it very well, and I had a fear that the next person might not do it as well as me. I believed (and possibly rightly so) that other agents would not recognize the fact that the supervisor of an Extra-Territorial Squad's main duty was not the investigation but negotiation. I kept telling myself that nobody else could do it as well as I could.

As I left LAX on this particular flight, the birthday guilt added to my stress. I also had to explain to my children that I had to change my promise because of an emergency overseas. My "baby," Madison, the little girl who had gotten lost in the casino, was now nine years old. She cried truly sad tears. I couldn't figure out why she was so upset. It was only going to be gone a couple of weeks. I thought maybe she was tired. She probably had a lot on her mind. I could not fathom then how important a father was to his children—or to his wife.

Landing at Singapore Changi Airport, one of my favorite hubs, the next day, I set about to find the lounge and charge the batteries on all my portable devices. On the way, I booted up my cell phone to pick up voice mail. As I walked through the busy terminal looking at signs for directions to the nearest business-class lounge, I went through my voice-mail messages. The first two were simply work calls about the administrative and logistical issues of my trip. The third changed my life forever. I can still hear it.

It was Madison. She was sobbing. I stopped in my tracks in the airport and almost got rear-ended by people walking briskly behind me. It took her several seconds to get the first word out, and I was terrified that something horrible had happened.

"Daddy," she sobbed, "please come home!"

As I heard the words "please come home," I was already thinking to myself that I could probably disregard this message, because she was going to pose me with an impossibility—leaving an assigned FBI trip. But she continued, and her words cut me like a razor.

"Daddy, please come home, we need you here, *please*. When you get this, *please* find a plane that's flying back home, and please come home on it." Her words sounded desperate.

I was frozen in the center of the busy terminal. But I can't remember anybody around me. It was as if I were alone in the world. I could almost hear her voice echoing off the walls. Every word she spoke cut me to the core. That question was one I wouldn't even ask myself, much less wanted to hear from anyone I loved. *Why couldn't I just turn around?* It was as if it hit me in the one vulnerable place.

I remember from history that Henry VIII loved jousting but one day left his visor open *just a crack*, and out of all the places in the world to be hit, the opponent's lance found that very crack and hit him right above the eye, nearly killing him and leaving him with lifelong injuries and possibly mental illness. Madison's question felt like it had hit me in the one place my armor didn't cover. How could a nine-year-old change what I knew to be the right thing to do? But she wasn't finished. It was the longest call I ever heard. Even though it was just a few sentences.

She continued to sob. "I love you, Daddy, and I miss you. Isn't there anybody else who could do your job? There's lots of FBI agents; you're my only dad." I could hear my heart beating in my ears. She finished the message with a meek "I love you; please come home."

Anybody else who could do my job?

So there I was, standing as if I had been punched in the stomach in the middle of an airport seven thousand miles from home, unable to remember why I was there. I replayed the entire message. In hindsight, I believe I was simply trying to find a good rebuttal so I could continue my flight to Jakarta. The result was not a rebuttal, but tears welling up in my eyes. It was not because I convinced myself that it was the right thing to do that I continued on to Jakarta; it was that I might not have had the bravery it would have taken to turn around and explain my departure to the FBI.

Hours later, I keyed into my room at the hotel Pan Pacific in Jakarta. I dropped my bags and pulled out my phone and listened to Madi's message again. I knew I was in the wrong place. I couldn't deny it. It was the most bizarre feeling in the world. I was right where the FBI wanted me, needed me, doing a job that I did extremely well, and yet I knew I shouldn't be there.

But as time heals all wounds, it also puts scabs on open wounds that should be sutured. In the days following, my realization that I was in the wrong place was replaced by another realization: I had a job to do; I was the supervisor of the Extra-Territorial Squad. It was difficult work, but I was good at it, and I enjoyed the challenge. I picked up Christmas presents before I flew home and got on the plane anxious to spend the rest of December and into January with a much-deserved respite from travel and a vacation from the FBI, but the phone message still echoed in my ears.

Clearing customs at LAX, I was met by stone-faced agents from the Rapid Deployment Team (RDT).

"What's wrong?" I asked.

They told me that there was a threat to bomb airliners flying from Europe to the United States over the Christmas and New Year's holiday.

"There's always a threat to do that," I protested.

"Steve," one said gravely, "this looks like it may be for real."

They drove me back to the federal building, and instead of picking up my car, transferring my luggage into it, and driving home, my presence was requested at the command post. "Command post." That told me what I didn't want to know. The FBI in Los Angeles does not have a permanently manned command post. It is only opened in times of emergency. I walked into a beehive. I was twelve hours behind on the threat, and things were already at full tilt. Reading the briefing files for the past twelve hours, I realized that this actually was a planned attack and had not yet been completely interdicted. I don't know what Scotland Yard was doing over there, but they had some pretty big "saves." The flights were from Paris and London to Los Angeles, so most of the victims would be Los Angeles persons or people who had business in Los Angeles. We were the only US FBI office involved in the investigation, and it was going a mile a minute. I became one of the assigned case supervisors and was given a twelve-hour shift in the command post. Agents were en route to Paris and London, and Scotland Yard was picking up suspects as we spoke. During one of the arrests, one of their female officers was stabbed to death by a suspect. This was the real thing.

I do not think that the public, at least in the United States, realizes how close we came that Christmas to a major disaster. The bombs on the planes were scheduled to detonate as the planes were on final approach, which would've thrown half a million pounds of airliners, people, and burning fuel into highly populated neighborhoods. It would have been cataclysmic.

After a few hours in the command post, I was allowed to drive home, change my clothes, and prepare for the next couple weeks of work. It was a week before Christmas. I fervently hoped, and even believed, that the rush would be over in two to three days. However, rather than slowing down, the case was speeding up. My shift was 10:00 AM to 10:00 PM, which meant I had to leave the house around 8:30 in the morning, about the time the kids were getting up, and I would return home around 11 PM, after they were asleep. I was exhausted when I walked in the door.

There is no way to explain the toll twelve hours in an active command post working on a possible terrorist attack will take on you. Working those hours also ensured that I couldn't find stores before or after work to do Christmas shopping. The family did not have a Christmas tree until December 23, when Michelle finally gave up on me and found a very small Christmas tree to put in the living room. I did not make it home on Christmas Eve until 7 PM, after all the stores were closed.

Christmas Day was wonderful, regardless of the situation, but certainly subdued. I returned to work on December 26 angry. I was angry at the FBI. I was angry at my job. I was angry at me. The FBI never lied to me about what the job entailed. As the old saying goes, "I knew the job was dangerous when I took it." Nobody had ever been shy about saying that I would be working Christmases, and I had worked several in the past. But this one seemed to be a backhanded slap. By December 28 the case had wound almost completely down, and we closed the command post.

On January 2 we held a case debrief. There were about fifty people in the meeting. The Counterterrorism ASAC for the past few years and one of the best bosses I ever had, Jake Parker, and I sat on desks informally in the emergency operations center (EOC), facing the rest of the people.

I, however, was somewhere else mentally. I had hit a wall. Jake would occasionally have to look over at me and ask me to answer a question that I hadn't even consciously heard. I would ask them to repeat the question and then give a halfhearted answer. The rest of the time I sat with a thousand-yard-stare, fighting off what I knew I needed to do. I felt like a man standing on the edge of a building, believing that the only thing that will end the pain of this life is to jump off, and at the same time the rational side of him is begging him not to do it. There was a massive conflict going on inside of me. I think only my secretary, Meghan Flynn, detected a problem. She looked at me from across the room, quizzically. I just shook my head slowly.

Two hours into the one-hour meeting, it was approaching noon. Jake apologized for going long but said that we would be finished by one o'clock. I realized then that this meeting was a metaphor for my entire career to that point. An hour turns into three, important things are missed, and there are fifty other people staring at me who could do what I'm doing. As we continued from that point, I decided to "jump." I gave my boss what must have been a strange look, and he returned a "What the hell is wrong with you?" face. There could be no compromise, I realized, between the position I had in the FBI and the position I had with my family. One would live and one would die.

Wordlessly, in the middle of one of Jake's sentences, I stood up, closed my briefcase quietly, and started to walk out of the room. Jake stopped talking and looked at me. I turned and looked at him and said, "I've got to go." I'm sure I appeared robotic. Jake was a fairly smart guy, and he sensed that this was not the time to ask any questions about that statement. As I walked out I began to feel an elation building inside of me as if I was walking out the front doors of a prison. I felt light on my feet and I wanted to shout. There was resolve in me at that point that I don't think knew any bounds. On the executive floor I walked past the secretary and directly into the office of the acting director of the Los Angeles field office as he was putting on his coat to go to lunch.

"Henry," I said bluntly, "I quit."

Henry turned around confused and asked, "Quit what? The FBI? Being a supervisor? Or counterterrorism?" I didn't particularly like Henry, but he certainly knew how to size up the situation.

"I don't know, Henry. You're going to help me with that decision." If I were Henry I probably would've thought seriously about calling a doctor. Instead, he began taking off his coat and told me that he "wasn't that hungry anyway." Over the next half hour, Henry Andrews, who I didn't like and who I knew didn't like me, became a counselor to me. Two men who had hated each other in the office and had done much to submarine each other became friends in the next hour.

Minutes later, Jake arrived at Henry's office. Nobody had told him where to find me, but he apparently knew. Jake, Henry, and a third SAC, Bill Stubbs, took me to lunch. It was by far the most human meeting I ever had with management. Bill explained how he had "donated a marriage" to the Bureau, and it was the worst bargain he had ever made. The national divorce rate is about 50 percent. The law enforcement divorce rate is 70 percent. While the FBI claims to keep no statistics on their divorce rate, my observations make me think that 70 percent might be low for the FBI. All three men expressed their desire to do whatever they could to help me keep my marriage together. I told them I wanted a job in the Bureau where all I had to do was come to work in the morning and go home in the evening. They couldn't think of a job like that.

The job that I was giving up hadn't existed when I came into the Bureau, but if it had, it would have been my highest goal. It was beyond my wildest dreams that I achieved that position. I am reminded of a quote that I had copied down and stuck on my bulletin board in my office, paraphrased from Oscar Wilde: "The only thing worse than not achieving all your dreams, is achieving all your dreams."

Had I followed through on everything that I initiated at that point, I would have saved myself misery that I had never imagined. But like an alcoholic who goes to a few meetings and then falls off the wagon, I did not keep my eye on the ball.

18
Insanity

EINSTEIN SAID INSANITY is doing the same thing over and over again and expecting different results. He was right, and by 2004, I was completely insane.

I had worked out a transfer to the Aviation Unit with Jake and Henry. I would be back flying. Hopefully, mainly helicopters, as they didn't fly far from home. But as I was waiting for my transfer to the Aviation Unit, an FBI position posting caught my eye. The Bureau was looking for an assistant legal attaché at the United States Embassy in Nassau, the Bahamas. The assignment would be for the summer, and the ALAT in that office would be reporting to the legal attaché in Barbados, which was fourteen hundred miles away. Essentially, I would be my own boss and have the territory from Bermuda to the British Virgin Islands. My love of the Caribbean was not a secret.

I called Michelle about the job and proposed that the family go with me and have a two-month vacation in the Bahamas. Michelle was not very receptive. I argued that the kids would be out of school and we would be able to have a two-month paid vacation in the Bahamas. Michelle was dubious that anything that involved the FBI could be a "solution" to our problems. But I got the kids excited about it, and she finally acquiesced. But for Michelle, it was too little, too late.

Arriving in the Bahamas, it truly was what I had hoped it would be. I worked an eight-hour day, and my commute was a short walk across the street to the embassy from our hotel, the Colonial Hilton. The Hilton was a beachside property that had been the mansion of the colonial governor of the Bahamas when the islands were a British territory. Michelle and the kids spent the days at the beach. Weekends were our own. I could not understand when Michelle became more and more depressed. But after the first week or so, it became very clear to me that Michelle's feelings about me had changed. She loved the kids, doted on the kids, but could not find anything civil to say about or to me. The resentment in her heart was too much. Though I didn't realize it at the time, she was like a spring that has been stretched too often and too far. After a while it simply does not rebound.

I didn't realize the extent of the damage I had already done and that absent heroic measures, it was too late. What we needed was not a fantasy vacation; what we needed was a real life, in our own house, talking to each other and rebuilding. But I didn't understand that. I was also learning that one of the things a *man* needs most in a relationship is to be loved and admired by his wife. After years of not having her needs met, Michelle could no longer meet that need for me. I began to wonder whether she even loved me. Rather than humble myself and try to find out how things could change on my end, I began, as I had so many times before, to look for an escape.

At this, the most inopportune time ever, I received a call from my old SWAT buddy from the Thirties, James Benedict, who had taken over the Rapid Deployment Team, on which I was still an investigative supervisor. James explained that the Los Angeles RDT had been selected to cover the 2004 Athens Olympics, and

James was creating a team of specialists and supervisors to be on call for any acts of violence against American athletes, teams, or entities during the games. We would be stationed at a large villa on the island of Crete that had been converted into a small hotel with only fifty rooms. He offered me the job of supervising the investigative branch of that group. He also told me that most of my SWAT buddies would be there, as would my friends on the dive team and the bomb squad. It was as if he was offering me a summer camp with my best friends.

Had I been "sane," according to Einstein, I would've told James that this might be the last straw in my marriage and that there was no way I could even consider going. But I wasn't Einstein. I told him that I would consider it. I considered it for two days, during which time Michelle made it very obvious that her feelings about me were lukewarm at best. I wanted nothing more than to be away from her. I told her about the Crete trip and she reacted extremely negatively. It was a stronger, more negative reaction than anything I had ever heard from her.

I offered to fly her out to Crete so that we could spend the time together. This did not change her mind. When we got married, Michelle and I had a slogan that we would repeat to each other frequently. It was "divorce is not an option." Because of this, I was surprised when she said, "If you go to Greece, I might not be there when you come back." I called her bluff. That was a mistake.

We returned from the Bahamas on July 30, and the next day I joined the RDT for the trip to Crete. On the plane was a relatively new agent who I had first seen during the command post at the 9/11 attacks. She was an attractive, outgoing blonde, and I learned that she and I would be working together in Crete. Once on the island, she and I became friends, and I ended up not being able to bring Michelle to Crete after all, due to rules against dependents accompanying the agents on this trip.

Over the course of the next six weeks in Crete, I crossed boundaries I had laid down for the protection of my marriage that I knew were sound: I would never, ever be alone in a compromising place or situation with another woman. Yet during my time in Crete I broke this rule often, discussing my marital problems with an attractive single woman over drinks. There was no doubt in my mind how reckless I was being. On one hand I desperately didn't want anything to happen. But on the other hand, I was intentionally putting myself in situations where bad things could happen. The girl was fifteen years my junior, but she seemed to like and admire me, which was incredibly refreshing after months of living with somebody who was truly (and understandably) angry at me. She had seen the cases I worked and was complimentary about my skill as an agent. She made me feel good about myself at a time when my own wife could barely be in the same room with me, it seemed. She did not encourage the relationship, but I did nothing to discourage it. It was never a physical relationship in any way, but my affections were in play, and that was just as bad. It was also alienating me from my friends on the team, and especially my administrative assistant, Meghan, who knew Michelle and was incensed with me.

When the Olympics concluded, no attacks had been launched at US athletes, and the attacks I had made on my marriage had apparently not been fatal. Or so I thought. Contrary to her threats, Michelle was at home when I returned and had every intention, at that moment, of making our marriage work. But she was obviously still dealing with anger toward me. She was especially bitter that I had broken my promise to take her to Crete.

The woman from Crete and I continued to correspond by e-mail occasionally. I considered it innocent; they were friendly conversations, not romantic in character. And one day, I left one of those communications on the screen of my computer in my office at home. Michelle found it. That likely was the beginning of the end.

I was flying again at Point Mugu and felt that I had made a huge sacrifice for the family. Instead of having Gulfstream jets coming to pick me up, I could not even qualify to copilot them. The best secretary in the FBI, Meghan Flynn, was now my boss's secretary. I thought that I had made a huge gesture and that it was time for Michelle to give back. Instead, Michelle had become a different person than I had known previously. She began to act in ways I could not understand, was nearly always angry at me, and had very little tolerance for anything about me. I was miserable at home. By Thanksgiving 2006 Michelle had lost at least 20 pounds and become frighteningly thin. Just before Thanksgiving 2006, she demanded that I move out of the house. By that point, I was only too glad to oblige.

Our separation was theoretically intended to bring us together, but my interest in getting back together was compromised by my interest in seeing "what else was out there." I was not involved with anybody (especially not at the FBI), but I craved a way out of the mess I had created. After almost a year, I found a divorce lawyer and told Michelle I wanted out. I had convinced myself that this was okay in God's eyes. When you want something enough, you can rationalize anything. Once I had made the decision to end the marriage, I found the perfect assignment for me.

A job canvas was sent out to all undercover agents requesting a trained scuba diver. That sounded interesting. I responded and found that it was an assignment in the Caribbean, where the FBI needed a scuba instructor in a resort. It would be a minimum three-month assignment with the possibility of three-month extensions as the case went on. For a "newly single man," there was nothing more exciting. As a candidate for the assignment, I was sent back to Virginia for the standard three-day undercover psychological evaluation. It was a series of psychological tests followed by a recommendation for or against the participation in the undercover.

Going to these is kind of fun, because the locations are not known FBI locations but undercover locations that look like normal offices but are in reality FBI operations. When you go through a certain door, you find the FBI behind it. It feels very cloak-and-dagger and scratches an itch that many of us in the FBI have.

When I went through that particular back door into the FBI office that day, I found my evaluator to be Special Agent (Dr.) Ira Bahr, a classmate of mine at the FBI Academy. Ira would have a leg up on evaluating me, as he had lived down the hall from me for four months almost twenty years prior. If he remembered anything at all he should have remembered that I was stable. I completed the usual written tests and spent a couple days with Ira, going to breakfast lunch, and lunch the next day together, and even driving his new Corvette around town. We talked for hours about my situation, about Michelle, about the impending divorce, about Greece, about counterterrorism, and about my family.

In our final meeting, Ira's job was to debrief me on what he had found. He told me that he was going to recommend me for the undercover assignment. However, he said very seriously that he was doing so "only because the French Foreign Legion doesn't take Americans anymore." He explained that it was very obvious to him that I was running away from something. Nevertheless, I was elated that I had been recommended for the undercover, and I was planning my next six months of exciting discovery.

That night, I celebrated with one of my favorite business trip rituals. I always treat myself to barbecued ribs, a cold microbrew draft beer, and the latest issue of any of three or four magazines about historical airplanes (yes, I am also a geek). That night was no different. I had opened up my magazine, I had taken my first sip of my beer, and I was savoring some fine baby back ribs. Then my phone rang.

The caller ID told me that it was Michelle. I was surprised that she was calling. I pushed IGNORE and started on my ribs. A few minutes later, a beep told me that I had received a voice message from my answering machine. The length of time between the ring and the notification told me that it was a long message. My curiosity got the best of me and I played it back. Michelle began by saying that her counselor had told her not to call me. However, she said that she needed to talk to me one more time. That actually bolstered me even more, knowing that I had an "out" for whatever she was about to say. "Your counselor *said* not to call. . . ."

"Please do not divorce me." The way she said it, and the humility with which she said it, startled me. It actually felt like a punch in the gut.

"I love you." I hadn't heard that in over a year.

"I will do anything to save our marriage," she pleaded. This sounded like the girl I fell in love with. But I knew in my heart it was too little, too late.

I didn't believe her, but I was surprised at her humility, after such vitriol between the two of us. I hadn't heard this Michelle in several years. But I knew it was a temporary, emotional thing, so I texted her back, "How serious are you?"—fully intending to put a condition on a reconciliation that she could not accept. Then I would feel blameless.

A half hour later, I got the response: "I'm completely serious. I'll do whatever it takes." Wow. That caught me by surprise. I was having that old conflicted feeling again. I wanted my freedom, but here was something I could not ignore. What I didn't know is that after receiving my "How serious are you?" message, Michelle had called friends, family, and people she trusted to make sure she said the right thing. And she prayed. That wasn't fair.

I went back to the hotel that night confused by my own emotional reaction. I knew I wanted out. But something was screwing up the whole plan. The problem that I would not admit to myself was that I loved Michelle. I mean, I honestly had a deep, deep affection for her and cared about what happened to her. I had managed to numb those feelings for a while, but I was having trouble staying numb. I remember the first time that scared feeling entered my head twenty years before, when I realized I didn't want to be without her, even as I didn't want to lose being single. Regardless of her faults or my faults, I was head over heels in love with this woman. She was a part of me. But she wasn't the same, I thought.

The next day I was to take a flight out of Dulles, and I arrived at the airport several hours early so that I could go to the Udvar-Hazy Center of the Smithsonian National Air and Space Museum, which is just by the airport. It's a spectacular place for airplane geeks like me. While walking around the airplanes, I was thinking more about Michelle than I was the planes. So finally, I called her.

I don't know what happened to me that day. But it started during that phone call. All the hopes and dreams for a new start, a new undercover assignment, a new life, and all the plans I had made for my new future vanished during that call. Somehow, the bitterness was gone, the grudge disappeared, and I missed her. All I wanted from that moment was to get back with the woman I loved. I am convinced that God did something special that day. I flew home, and we moved back in together. We stayed in separate rooms, but we began dating. We took it slowly, and it was a long time before we were back in the same bedroom, but we have never gone back.

For the next year, we got reacquainted and fell in love again. Stronger, more resilient, more forgiving love. Love based on a decision, on a commitment, not just a feeling. A year after getting back together, we went on a "honeymoon" for our *second* marriage. We went to Crete, to the same village in which I had stayed during the Olympics. Only this time, it was with the woman I loved. This was the trip I had promised her years before.

We had unfinished business to attend to.

19

Sparky, Why Don't You Head West?

MY "SECOND TOUR" as a pilot at Point Mugu was in many ways more fun, as we had new, exciting aircraft to fly and my best friend, Dodger, had become a full-time pilot. But as I approached fifty, my career in the FBI had become secondary in my mind to Michelle and the kids. I had gotten used to running large investigations; taking on large, challenging tasks; and doing things that scratched my adrenaline itch. But it was obvious to me that doing that type of work in the FBI was not going to work anymore. And flying, as much as I loved it, was no longer intellectually fulfilling. I wanted to do more.

Four months before I turned fifty, I got a call from a corporation who needed someone to run security and develop security policy for their facilities and people in the Los Angeles area, England, Italy, Switzerland, Germany, Argentina, Thailand, and China. The pay was good; it came with a company car, education benefits for my three kids (then approaching college age), and the promise of reasonable international travel—travel on which Michelle could

307

accompany me. Plus the office was ten minutes closer to my house than Point Mugu. I accepted.

In many ways, leaving the FBI was more difficult than joining. When I entered the academy, I was twenty-five years old. When I retired, I was fifty. Half my life, from the delivery room to my retirement party, was as an FBI agent. Two-thirds of my adult life has been as an agent. When I arrived at the academy, I didn't know how to be an agent. When I left the Bureau, I didn't know how *not* to be an agent. It was more than what I did; it was *who I was*. It was as familiar to me as seeing my face in the mirror. And for the first time, or so it seemed, I was seeing the face of somebody else in the mirror.

The last time I drove to the FBI office as an agent was to turn in my guns. It was more, much more, than simply giving back objects that had some kind of monetary value. They were talismans of who I was. They were status symbols. When I left SWAT, I remember turning in my Springfield Custom .45 semiautomatic pistol, which only SWAT agents were issued. In the office, seeing that pistol on an agent's hip signified he was on SWAT. It was like a letterman's jacket. Now, I had to give the rest of my weapons back. It was heart-rending, like I was driving a cherished family pet to the edge of town and pushing it out of the car and driving away.

I walked through the office trying not to dwell on what I was doing for fear I'd get emotional. I was afraid people would realize what I was going through—and then I was afraid people wouldn't. At the firearms room, I unceremoniously placed my Glock 23 pistol, my Remington 870 shotgun, and my MP5 9mm submachine gun on the table as the firearms personnel signed the receipts indicating that I had turned them in. I said nothing, because I didn't want this to last a second longer than it had to.

Driving away from Westwood that last time was not difficult. At that point in my life, the sight of the federal building could still turn my stomach and make me nauseous. Not because I didn't love the Bureau or the job, but simply because of the stress that came with the job. Stress from the days in those twenty-three years in Los Angeles when I knew I needed to be home, but knew I couldn't leave the office. Stress from the fear of people dying if I made a mistake. Stress from SWAT, from the tryouts and the training to the operations. Stress from working days when I was sick from chemo and didn't know how long I would live.

But as I walked out of the FBI office as an agent for the last time after giving back my weapons, I thought back to the FBI academy on March 18, 1984, when I first put my pistol in my holster and walked out the front door, unsure of what was ahead of me. And now I knew.

It was the greatest single gift God had ever given me, at least among things that don't live and breathe. It defined me and likely will until I die. My FBI career was the most exciting adventure I will ever have, and just as with my love for Michelle, finding words to express my love for my career is difficult. It wasn't the FBI organization, the bureaucracy, or even the badge. It was the people and what the Bureau let me do. No, it was what the FBI *required* me to do. It required of me more than I thought I had in me, and it made me stronger, yet showed me my weaknesses more clearly than any other endeavor besides fatherhood. I could not have comprehended, on that brisk March day in 1984, what my FBI career would be. I lived more and did more than I thought possible in my twenty-five-year careers.

As I left the building that day, I saw near-brand-new agents walking in, doubtless with still-shiny guns and badges, chatting excitedly about their cases, and I wanted to ask them, *Do you have any idea what you're in for?* I smiled for them as I left, because *I did.* I knew the gut-wrenching struggles and I knew the painful growth in store for them. And I realized that this was a good time and the right time for me to leave. When I eventually give my daughters away at their weddings, I will have already experienced a little of that feeling. I will miss them, and I will grieve in a way that they are no longer my babies in my arms, but I won't hold on to them. It would be terrible for them and worse for me.

That afternoon, at Point Mugu, I turned in everything else the FBI wanted back, including, sadly, the keys to my jet-black, 4.6 liter Mustang GT. I would miss that car, too. But the Bureau does make one thing easier for the retiring agent. Two months before retirement, I sent in my badge and credentials to FBIHQ, and the department responsible for court exhibits created a wonderful plaque that includes my credentials and the badge I carried throughout my entire career. Not having to drop your badge on your boss's desk on your very last day is one of the great subtle kindnesses of the process.

But the final act remained. It was my fiftieth birthday. The day before, I had flown my last scheduled mission, a two-ship formation flight out to San Nicolas Island about a hundred miles into the Pacific Ocean in preparation for an FBI operation. But on this day, I would make my last helicopter flight.

Nobody said a word in the office as I started to gather my flight gear. It was obvious that they were allowing me my privacy, letting me have my thoughts. The helmet I would wear was one that I had been issued more than twenty years before. It had been rebuilt several times and fit me like a glove. It would be retired with me, to a bookshelf above my desk at home—at least until it's needed again.

I sat at my office desk and cleaned the visor one last time before I went out. Under the helmet and survival vest, my flight suit for the day would be my usual: T-shirt, jeans, and sneakers. I know, I know, I know. You would think that somebody with the name "Sparky" would have learned long before that this was not a good idea. Frankly, though, if something had happened on that last flight and I hadn't survived for whatever reason, it would have been something of a backhanded gift.

I found the helicopter on the pad, already outside of the hangar, washed and gleaming in the sun. I knew it would likely be the last time I ever flew her, and I had truly come to love that particular ship. The preflight of the helicopter took an unusually long time, as I ran my hand over every part of the aircraft. When I could no longer find a reason to delay it any longer, I climbed into the pilot's seat as easily and instinctively as putting on my T-shirt. I donned my helmet, snapped into the harnesses, and sat silently, taking in her smells and remembering our adventures, the cases we'd worked, and the places we had gone.

Out of my peripheral vision, I caught movement, and I glanced into the hangar, where several of the pilots were standing deep in the shadows watching, not wanting to intrude. This didn't cause me any emotion, of course, but I dropped my gray sun visor anyway—because of the glare.

Going through the checklist slowly, I lit the engine off as I had done so many times before. I held the controls more gently than I ever had, caressing them, not just moving them. My liftoff that day was possibly the smoothest I had ever made. I hovered sideways off the pad as always and sat in that hover for a good thirty seconds before I called tower.

"Tower, Rock Four-five, base of the tower for a Mugu Rock departure, low-level."

The response was immediate: "Rock Four-five, approved. Wind two-one-zero at five, depart eastbound via taxiway alpha. Report the Rock outbound."

Rather than just turn right to the easterly heading, I did a complete 360-degree pedal turn in place, then turned toward Mugu Rock. I accelerated down the taxiway at ten feet, rising to twenty feet and accelerating through one hundred knots by the end of the taxiway. A slight right turn put me almost immediately over the colony of seals in the lagoon, then over the breakers.

The trip down the coast at fifty feet was spectacular, as usual. The first beach I passed was Thornton Broome beach, where I had proposed to Michelle twenty years before. Sunbathers waved at me as I skimmed the waves. The breakers were hitting the rock barriers down the coast, and the mist rose halfway to the helicopter. I zoomed a hundred feet over the surfers at Zuma Beach, where I had nearly ditched a burning airplane just months before my wedding. Then I roared on past the homes of the stars at the Malibu Colony and on to Santa Monica. From there, it was east over Beverly Hills and Hollywood.

The memories were almost too much to absorb. I flew through downtown, where I had learned to land on tall buildings, and headed directly for the Hollywood sign. On top of Mount Lee, the edifice on which the sign is situated, is a helipad we had used for decades as a perch when we took breaks while the people we were following had lunch or watched a movie.

I couldn't help myself, and I landed there and shut down. From this place, one can look into the Los Angeles basin or walk to the other side of the mountain and look down at Burbank and Van Nuys in the San Fernando Valley. It is weirdly silent there, except for the whisper of the wind. Though you can see millions of cars, for some reason you cannot hear anything but a barely discernible hum from the freeways.

After a few minutes with my own thoughts, walking around and watching hawks soaring on the updrafts, I cranked up and headed back to base. But on the way, I engaged in one last ritual, a ritual that I had started twenty-three years before.

Thousand Oaks is on the route between Los Angeles and Point Mugu. Most of the time that meant that on the way home I would be flying near to or over our home. And when in a helicopter (sometimes even a plane), I would fly low over the house to let the family know I was on my way home. Michelle said that when I buzzed the house, she and the kids could almost time my arrival at home—an hour and a half later, give or take five minutes, I would walk in the door.

On this day, I didn't just buzz the house; I stayed for a while. I circled lower and lower, slower and slower, looking down and seeing Steve Jr., Meagan, Madison, and Michelle waving up at me for the last time. I only turned to Point Mugu when I was having trouble seeing through misty eyes.

Coming in over the pad for the last time, I set the helicopter down as gently as I ever had and sat as the engine cooled for several minutes before shutdown. All the pilots were waiting. After the blades stopped, I got out to handshakes and backslaps and was awarded a ride back to the hangar in the unit Jeep. Minutes later, we adjourned to nearby Camarillo Airport, to a hangar that belonged to Dodger, for beers, cigars, stories, and the ceremonial but unexpected drenching with an amazingly large half-barrel of cold water. It was fitting that I spent my last afternoon in the Bureau in the company of my friends. Not surprisingly, they are the greatest assets the Bureau has.

The beer and the cigars were wonderful, but they could not ease my sadness. Dropped off at my house by Dodger, I walked in, and there waiting for me, already crying *for* me, was Michelle, the only person who could not just salve my sadness but ease it. I knew this day was inevitable. But to face it without her would have been more than I could have taken.

FBI Glossary

A&D: A law enforcement abbreviation for the warning "armed and dangerous."

ALAT: Assistant legal attaché, an FBI agent assigned to a US embassy as a liaison between the host country and US law enforcement.

ASAC: Assistant special agent in charge, an FBI executive responsible for a division (such as terrorism, or white collar crime) within an FBI field office.

breacher: A SWAT team member responsible for forcing open doors during an operation.

breech: The end of a firearm barrel into which the ammunition is fed (and sometimes ejected.)

class date: The date on which an FBI recruit is to report to the FBI Academy for training.

code 3: A police code indicating that a law enforcement vehicle is en route to a location utilizing lights and siren.

code 4: A police code indicating that no further assistance is needed and the situation is under control.

cold bore: The first shot fired from a gun on a given day; usually used in reference to sniper rifles. Also known as a cold shot.

cold car: A vehicle that cannot be traced back to the individuals using it in a law enforcement or criminal operation—for example, a stolen car used in a bank robbery. In FBI undercover operations, it's a non-Bureau car (frequently seized from drug dealers) that is registered to a fictional person or company; it's frequently a luxury or sport vehicle.

condition lever: The mechanism on a firearm that determines the firing condition of the weapon, such as single-round, burst, full automatic, or safe.

crown: The opening at the end of a firearm's barrel, from which the bullet exits.

decomp: Law enforcement shorthand for "decomposition."

desk: FBI slang for a supervisory position.

drop: The delivery of an item to a prearranged location—for instance, the ransom in a kidnapping case.

dry cleaning: FBI slang for a subject's attempt to identify and/or lose a surveillance.

EC: Electronic communication, the basic forms of FBI communication, including everything from memos to teletypes.

emergency operations center: The facility in which FBI command posts are run.

execute: A law enforcement order to initiate an assault.

eye: The primary surveillance position; the agent closest to the subject of a surveillance.

first office agent (FOA): The FBI term for "rookie"; an agent serving in his or her first office assignment.

go to ground: To hide or otherwise attempt to evade law enforcement.

green: The predetermined entry point for the SWAT team at the site of a SWAT operation.

grounder: The ground teams in a surveillance operation, as distinguished from aircraft surveillance.

GS-13 agent: The most senior FBI agent position (from their pay grade).

head west: Aviation slang for "you are relieved" or, most frequently, "return to base."

HRT: The FBI's elite Hostage Rescue Team, made up of agents with a background in military special operations.

hydra-ram: A miniature version of the "jaws of life" used by the fire department, employed by SWAT breachers to open security-bar doors.

initial appearance: The federal court system's version of an arraignment.

KMA agent: An FBI agent eligible for retirement (acronym for "Kiss my ass").

lead: An investigative request from one FBI office to another. It can be anything from a records check to a request to locate and arrest a subject.

mags: Ammunition magazines.

major case prints: A comprehensive form of fingerprinting that includes prints of the palms, the whole hand, each finger, and every fingertip.

MO: "Modus operandi," or "method of operation"; in law enforcement, it describes a subject's known behavior and preferred methods for committing a crime.

OP: "Office of preference," the FBI office to which a new agent indicates he or she would prefer to be assigned. Many people believe that telling the FBI that you want to go to an office will guarantee that you will *not* be sent there.

operator: A member of a SWAT team (taken from the military term for a special forces team member).

out of battery: A condition in which the bolt and/or firing pin of a gun cannot contact the bullet face, rendering it incapable of firing.

pedigree: A fictional history assumed by an agent working undercover. It must be complete, including such details as marital status and backstopped (legitimized) credit history.

pegged: In aviation slang, it's the position of an indicator needle that is maxed out and leaning against the edges of the gauge.

PIC: Pilot in command, the FBI term for pilots who have passed not only FAA check rides but also more demanding FBI check rides.

rabbit: A suspect who runs.

REILs: Runway end identifier lights, the instrument approach lights used to define the runway at night.

SAC: Special agent in charge, an FBI executive in charge of an entire field office—except in very large offices, where there may be several, each in charge of an entire investigative division.

SAR: Search and rescue, military rescue helicopters and crew designated for recovery of the crews of craft in distress.

sit down: A command issued to ground surveillance team members, indicating that they should pull over and park where they are—for instance, because a surveillance subject has pulled to the side of the road.

soft clothes: FBI and law enforcement slang that can indicate several different types of clothing—casual (as opposed to the usual suits worn in office situations), civilian (as opposed to SWAT uniforms), and very casual (such as cutoff jeans and flip-flops utilized in covert or undercover operations).

SOG: Special Operations Group, the FBI's covert surveillance teams.

special: A case so large that agents are pulled from other offices for periods from a month to a year to work it.

ten-four: Normally written as 10-4, a police code that means "affirmative."

subject: The FBI's preferred term for a suspect.

technical install: The installation of covert cameras or microphones as an investigative technique.

TOC: "Tactical operations center," a SWAT operation's mobile command post.

Top 12: The FBI's twelve largest offices.

truck stop cutie: A prostitute who works at truck stops, going from sleeper cab to sleeper cab.

twenty: Short form of 10-20, the police code for "location," as in "What's your twenty?"

UC: Undercover operation or undercover agent. As in "I'm busy doing a UC today" or "We need a UC who can speak Spanish."

UCA: Undercover agent.

UFAP-murder: A law enforcement abbreviation for the criminal charge "unlawful flight to avoid prosecution for murder."

wire: A wiretap.

yellow: In a SWAT operation, the final point of cover and concealment before the site of the operation.

Index